LOTUS™ 1-2-3™ FROM A TO Z

Andrew T. Williams

A Wiley Press Book
Wiley & Sons, Inc.
New York • Chichester • Brisbane • Toronto • Singapore

Trademarks

1-2-3 is a trademark of Lotus Development Corporation.
Compaq is a trademark of Compaq Computer Corporation.
dBASE II is a trademark of Ashton-Tate, Inc.
DIF is a trademark of Software Arts, Inc.
Epson MX is a trademark of Epson America, Inc.
Hercules Graphics Card is a trademark of Hercules Computer Technology.
IBM PC is a registered trademark of International Business Machines, Inc.
Multiplan is a trademark of Microsoft Corporation.
SuperCalc2 is a trademark of Sorcim, Inc.
Texas Instruments Professional Computer is a trademark of Texas Instruments, Inc.
VisiCalc is a trademark of VisiCorp, Inc.

Library of Congress Cataloging in Publication Data

Williams, Andrew T., 1943-
  Lotus 1-2-3 from A to Z.

  "A Wiley Press book"
  Includes index.
  1. Lotus 1-2-3 (Computer program)
  I. Title. II. Title: Lotus one-two-three from A to Z.
HF5548.4.L67W53   1984   001.64′25   83-26057

ISBN 0-471-87919-3
Printed in the United States of America

85 86 10 9 8 7 6 5 4 3 2 1

Dedication

To the memory of my parents.

Acknowledgments

Many people contributed directly or indirectly to the making of this book. It is a better book for their help. In particular, Linda Williams helped turn half formed ideas into concrete prose by her willingness to listen, to make suggestions (tactfully), and, when called upon, to read parts of the manuscript. One could not have a better partner in this enterprise.

Special thanks to my editor at John Wiley & Sons, Theron Shreve, for encouragement throughout the project and to David Sobel, the Managing Editor who carefully guided me through the preparation of my manuscript for electronic production. The team work of these people and the staff of the Publisher's Network allowed me the opportunity to become directly involved with the latest book production techniques. Thanks are also due to the Developmental Editor who did her best to correct my inconsistencies and to the outside reviewer who carefully read the manuscript and made many helpful suggestions.

Finally, thanks to Steve Miller, the Publishing Coordinator at Lotus Development Corporation. His aid throughout the drafting of the manuscript was invaluable.

CONTENTS

PREFACE

Lotus 1-2-3 started a revolution in microcomputer software. It was introduced in the Spring of 1983, and it quickly became the best selling program of any type for the IBM Personal Computer. In a market where IBM PC "compatible" has become a buzz word, the real compatibility people seek is 1-2-3 compatibility. Both *InfoWorld*, a microcomputer trade publication, and *Fortune*, the widely read business magazine, named Lotus 1-2-3 software Product Of The Year for 1983.

Lotus 1-2-3 does two things to deserve this praise. The first is to successfully integrate an electronic spreadsheet, database functions, and graphics in one package. Users like the ability to move back and forth between these modes—to analyze information both numerically and graphically, and to use the database functions to sort the rows of a worksheet into a new order or to search for entries that meet a particular criterion. But integration isn't enough. There are other integrated products on the market, and they haven't met with Lotus' phenomenal success.

The real key is that 1-2-3 is an elegantly designed program. It provides all of the features found on any other electronic spreadsheet program (and more). But what sets Lotus apart from a Multiplan or a SuperCalc is that—in spite of its power—Lotus is easy to learn and easy to use.

There are three major areas in which Lotus surpasses the competition. First, Lotus introduced an "expanding cursor." Many spreadsheet functions—copying, moving, printing, etc.,—require you to designate a range of cells for action. Lotus displays the selected cells in reverse video (dark characters on a light background). The expanding cursor makes the task of selecting ranges particularly easy.

Next, Lotus makes extensive use of full English word command names and long, informative prompt messages. By reading the screen, you always know what choices are available and what response 1-2-3 expects.

Finally, 1-2-3 introduced a tremendous library of help screens. These screens display help that is keyed to your particular need at a particular point in the program.

Any one of these innovations by itself would not have made for a great program. But when augmented with dozens of other less sweeping features, the combination adds up to a level of ease of use that has simply not existed before.

How To Use This Book

Lotus™1-2-3™ From A To Z is a complete guide to Lotus 1-2-3. The structure of the book mirrors the structure of the commands and modes of 1-2-3. Part A covers the basics of getting started with 1-2-3. Part B is about the worksheet mode, the 1 of 1-2-3. The major commands—Worksheet, Range, etc.,—are discussed in separate chapters. Part C is on the Database command, the 2 of 1-2-3, and Part D is on the Graph command, the 3 of 1-2-3. Appendices A and B cover key assignments on particular machines and an advanced feature of 1-2-3 called the Typing Alternative. Appendix D explains how to use Symphony's Telecommunications environment.

Each 1-2-3 command is discussed, and examples are given to illustrate the major points. Each command and each major subcommand are outlined in command trees. These diagrams show exactly what will appear on the screen at each point in a command. The command trees give you a quick, overview of a command and the choices it presents.

To get a step-by-step treatment, you can read straight through *Lotus™1-2-3™ From A to Z*. You may, however, want to skip ahead and read those parts of Chapter Six (The File Command) and Chapter Seven (The Print Command) that describe the basic techniques of saving and printing electronic spreadsheets. You can also turn directly to the chapters on the Data command and the Graph command should you need those features before you complete your study of the Worksheet commands.

Most chapters contains a Hands On section. Be sure to take the time to do these exercises. By actually using a command, you gain a mastery that cannot be achieved by reading the text alone. Each chapter concludes with a Self Test. The questions in the Self Test highlight the major concepts covered in the chapter. Use them to review your understanding.

Finally, in Chapter Eight there is a list of ten tips for constructing 1-2-3 worksheets. You will want to consult that list as soon as you begin constructing worksheets. The tips bring together in one place the most important principles of spreadsheet construction.

Symphony

The Bridge To Symphony

In 1984 Lotus 1-2-3 acquired a big brother, *Symphony*, an even larger integrated spreadsheet program from Lotus Development Corporation. In many ways Symphony is an advanced version of 1-2-3, and thus many people who buy 1-2-3 will want to know how it compares with Symphony. Throughout *Lotus™1-2-3™ From A To Z* you will find boxes like this one containing text about the similarities and differences between the two programs. Taken together these boxes form **The Bridge To Symphony**. Should you need to, you can use The Bridge To Symphony to make the trip from 1-2-3 to Symphony quickly and with a minimum of effort.

The Bridge To Symphony begins in Chapter 1 with a detailed overview of Symphony as it compares to 1-2-3. Readers who use databases will find the detailed instructions in Chapter 9 for using the Forms Generate command of particular interest. And everyone should read the Epilogue which poses the question "Do you really need a Symphony when you can make such beautiful music with a Trio?" This is an important issue so if you are considering buying Symphony in place of 1-2-3 or considering trading in your 1-2-3 package for Symphony be sure to read the Epilogue. Finally, Appendix C gives step-by-step instructions for using Symphony's Telecommunications environment to send and received spreadsheet information.

As you work your way through *Lotus™1-2-3™ From A To Z*, you can read the Symphony material as you go along or you can skip over it. The material is self-contained and neither your understanding of Lotus nor your understanding of Symphony will suffer if you leave the Symphony material until later.

PART A
GETTING STARTED WITH LOTUS 1-2-3

Before you begin to construct electronic spreadsheets with Lotus 1-2-3, you must do and learn a number of things. Part A covers that "preconstruction" material.

Chapter one, "The ABC's of Lotus 1-2-3," is an overview of the worksheet, graphics, and database features of 1-2-3. The chapter shows how infomration can be organized into a worksheet and how that worksheet can be sorted with 1-2-3's Database commands. The Graph command is then used to display numerical information pictorially so important relationships can be quickly understood.

Chapter two, "Getting Ready to Use 1-2-3," explains what you must do to prepare the magnetic diskettes that come in the Lotus package for use on your microcomputer. This chapter also gives you a tour of the Lotus Access System, your computer's keyboard, and the 1-2-3 screen as it appears on your computer's monitor. A very important part of chapter two is an explanation of how the Lotus menus work and how to position the cursors (the active parts of the screen) where you want them. The chapter concludes with a "Hands On" session in which you create your first Lotus 1-2-3 electronic spreadsheet.

CHAPTER ONE
THE ABC'S OF LOTUS 1-2-3

OBJECTIVES

- To become acquainted with electronic spreadsheets.
- To become familiar with the three elements of Lotus 1-2-3; the worksheet, the database, and the graphics function.
- To preview the things to come in *Lotus™1-2-3™ From A to Z*.

INTRODUCTION

What is an Electronic Spreadsheet?

An *electronic spreadsheet* is a microcomputer program that allows you to solve problems involving numbers. It is organized into columns and rows like an accountant's spreadsheet, except that it is much larger. From top to bottom, 1-2-3 has 2,048 rows and from side to side, 256 columns. In addition to its great size, it places the lightning fast, error-free calculating ability of a microcomputer at your finger tips.

Electronic spreadsheets allow you to do your job faster, and more efficiently. Because they obviously improve productivity, electronic spreadsheets are largely responsible for the explosive popularity of microcomputers. They give everyone who uses them—executives, managers, owners of small businesses, investors, consultants, researchers, and home owners—an electronic blackboard, a piece of electronic chalk, and an electronic tool kit with which to solve virtually any problem involving numbers.

The great power of an electronic spreadsheet lies in the fact that it provides you with a *generalized* problem-solving tool. One that lets you find solutions to your problems in your own way, using your knowledge of the situation, and your creativity.

What is Lotus 1-2-3?

Lotus 1-2-3 is an *integrated electronic spreadsheet* that has set the microcomputer software market on its ear. According to *Softalk For The IBM PC*, it took only 32 days for 1-2-3 to vault into first place on the sales charts. Since then, 1-2-3 has become available on many microcomputers in addition to the IBM PC. But in those first few weeks, demand was so strong that *Softalk* reported: "Buyer acceptance of the program borders on the mania produced in the Apple or Atari markets by a breakthrough in arcade-game programming."

All the fuss centers on the elegant way 1-2-3 integrates the three most popular analytical programs—the electronic spreadsheet, a database, and graphics—into a single, powerful, easy-to-use package. It makes analyzing any financial or numeric problem as easy as...well...1, 2, 3.

The best way to get a feeling for what 1-2-3 is all about is to see it in action. In the following pages, you will examine a worksheet, a database, and some graphs. You don't need to know how 1-2-3 works yet. That's what you you will learn in the rest of the book. For now, try to get the flavor of the program, and try to imagine the many ways you can put its features to work for you.

THE WORKSHEET: THE 1 OF 1-2-3

Lotus 1-2-3 is a powerful, sophisticated electronic worksheet. As a pure worksheet program, 1-2-3 has more features and functions than such popular programs as VisiCalc, Multiplan, or SuperCalc2.

Table 1-1 shows a simple 1-2-3 worksheet. It gives some information about two of life's great constants: death and taxes. The information in the table is arranged into rows and columns, and you can easily read off interesting facts, such as the per capita income in Switzerland ($15,455) or the female suicide rate in the United Kingdom (7.9 per 100,000 population). The averages and the standard deviations for each column are shown across the top of the table.

Commands

The 1-2-3 software includes many commands for constructing, modifying, and analyzing electronic spreadsheets. The commands make the construc-

TABLE 1-1
Death and taxes. Information about income, taxes, and suicide rates in seven countries.

Country	Income Per Capita	Taxes Per Capita	Average Tax Rate	Suicide Rate	
				Male	Female
Average	$10,113.29	$2,228.71	22.04%	32.5	15.1
Standard Deviation	$2,732.85	$740.84	5.21%	10.5	5.2
Switzerland	$15,455.00	$2,802.00	18.13%	43.5	17.9
United States	$E,612.00	$2,199.00	25.53%	26.8	8.8
Austria	$9,114.00	$2,104.00	23.09%	45.3	18.8
France	$E,980.00	$2,605.00	29.01%	29.8	11.5
Denmark	$12,956.00	$3,395.00	26.20%	39.9	22.6
Japan	$E,460.00	$1,059.00	12.52%	29.3	17.9
United Kingdom	$7,216.00	$1,437.00	19.91%	12.9	7.9

tion process quick and efficient, and they make the resulting tables clear and easy to understand. One example is the extensive set of *Format* commands 1-2-3 has for enhancing your worksheets' appearance.

In Table 1-1, the Format command is used to display currency in the first two columns with dollar signs, commas, and two places to the right of the decimal point. Likewise, the percent signs and the two decimal places in the third column are accomplished by setting the Format command for those cells to percent. Other Format commands used in Table 1-1 include justifying text to the right edge of a column and displaying one place to the right of the decimal in the last two columns.

In addition to the Format commands, 1-2-3 has many worksheet commands. An important one is the *Copy* command. It takes the contents of a cell or group of cells and copies it into other cells. In Table 1-1, the Copy command was used to copy the formulas for average and standard deviation from the "Income Per Capita" column to the other columns. The formulas calculate the statistics for a corresponding group of cells in each column and are only entered once. The Copy command saves a great deal of time and avoids any errors that can occur when the same formulas are entered over and over. You will make constant use of the Copy command when building and modifying electronic spreadsheets.

Perhaps you would like to add Germany to the list of countries, and, for some reason, you would like to place it between France and Denmark. With an old-fashioned manual spreadsheet, you would have to either redo the entire worksheet or write new entries between the existing ones. With 1-2-3 you just use the *Insert* command to insert a new row. When it inserts the blank row, 1-2-3 adjusts all the formulas and functions on the worksheet to take account of this new information.

Maybe you aren't interested in the information on the Average Tax Rate column and would like to eliminate it from the table. It's simple: just use the *Delete* command to delete the unwanted column. At the same time, columns to the right move over to fill the space.

Never again will you have to resort to microscopic writing to fit a row into the middle of a table. Never again will you have to use scissors to remove unwanted rows or columns and glue to reassemble the worksheet. Press a few keys, and "poof"; your electronic scissors insert or delete rows or columns anywhere on the worksheet.

Built-in Functions

While the worksheet commands place the electronic power of your micro-computer at your finger tips, 1-2-3 has another group of features that makes constructing and using worksheets a breeze. These are the *built-in functions*. They instruct 1-2-3 to perform mathematical calculations on the contents of specified cells. The built-in functions range from a simple summation function that totals a set of numbers, to complicated financial functions such as calculating the internal rate of return of a series of cash payments.

Table 1-1 uses only two of 1-2-3's more than 40 built-in functions. The average function at the top of the table finds the average for each column over all the countries, and the standard deviation function in the next row finds the standard deviation of the amounts in the columns.

1-2-3 doesn't limit you to the predefined built-in functions, but allows you to define your own relationships by creating algebra-like formulas. This was done in the Average Tax Rate column where each entry is calculated by dividing the entry in the Taxes Per Capita column by the corresponding entry in the Income Per Capita column. As noted earlier, the Format command was used to display the result as a percentage followed by a percent sign.

THE DATABASE: THE 2 OF 1-2-3

What is a Database?

A *database* is a collection of information arranged in a way that makes specific information easy to find. An address book is a familiar example of a database as is Table 1-1 on death and taxes. Your address book is arranged by name, and you can quickly find the street address, telephone number, and other information you have written under a particular name. The death and taxes table is arranged by country, and you can find all the information that relates to a particular country by reading across the corresponding row.

A 1-2-3 database is just like your address book, except that it must fit into the row/column format of an electronic worksheet. This gives rise to some specialized vocabulary.

In a database, each row is called a *record*. A record contains all of the information about a single topic. In your address book, the information is about a single individual. In Table 1-1, the information in a record (or row) is about a single country.

In a database, each column is called a *field*. Each field contains a particular type of information. In your address book, the name may appear on the first line of each entry followed by the street address, the city, the state, and the telephone number. The *location* for each type of information—(name, address, telephone number)—is a field. In Table 1-1, the columns are the fields. All information about Income Per Capita, for example, is located in a single column.

Sorting a Database

Lotus' database has many advantages over an address book or a pile of 3 x 5 cards. In particular, a microcomputer excels at tedious, repetitive tasks like rearranging or sorting the rows of a worksheet based on the contents of different columns.

For example, you may have noticed the countries in Table 1-1 are not presented in any particular order. With seven countries, this isn't much of a problem, but what if you had a table of 100 countries? Finding the entry for Ethiopia might be difficult. It is a simple matter with 1-2-3 to define Table 1-1 to be a database and then to use the database *Sort* command to rearrange the rows alphabetically (see Table 1-2 on following page).

You can also answer many interesting questions by sorting the information in Table 1-1 in different ways. For example, which country has the highest taxes per capita? Table 1-3, which is sorted on the Taxes Per Capita column, quickly gives you the answer: Denmark with $3,395.00. Which country has the lowest male suicide rate? Table 1-4 yields the United Kingdom with 12.9 per 100,000 population. (See Tables 1-3 and 1-4 on following pages.)

Lotus will sort a database on any column in either ascending or descending order. Furthermore, it can sort the database on one column (the *primary key*) and at the same time, sort each subcategory by another column (the *secondary key*). Thus subcategories of information can be ordered at the same time the whole database is rearranged.

The 1-2-3 database has may additional features. You can set up a test or

TABLE 1-2

Table 1-1 sorted alphabetically by country.

Country	Income Per Capita	Taxes Per Capita	Average Tax Rate	Suicide Rate	
				Male	Female
Average	$10,113.29	$2,228.71	22.04%	32.5	15.1
Standard Deviation	$2,732.85	$740.84	5.21%	10.5	5.2
Austria	$9,114.00	$2,104.00	23.09%	45.3	18.8
Denmark	$12,956.00	$3,395.00	26.20%	39.9	22.6
France	$8,980.00	$2,605.00	29.01%	29.8	11.5
Japan	$8,460.00	$1,059.00	12.52%	29.3	17.9
Switzerland	$15,455.00	$2,802.00	18.13%	43.5	17.9
United Kingdom	$7,216.00	$1,437.00	19.91%	12.9	7.9
United States	$8,612.00	$2,199.00	25.53%	26.8	8.8

TABLE 1-3

Table 1-1 sorted by Taxes Per Capita, highest to lowest.

Country	Income Per Capita	Taxes Per Capita	Average Tax Rate	Suicide Rate	
				Male	Female
Average	$10,113.29	$2,228.71	22.04%	32.5	15.1
Standard Deviation	$2,732.85	$740.84	5.21%	10.5	5.2
Denmark	$12,956.00	$3,395.00	26.20%	39.9	22.6
Switzerland	$15,455.00	$2,802.00	18.13%	43.5	17.9
France	$8,980.00	$2,605.00	29.01%	29.8	11.5
United States	$E,612.00	$2,199.00	25.53%	26.8	8.8
Austria	$9,114.00	$2,104.00	23.09%	45.3	18.8
United Kingdom	$7,216.00	$1,437.00	19.91%	12.9	7.9
Japan	$8,460.00	$1,059.00	12.52%	29.3	17.9

TABLE 1-4

Table 1-1 sorted by Male Suicide Rate, lowest to highest.

Country	Income Per Capita	Taxes Per Capita	Average Tax Rate	Suicide Rate	
				Male	Female
Average	$10,113.29	$2,228.71	22.04%	32.5	15.1
Standard Deviation	$2,732.85	$740.84	5.21%	10.5	5.2
United Kingdom	$7,216.00	$1,437.00	19.91%	12.9	7.9
United States	$E,612.00	$2,199.00	25.53%	26.8	8.8
Japan	$8,460.00	$1,059.00	12.52%	29.3	17.9
France	$E,980.00	$2,605.00	29.01%	29.8	11.5
Denmark	$12,956.00	$3,395.00	26.20%	39.9	22.6
Switzerland	$15,455.00	$2,802.00	18.13%	43.5	17.9
Austria	$9,114.00	$2,104.00	23.09%	45.3	18.8

criterion and then find the entries in the database that meet it. For example, you could search the database for all countries that have male suicide rates of less than 30 per 100,000 and that have per capita incomes of greater than $8,500. (In Table 1-1, that would be France and the United States.) You can also extract records from the database and have copies of the information appear elsewhere on the electronic spreadsheet. This is useful for tasks such as creating mailing lists or identifying particular types of clients. Later in this book, you will learn how to use these and many other Data command features.

GRAPHICS: THE 3 OF 1-2-3

The information in Table 1-1 tells you about death and taxes, but graphs would make it easier to see the relationship. Lotus can draw five different types of graphs; line, bar, stacked-bar, pie, and XY. A useful graph for seeing the relationship between suicide rates and taxes is the XY graph displayed in Figure 1-1. It plots Taxes Per Capita along the horizontal (or X) axis and the Male Suicide Rate along the vertical (or Y) axis. The graph is clear; each point is labeled with the country's name, and optional grid lines have been drawn in. As you probably suspected, higher taxes per capita are generally associated with higher male suicide rates.

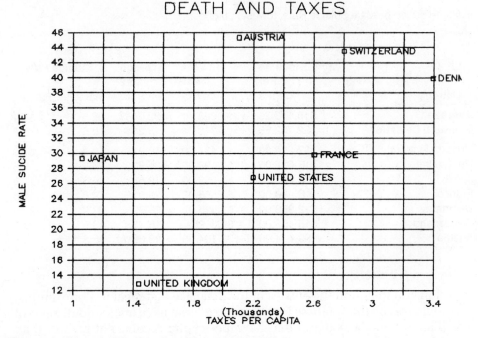

Figure 1-1. XY graph of death and taxes in seven countries.

But the story doesn't end there. Perhaps you would like to see the relationship between death and income. With 1-2-3, you can quickly respecify a graph and immediately view the results. Figure 1-2 shows the relationship between Income Per Capita and the Male Suicide Rate. If anything, the relationship is closer than between Taxes Per Capita and the Male Suicide Rate. If high taxes and high suicide rates go together, then so do high incomes and high suicide rates.

Of course, the preceding paragraphs aren't a definitive treatise on the relationship between death and taxes, but they do provide good examples of Lotus 1-2-3's power and flexibility. The worksheet commands and the built-in functions let you construct the original worksheet quickly and easily. You can then use the Database Sort command to reorder the information.

Finally, the Graph command can present the numerical information visually. Many people can grasp complicated relationships more easily in graphic form, and 1-2-3 provides them with a quick, powerful, easy-to-use visual tool.

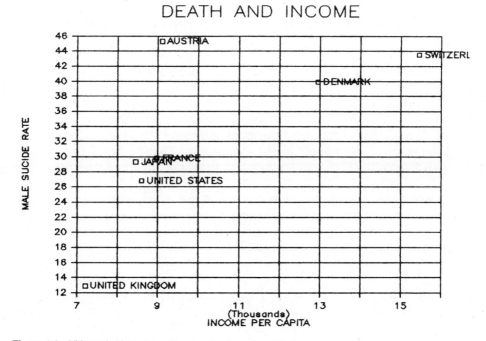

Figure 1-2. XY graph of death and income in seven countries.

PREVIEW OF COMING ATTRACTIONS

You have now been introduced to the worlds of 1-2-3, but this introduction has just scratched the surface. You know what the three parts of 1-2-3 are, and you have a general idea of what they can do. You should also have some idea of 1-2-3's many features.

You are probably anxious to start learning to use 1-2-3 to solve your problems. Before you get started, you have to prepare the program diskettes for use on your computer, and you have to learn some fundamental skills such as how to move around a 1-2-3 worksheet and how to enter information. Gaining these skills is the subject of the next chapter.

After you have done the necessary groundwork in chapter two, the remaining three parts of *Lotus™ 1-2-3™ From A to Z* will teach you all you need to know to construct your own 1-2-3 worksheets, databases, and graphs.

Part B explains all of 1-2-3's worksheet commands. You will learn to change a worksheet's appearance with the Format commands, to use the Insert and Delete commands when constructing a worksheet, and to save and print worksheets with the File and Print commands.

Part C explains 1-2-3's Database command. You will learn how to create a database, to sort it, and to find and extract entries that meet a specific criteria.

Finally, Part D explains how to create line, bar, stacked-bar, pie, and XY graphs with 1-2-3's Graph command. You will also learn to use the many options of the PrintGraph program to print professional-looking copies of your 1-2-3 graphs.

Before you get to the main feature, let's take a quick look at 1-2-3's big brother, Symphony. Throughout this book, there are sections like the following that present information about Symphony. These boxes connect the information about 1-2-3 directly to Symphony. Taken together, they form *The Bridge To Symphony*.

Sometimes the information in the boxes is about the specific differences between the way a particular task is done in 1-2-3 as compared to Symphony. At other times, the boxes introduce you to special features found only in Symphony. In either case, if you are interested in Symphony, please read the boxes; if you wish to skip them, feel free to do so.

After you have learned about Symphony, you can do a brief exercise to test your understanding of the information presented in this chapter. Each chapter ends with a self-test to see if you remember the major points presented in the chapter. The answers follow each self-test. (Don't peek!)

Symphony

Symphony adds a 4 and a 5 to the 1, 2, and 3 of Lotus 1-2-3. The 4 is word processing and the 5 is telecommunications. The word processing has most of the features of a stand-alone word processing program. You can use it to write memos, letters, and reports, and you can use it to edit labels and headings and to write detailed instructions on your worksheets. The telecommunications feature lets you send and receive information. You can communicate with other microcomputers, and you can communicate with mainframe computers. The information you receive is immediately available in worksheet form for you to analyze, edit, or print.

The Differences Between 1-2-3 and Symphony

Symphony contains *all* of the features of 1-2-3 so that everything you learn about 1-2-3 will be useful to you when using Symphony. In fact, the best way to learn to use Symphony is to master 1-2-3 first.

The major difference between the two programs has to do with what Symphony calls *environments* and the way Symphony manages its environments, which is through the use of *windows*. Environments correspond to the (worksheet), 2 (database), and 3 (graphics) of 1-2-3. Symphony has five environments; Sheet, Doc, Graph, Form, and Comm. Each environment treats the underlying information in a different way. The Sheet, Form, and Graph environments are very like 1-2-3's worksheet, database, and graphics modes. The Doc (for document) environment is for word processing and the Comm environment is for telecommunications.

Windows are the key to understanding how Symphony manages these five environments. A *window* is the lens through which you view the information you are working with. Different lenses give a different "appearance" to the underlying "reality" which is that everything you do with Symphony is done on a vast spreadsheet of 256 columns and 8,192 rows. All information, text, database specifications, and so forth, is stored in spreadsheet cells.

The appearance or environment is how Symphony treats the underlying information and how that information appears on the screen. The environment also determines the tools Symphony gives you for manipulating the information. In a Sheet environment, it is treated as standard spreadsheet entries and you are given access to spreadsheet tools. In a Doc environment, the underlying cell structure of the worksheet seems to disappear and the blank screen is ready for word processing. Here the tools are word processing tools such as search and replace. The text in a Doc environment is, however, stored in spreadsheet cells, and it can be viewed in those cells by switching to the Sheet environment.

Each time you create a window you assign it an environment. It is impossible to have an environment without a window, and every window must have its designated environment. Thus you may have a Doc window, a Sheet window, and a Form window—all defined on the same or different ranges of cells. You can create as many windows as you like with which to view Symphony's worksheet. (Windows are named to keep them straight.)

The key to Symphony's integration is that while windows are assigned environments, you can change a window's environment at the press of a key. Thus you can create a worksheet in the Sheet environment, switch to Doc to add some text, then switch to Graph to display a graph, based on the information in the worksheet, side by side with the text and the spreadsheet.

Symphony is considerably harder to master than 1-2-3 simply because you have to master the management of windows, and because the program has many more options for each command. These additional options contribute to the overall power of Symphony, but, at times, they can also be confusing. The way to master Symphony is one step at a time—and the first three of those steps are 1-2-3.

SELF-TEST

QUESTIONS

1. What are the three major functions of Lotus 1-2-3?
2. What are two commands that can be used to *construct* a 1-2-3 worksheet?
3. How many different types of graphs can be created with 1-2-3? Name two of them.

ANSWERS

1. Spreadsheet, database, graphics.
2. Format commands (currency, percentage, etc.) and the Copy command.
3. 5. Bar, stacked-bar, XY, line, and pie (any two).

CHAPTER TWO
GETTING READY TO USE 1-2-3

OBJECTIVES

- To learn how to prepare the Lotus program diskettes for operation.
- To learn to load the programs on the Lotus System Disk into your microcomputer's memory.
- To learn to use the Lotus Tutorial Disk to speed your introduction to the program.
- To learn about the functions of the Lotus Access System.
- To become familiar with the Lotus 1-2-3 screen.
- To become familiar with the ways Lotus 1-2-3 uses the keyboard keys.
- To learn to move the cursor around the command line, the entry line and the worksheet.
- To learn to enter values and labels into a worksheet.

"READ THIS FIRST"

You must learn and do a number of basic things before you can begin constructing worksheets with Lotus 1-2-3 or even before you can load the program into your microcomputer. This chapter provides fundamental information needed to get ready to use 1-2-3.

The first time you remove the Lotus 1-2-3 manual from its slip case, a small pamphlet will fall into your lap. It is titled *Getting Started*, and it comes with the admonition "READ ME FIRST." That's a good idea as the tasks outlined in the pamphlet *must* be completed before you can use Lotus 1-2-3. (If the pamphlet falls to the floor and slides under a six-ton safe, don't worry. The same information is in the "Getting Started" section of the manual.)

Every microcomputer uses programs, generally called the Disk Operating System (DOS for short), to manage the flow of information between the computer's memory and the magnetic diskettes where programs and data are stored. Before you can use 1-2-3, you must copy the appropriate DOS program files onto the program diskette. This process is called "installing DOS." The installation procedure required to make Lotus 1-2-3 operational is what is described in detail in the *Getting Started* pamphlet.

Symphony

The steps you must go through to prepare the Symphony diskettes for use on your microcomputer are similar to the steps described on the following pages for 1-2-3. The instructions in the Symphony manual are clear, and when you are running Symphony's Install program, you will have frequent opportunities to ask for help messages, should you need them.

The Program Diskettes

A sealed package at the back of the Lotus manual contains the five diskettes that make up the 1-2-3 program. You will install DOS on these diskettes. They are labeled: System Disk, System Disk (backup copy), Utility Disk, PrintGraph Disk, and Tutorial Disk.

Symphony

The Symphony package contains the following disks: Program Disk, Program Disk (backup copy), PrintGraph Disk, Install Program Disk, Install Library Disk, Tutorial Lessons Disk, and a Help and Tutorial Disk.

The System Disk and the System Disk (backup) are identical. They both contain the programs actually used to create the 1-2-3 electronic spreadsheets. They are often referred to as the "program disks." After you have completed the installation procedure, you will use the System Disk whenever you use 1-2-3, and you should store the backup copy in a safe place.

You must have a backup copy of the System Disk because magnetic diskettes are subject to failure from stray magnetism, static electricity, dust, or simply old age. If something happens to the System Disk, replace it with the backup copy, and use the card in the back of the Lotus manual to order a replacement. There is a nominal charge for this service.

The Utility Disk contains the library of device drivers as well as the programs used by the Lotus Access System. After installation, the Utility Disk will also contain the programs used to format, copy, and compare data diskettes.

The PrintGraph Disk prints the graphs created with the Graph Save command. When required, messages will appear on your computer's screen prompting you to insert the Utility Disk or the PrintGraph Disk into the appropriate disk drive. These prompts appear whenever 1-2-3 requires programs contained on these diskettes.

The last diskette in the package is the Tutorial Disk. It contains six sophisticated, self-paced tutorials designed to introduce you to the major features of Lotus 1-2-3. The tutorials are excellent, and you should work through them early in your introduction to the program.

A word of caution: the tutorials won't turn your computer into a space-age teaching machine. They are best described as demonstration programs. When using them, Lotus only accepts a press of the correct key, so you can't learn from your mistakes, and you can't learn by experimenting on your own. You may even lose interest and fail to read all the text presented on the screen. In any case, the tutorials are *only* an introduction to the program since many of 1-2-3's features aren't discussed in these programs.

After you have completed the installation procedure, you can run the tutorial by inserting the diskette into the system disk drive (usually the left-hand disk drive) and typing the word **TUTOR** followed by pressing the **[ENTER]** key. Note that instructions that are printed in bold type, such as " **TUTOR**," are to be entered from your computer's keyboard letter by letter: **T-U-T-O-R**. Words in bold type and brackets, such as **[ENTER]**, refer to specific keys on the keyboard.

On some computers, the **[ENTER]** key is called the "return" key or the "broken arrow" key. Whatever it is called, it performs the same function. Pressing the **[ENTER]** key causes an action to occur or information to be entered into the worksheet. Consequently, this key will be referred to as the **[ENTER]** key, regardless of the terminology used by a particular brand of computer. (See Appendix A for machine-specific information about the keyboards of different microcomputers.)

Installing DOS

Exactly what you must do to install DOS depends on whether you have a hard disk system or two floppy disk drives. If you have a hard disk system, follow the instructions for copying the Lotus program files onto the hard disk. If you have a two disk drive system, follow the instructions for placing DOS files onto the appropriate diskettes.

The instructions are in the *Getting Started* pamphlet under the title "Transferring DOS Programs," and they are clear and explicit. As you go through the installation, a series of messages appear on the screen to prompt you through the procedure. However, if you aren't familiar with a microcomputer and the general procedure for installing DOS, you should carefully read the entire instructions *before* trying to perform the installation procedure.

Installing Device Drivers

After you have installed DOS on the program diskettes, you have one more step to complete before 1-2-3 is ready to use. This step is to copy from the Utility Diskette to the other diskettes those particular "device drivers" required by your computer system. If you think of your microcomputer as a stereo system where each component must be connected to other components by the correct cables, then the device drivers are the connecting cables. They let 1-2-3 work with the particular pieces of hardware you have chosen for your computer system.

Typically, your system will have either a monochrome monitor (no graphics) or a graphics monitor (which may or may not be a color display). Alternatively, your system will use two monitors; one to display graphics and one to simultaneously display the worksheet. Your computer may also have special circuit boards (or "cards"), such as the Hercules Graphics Card, that let 1-2-3 display graphics on the IBM Monochrome Display. Whatever the combination of equipment in your system, 1-2-3 has drivers that can be installed to take full advantage of your hardware.

If you follow the instructions given in the screen prompts and the pamphlet *Getting Started*, you should have no trouble installing the drivers required by your system. However, if after following the directions you do experience difficulties, return to the beginning and repeat the process. If you still have problems, seek help from the dealer who sold you Lotus 1-2-3.

LOADING THE LOTUS SYSTEM DISK

After you have installed DOS and the appropriate device drivers, you are ready to load 1-2-3 into your computer. There are two ways to do this and the one you choose depends on whether your computer is on or off.

If your computer is off, insert the Lotus System Disk into the default or system drive and close the disk drive door. The default drive is usually the left-hand disk drive of a two-drive system. Once the System Disk is in the correct disk drive, turn the computer on. After a few moments during which your computer performs its power-on self-tests, 1-2-3 will be read into memory.

If your computer is already turned on, insert the System Disk into the default drive and press the **[CTRL]-[ALT]-[DEL]** keys simultaneously. This sequence of keystrokes, called the "system reset," will cause your computer to read into memory any program on a diskette in the system disk drive. (Note: When two or more key names are connected by dashes, the keys are to be pressed and held down in the order indicated. If they are not connected by dashes, the keys are to be pressed and released in sequence.)

The Date/Time Prompts

The first thing that will appear on your screen is the "Date Prompt," Figure 2-1A. After you enter the date, the "Time Prompt," Figure 2-1B, appears. Supply the current date and the correct time in the format required by your computer. If you don't know the format (DD/MM/YY, for example), check your computer's disk operating system manual. Complete the entry with a press of the **[ENTER]** key.

```
A>date
Current date is Tue 1-01-1980
Enter new date: _
```

Figure 2-1A. Date Prompt.

```
A>date
Current date is Tue 1-01-1980
Enter new date: 3-08-85

A>time
Current time is    0:00:33.39
Enter new time:_
```

Figure 2-1B. Time Prompt.

If you want, you can bypass the date and time prompts and accept the default values (usually something arbitrary like midnight January 1, 1980). This is not recommended because Lotus 1-2-3 adds the time and the date to each file that the program stores on a data diskette. This useful information can tell you when a worksheet was last updated, and it can tell you which of two versions of a similar worksheet is the original. Lotus also can sort all filenames on a diskette by the date they were created, but to use this feature, you must enter the correct date each time you load the Lotus System Disk.

Symphony

Setting the current date and time is particularly important when using Symphony since the program displays the date and the time on the bottom left of the screen.

Lotus At The Crossroads: The Access System

After you have responded to the date and time prompts, the menu for the Lotus Access System, Figure 2-2, appears on the screen. The Access System is a kind of crossroads. From here you can go directly into the worksheet program or you can branch off to perform a number of other tasks.

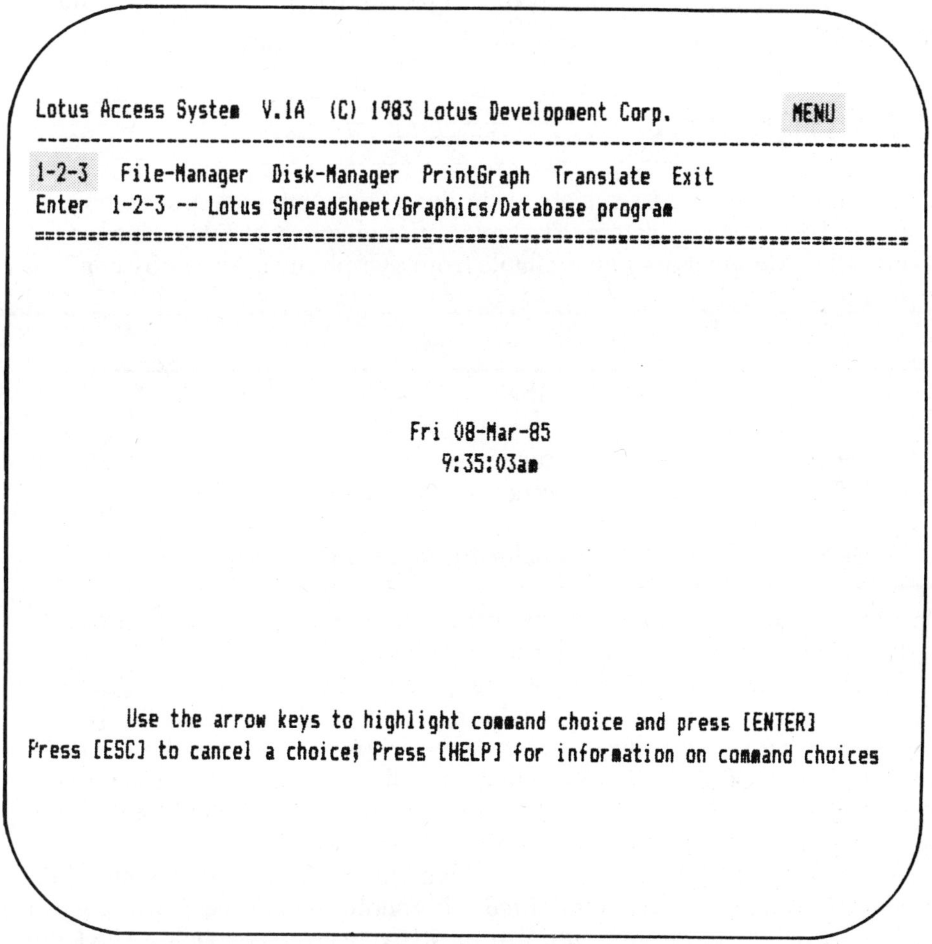

```
Lotus Access System V.1A  (C) 1983 Lotus Development Corp.          MENU
------------------------------------------------------------------------
1-2-3   File-Manager  Disk-Manager  PrintGraph  Translate  Exit
Enter  1-2-3 -- Lotus Spreadsheet/Graphics/Database program
========================================================================




                           Fri 08-Mar-85
                            9:35:03am






       Use the arrow keys to highlight command choice and press [ENTER]
 Press [ESC] to cancel a choice; Press [HELP] for information on command choices
```

Figure 2-2. The Lotus Access System menu.

The Lotus Access System menu is typical of the 1-2-3 menus you will encounter throughout the program. Like a restaurant menu that presents you with the dilemma of choosing between a Baked Alaska and Chocolate Truffles, a 1-2-3 menu gives you choices between options.

In this case, the options are 1-2-3, File-Manager, Disk-Manager, PrintGraph, Translate, and Exit. They are displayed on the command line of the menu. It is called the command line because these are the commands that you can currently issue to 1-2-3. The line below the command line is called the prompt line. It gives you additional information about the choice on the command line that is currently highlighted by the bright bar of light called the *command line cursor.*

| Symphony |

The Symphony Access system is similar in function and appearance to the 1-2-3 Access System. The only difference is that File-Manager and Disk-Manager are not available from Symphony's Access System menu.

In Figure 2-2, the command line cursor highlights 1-2-3, and the prompt line tells you that if you select this command, you will:

Enter 1-2-3 — Lotus Spreadsheet/Graphics/Database program.

The prompt line changes each time the command line cursor moves to highlight a different option on the command line.

You can select a choice from this or any other Lotus menu in two different ways: you can type the first character of your choice (for example, **[F]** for File-Manager), or you can point to your choice by using the **[RIGHT ARROW]** and **[LEFT ARROW]** keys to move the command line cursor to the right or the left until it highlights the desired option. Once highlighted, the option is selected by pressing the **[ENTER]** key.

As you can see from Figure 2-2, when the Access System menu first appears, the choice 1-2-3 is highlighted. This choice—to proceed directly to a 1-2-3 worksheet—is the one you are most likely to make. It is called the *proposed response;* the response Lotus "proposes" you select by having it appear highlighted by the command line cursor when the menu first appears.

Lotus always proposes a response when a choice is required. If the proposed response is the one you want, choose it by simply pressing the **[ENTER]** key. If the proposed response isn't the desired choice, you can choose another.

The choices on the command line of the Lotus Access System menu are described in the following paragraphs. If you select File-Manager, Disk-Manager, or Translate, a message appears prompting you to insert the Utility Diskette. If you choose PrintGraph, you are prompted to insert the PrintGraph Diskette. If you are using a hard disk, the correct programs will be loaded automatically.

1-2-3 The first choice on the menu is 1-2-3. If you make this choice, you will move out of the Access System and into a Lotus 1-2-3 worksheet.

File-Manager As you create worksheets, you will store the results on a data diskette for future use. When you select File-Manager from the Access System menu, follow the screen prompt and insert the the Utility Diskette. Then press **[ENTER]** and the screen will change to look like that shown in Figure 2-3. The screen displays the filenames of the files on the current data diskette or in the current directory if you are using a hard disk. A new menu also appears across the top of the screen.

```
LOTUS File Management System V.1A (C)1983 LOTUS Development Corp.    MENU
--------------------------------------------------------------------------------
Copy  Erase  Rename  Archive  Disk-Drive  Sort  Quit
Copy selected files from the current disk to another.
================================================================================
  FILENAME EXT   DATE     TIME    SIZE
  BA110    WKS  05-Jan-82  3:09pm  19200
  BA110APH WKS  05-Jan-80  1:54pm  19072
  BIO      WKS  03-Nov-82  7:28pm   6912
  BOOKTBL  WKS  09-Apr-83 11:35am  14967        Current Drive:     B
  BOOKTODO WKS  05-Apr-83  5:29am   5248        Number of Files:   36
  CAR      WKS  31-Oct-82 10:26am   6144        Total Bytes Used:  303104
  CCC      PRN  04-Apr-83  9:09pm   3200        Total Bytes Free:  19456
  CCCLIST  WKS  04-Apr-83  9:08pm   5376
  CH11TEST WKS  12-Jan-80  0:13pm  11904
  CH12MACR WKS  21-Apl-83  2:43pm   3840
  CH12TA   WKS  21-Apl-83  2:45pm   3840
  DATATBL  WKS  12-Jan-83 12:18pm   5120
  DATATBL  PRN  12-Jan-83 12:21pm   3456
  DEDSORTE WKS  09-Apr-83 11:41am  17920
  DEMOHOTE WKS  18-Nov-82  3:31am  24448
  DIV2     WKS  22-Sep-83  1:52pm   2560
  DIV3     WKS  22-Sep-83  2:31pm   6656
  DIVIDEND WKS  23-Sep-83  9:04am   6784
```

Figure 2-3. File-Manager menu.

The File-Manager allows you to perform operations on files by selecting options from the command line of the File-Manager menu in exactly the same way you selected the File-Manager option from the Access System menu. Once again, the line below the command line gives an extended description of the choice currently highlighted by the command line cursor.

Copy copies the selected files to another diskette. *Erase* erases selected files. The *Sort* option sorts the files on the diskette by any of the columns. (In Figure 2-3, the files have been alphabetized by filename.) The *Archive* option allows you to create a copy of a selected file under another name. This is called "backing up the worksheet," and you must do it regularly because worksheets and files can sometimes be damaged accidentally. Finally, *Quit* quits the File-Manager and returns you to the Access System menu.

When in the File-Manager, you can point to files you wish to mark by moving the bar of light in the filename's display up or down with the arrow keys. When the bar of light is on a filename, you can mark it for processing (erase or copy, for example), and you can mark several files for processing at one time. Also notice that the File-Manager tells you the total number of files on the current data diskette, the number of bytes used, and the number of bytes free on the diskette.

Disk-Manager   To use a magnetic diskette as a data storage diskette, it must first be *formatted*. This process of preparing a diskette for use by 1-2-3 is performed by choosing the *Prepare* option from the Disk-Manager menu. Once chosen, messages appear on the screen to prompt you through the formatting process. Another Disk-Manager option is *Disk-Copy*. It makes an exact copy of a diskette. This is how you backup all the worksheet files on a diskette at one time. Finally, *Compare* verifies that two diskettes are exact duplicates, and *Status* reports overall disk usage statistics.

PrintGraph   This option is used to transfer control to the PrintGraph Disk. Once the PrintGraph Disk has been loaded, a menu appears and you make the choices necessary to print the graphs you have created with the Graph Save command.

Translate   This option is the "Berlitz" of the Lotus Access System. With it you can take VisiCalc worksheets or files from the popular database management program, dBASE II, and translate them into 1-2-3 worksheets.

The Translate feature is very important because it extends the power of 1-2-3 to information created and stored by other programs. If you have a library of VisiCalc worksheets, for example, you can convert them to 1-2-3 files at the push of a few keys. If you want to use 1-2-3 commands and functions on information in a dBASE II file, you can import the file, process it, then export it for reuse with dBASE II.

You can also use the Translate option to import or export information in Data Interchange Format (DIF) files. DIF files have a standard organization, and they are popular for moving information between different software programs.

Exit The final option on the Access System menu is Exit. When selected, Lotus returns program control to your computer's disk operating system.

HELP!!!: The Lotus Help Facility

You may have noticed the message at the bottom of the screen in Figure 2-2. It reads, in part,

• Press **[HELP]** for information on command choices.

The **[HELP]** key is the gateway to a library of more than 250 interrelated help screens. When you press **[HELP]** the display is replaced by a screen of information keyed to your needs at the moment. If, for example, you press **[HELP]** while the Access System menu is displayed, the screen will change to that shown in Figure 2-4 on the next page.

There are several things you should know about Lotus help screens. First, the number in the line below and to the right of the Access System menu, 11 in this case, refers to page 11 in the Lotus 1-2-3 manual. If the information on the screen isn't enough, you know exactly where to look in the manual to get more help. Second, while the Access System help screen stands alone, most other help screens are connected to other help screens and to a master index of help screens. You can view one related help screen after another until you have satisfied your need for information.

Finally, you can press the **[ESC]** key at any time in any help screen, and 1-2-3 will return you to the exact point in the program from which you asked for help. Nothing will have changed, and you can continue your work.

KEYBOARD TOUR

When you are moving into a worksheet from the Lotus Access System, pause a moment to take a tour of your microcomputer's keyboard. Appendix A contains the assignments for the most popular microcomputers that currently use Lotus 1-2-3. While each microcomputer has the same functions, the exact names and locations of some of the keys differ, so consult the table that corresponds to your computer.

```
Lotus Access System  V.1A  (C) 1983 Lotus Development Corp.        MENU
-----------------------------------------------------------------------
1-2-3   File-Manager  Disk-Manager  PrintGraph  Translate  Exit
Enter  1-2-3 -- Lotus Spreadsheet/Graphics/Database program
=================================================================== || ============

The Lotus Access System provides an easy, menu-driven way to access both the
Lotus programs (1-2-3 and PrintGraph) and supporting functions.  Picking a menu
choice is easy. Just use the arrow keys to move to the selection you want,
then press the [ENTER] key.  Here are the Lotus Access System functions in
a nutshell:


          1-2-3  Use 1-2-3
    File-Manager  Use the File-Manager program
    Disk-Manager  Use the Disk-Manager program
      PrintGraph  Use the PrintGraph program
       Translate  Use the Translate program
            Exit  Exit the Lotus Access System


Want more information on Lotus Access System functions?  After you select the
function, press the [HELP] function key.  A screen of information concerning
the function will appear.


                        Press the [ESC] key to continue
```

Figure 2-4. Help screen for the Lotus Access System menu.

To keep the instructions concrete, the next few pages will refer to the keyboards for the IBM Personal Computer and the Texas Instruments Professional Computer. (See Figures 2-5 and 2-6.) These two machines are among the most popular computers running Lotus 1-2-3, and their keyboards are typical of other microcomputer keyboards.

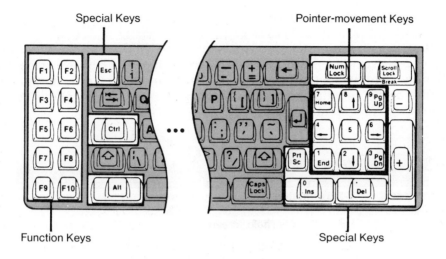

Figure 2-5. Layout of the keys on the IBM Personal Computer Keyboard.

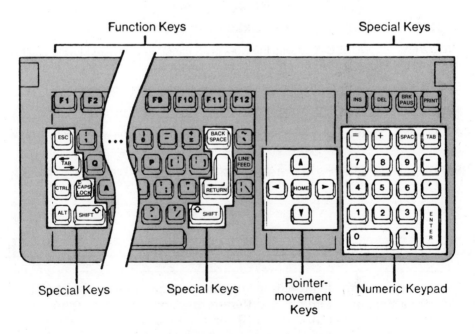

Figure 2-6. Layout of keys on the Texas Instruments Professional Computer Keyboard.

The Function Keys

The function keys are a set of keys (10 on the IBM PC, 12 on the TI PC) to which 1-2-3 assigns special commands. The IBM function keys are to the left of the keyboard, while the Texas Instruments' function keys are across the top. Both sets of function keys perform the same tasks. The functions Lotus assigns to the first 10 function keys are shown in Table 2-1.

TABLE 2-1

Lotus 1-2-3 function key assignments.

Function Key	1-2-3 Function
[HELP]	HELP: Displays help screen.
[EDIT]	EDIT: Places 1-2-3 into Edit mode. Allows you to edit entries under the worksheet cursor.
[NAME]	NAME: In Point mode displays the names you have assigned to ranges of cells.
[ABS]	ABSOLUTE: In Point mode changes a relative cell reference to an absolute cell reference or vice versa.
[GOTO]	GOTO: Moves the worksheet cursor to the designated cell.
[WINDOW]	WINDOW: Moves the worksheet cursor from one window to another when the screen is split into two windows.
[QUERY]	QUERY: Repeats the most recent Data Query operation.
[TABLE]	TABLE: Repeats the most recent Data Table operation.
[CALC]	CALCULATION: In Ready mode recalculates the worksheet. In Value and Edit modes converts formulas to their current values.
[GRAPH]	GRAPH: Draws a graph according to the most recent graph specifications.

Symphony

Symphony uses the ten function keys in combination with the **[ALT]** key for a total of twenty-three different functions. Many of the 1-2-3 function keys, **[CALC]** and **[ABS]** for example, perform the same functions in Symphony. There are, however, a great many function keys that are unique to Symphony (Figure 2-7).

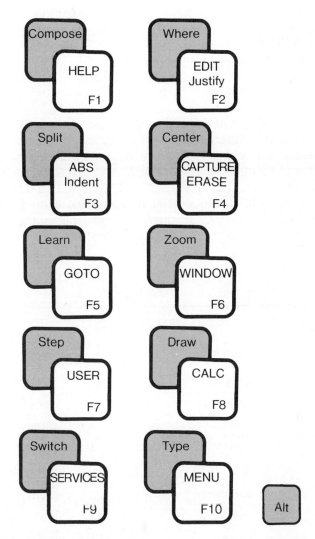

Figure 2-7. Symphony Function Key Assignments.

The most frequently used function keys are **[HELP]**, **[EDIT]**, and **[CALC]**. You have already seen the **[HELP]** key in action in the Access System. Use it whenever you're uncertain about what to do next. The help screens are particularly useful when trying to use a function or feature with which you are not familiar. The **[EDIT]** key lets you correct mistakes without having to completely retype the entry. The **[CALC]** key is used whenever you want to recalculate all of the formulas on a worksheet.

The other function keys have more specialized uses. For example, the **[NAME]** key is used to display the names you have assigned to ranges of cells. The **[GRAPH]**, **[TABLE]** and **[QUERY]** keys repeat the most recent graph, data query, or data table operation.

The Typewriter Keyboard

The large, central area of the keyboard is taken up by a typewriter-style set of keys. In addition to the standard keys for letters, numbers, and symbols such as @, #, and $, the typewriter keyboard has a number of special keys.

These keys include the escape **[ESC]**, control **[CTRL]**, and alternate **[ALT]** keys as well as the capital lock **[CAP LOCK]** key and the enter **[ENTER]** key. Most keys are referred to by the names printed on them, but on some keyboards, some keys (such as the tab, backspace, and shift keys) have only symbols. Table 2-2 shows the designation for these and certain other keys.

TABLE 2-2
Keys and their corresponding reference.

Key Symbol	Function	Will be Referred to as:
[↵]	entry or carriage return	[ENTER]
[←]	backspace	[BKSP]
[⇧]	shift	[SHIFT]
[⇥]	tab	[TAB]
[↑]	up arrow	[UP ARROW]
[↓]	down arrow	[DOWN ARROW]
[→]	right arrow	[RIGHT ARROW]
[←]	left arrow	[LEFT ARROW]

Among the special keys, the escape **[ESC]** key is a very important key in Lotus 1-2-3. Whenever you press it, you will *back up one step* in whatever command or function you are creating. The "undo" power of the **[ESC]** key is extremely handy, and you will use it often when constructing worksheets. If you would like to change what you have done and using the escape **[ESC]** key isn't enough, you can press **[CTRL]-[C]** or **[CTRL]-[BREAK]** (they are equivalent). When you do this, the *entire* command, entry, or formula will be canceled.

You should be aware of several differences between computer keys and similar keys on a conventional typewriter. The space bar, for example, is a real character: a space. Consequently, the space bar on a computer *can't* be used to move from character to character the way it can on a typewriter. If you try to use it this way, it will erase characters by inserting the space character in their place. The same situation occurs with the **[BKSP]** key. Each time it is pressed, it replaces a character with the space character.

The **[CAP LOCK]** key differs from the **[SHIFT LOCK]** key on a typewriter. On many computers, it shifts only the 26 letters of the alphabet to capitals. In particular, it doesn't shift the row of keys across the top of the keyboard from numbers to symbols. You must press a separate **[SHIFT]** key to have access to those symbols.

Finally, to the right of the IBM PC keyboard is a special key labeled **[PrtSc]**. (It also appears on many machines compatible with the IBM PC.) If the printer attached to your computer is turned on, **[SHIFT]-[PrtSc]** will produce a printout of everything currently displayed on the screen. You can use **[SHIFT]-[PrtSc]** instead of 1-2-3's Print command to get a quick "snapshot" of the screen's contents.

The Number Pad and Arrow Keys

To the right of the typewriter keys are the number pad and the arrow keys. The number pad is laid out like a ten-key adding machine and can be used for the quick entry of numbers. The arrow keys (up, down, left, and right) are used to move the different 1-2-3 cursors.

On some machines, such as the IBM PC, the number pad and the arrow keys are combined. To use one or the other, you must use the **[NUM LOCK]** key to shift between them. This generally means you must use the keys either for cursor movement or for number entry. (You can also use the **[SHIFT]** keys to move between numbers and arrows, or vice versa, depending on whether the **[NUM LOCK]** key is engaged.)

Other machines, such as the Texas Instruments PC or the Digital Equipment Rainbow, have a separate set of arrow keys. These machines conveniently let you use the arrow keys and the number pad without having to shift between the two functions.

On the IBM PC, some additional keys are located in the area of the number pad. The **[HOME]**, **[END]**, **[PgUp]**, and **[PgDn]** keys perform special cursor control functions, and the **[DEL]** key can be used to delete characters when editing an entry. Another key found on most keyboards is the **[SCROLL LOCK/BREAK]** key. Sometimes they are separate keys and sometimes they are shifted and unshifted versions of the same key. The **[SCROLL LOCK]** key is used by 1-2-3 for certain cursor control tasks. The **[BREAK]** key is used in conjunction with the **[CTRL]** key to cancel an entry or a command.

You have now been introduced to the different keys. Since much of the power and richness of Lotus 1-2-3 comes from the extensive use the program makes of the keyboard, you must become familiar with all the functions of all the keys. That is a formidable task, but don't worry; that familiarity will be a natural outgrowth of your increasing knowledge of Lotus 1-2-3.

Symphony

The Symphony Sheet (for "worksheet") environment doesn't have the back-lit row and column borders that characterize the 1-2-3 screen. Otherwise, they are functionally equivalent (Figure 2.8). Also, notice the window name, MAIN, in the lower right corner and MENU, in the upper right corner. The date and the time are also displayed in the lower left corner.

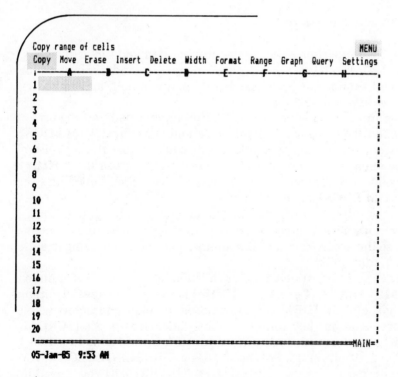

Figure 2-8. Symphony Sheet Environment Screen.

SCREEN TOUR

Now, turn your attention to the Lotus 1-2-3 worksheet screen. To get the screen to appear on your monitor, select the 1-2-3 option on the Access System menu. The next thing to appear will be the Lotus copyright notice accompanied by the instruction to "press any key to proceed." After pressing a key, the word "WAIT" flashes in the upper right corner of the screen while more of the 1-2-3 program is read into memory. After a few moments, "WAIT" is replaced by "READY," and a screen like the one shown in Figure 2-9 appears.

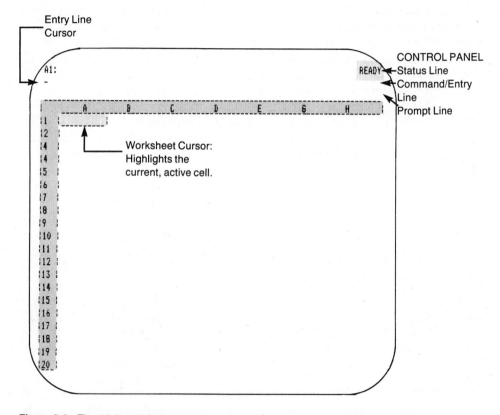

Figure 2-9. The 1-2-3 worksheet screen.

The 1-2-3 Worksheet

The first thing to notice about the 1-2-3 screen is that it is divided into two parts. The top part is called the *control panel*. It is in the same location as the Lotus Access System menu discussed above. (In fact, the Access System Menu is a specialized control panel.)

The larger part of the screen, below the control panel, displays a small fraction of the 1-2-3 worksheet. This area is bordered on the left by the numbers 1 to 20 and on the top by the letters A to H. In this section, you will learn about the worksheet. In the next section, you will learn about the control panel.

If you think of rows and columns intersecting to form a vast field of "cubbyholes", you will have a good idea of the structure of a 1-2-3 worksheet. Each cubbyhole, or *cell*, is formed by the intersection of a row and a column. Each cell has a unique name or *address* which is simply the letter of the column followed by the number of the row which intersect to form the cell. Therefore, the cell at the intersection of column E and row 5 is called "E5"; the one at the intersection of column B and row 20 is called "B20."

The 1-2-3 worksheet is made up of many, many rows and many, many columns. In fact, there are 2,048 rows and 256 columns for a total of 524,288 cells. This vast number of cells lets you construct many interrelated tables on a single worksheet, or single tables with many columns and many rows. The worksheet is so large, in fact, that if it were drawn out on a single sheet of paper, each cell 1/4″ high and 1″ long (about the size of a normal cell on the screen), the paper would be more than 21′ wide and 42′ high!

Of course, you can see only a few of the over one-half million cells at one time. In Figure 2-7, where each cell is nine characters wide, only 160 cells (8 columns and 20 rows) are on the screen at one time. Figure 2-10 shows the relationship between the actual 1-2-3 worksheet stored in memory and the visible portion displayed on your computer screen.

Think of your monitor as the window in the bottom of a glass-bottomed boat and the entire worksheet as the bottom of some exotic bay. Only a small fraction of the "bay", or worksheet is visible at one time and what is visible can be made to change as the "boat," or monitor moves. Later in this chapter, you will learn about the many ways 1-2-3 has for making any of the 524,288 cells appear on the screen.

The Worksheet Cursor   The most striking feature about the worksheet as it appears on your screen is the *worksheet cursor*, the bright bar of light in the upper left corner. The worksheet cursor highlights the one cell out of all the cells on the worksheet that is active at the moment.

Worksheets are constructed by placing text, numbers, or formulas into each cell. The cell currently available for receiving information is the one

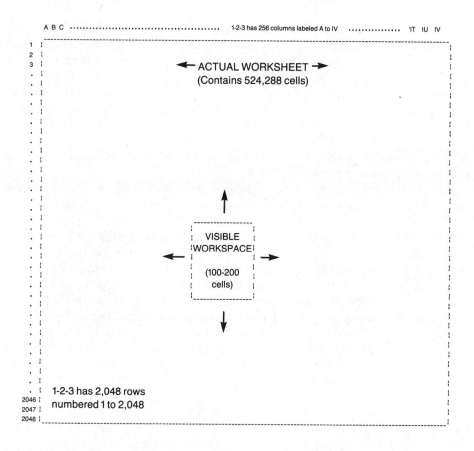

A B C ....   1-2-3 has 256 columns labeled A to IV   ....   'IT IU IV

← ACTUAL WORKSHEET →
(Contains 524,288 cells)

VISIBLE
WORKSPACE

(100-200
cells)

1-2-3 has 2,048 rows
numbered 1 to 2,048

Figure 2-10. Relationship between the portion of the worksheet visible on your monitor screen at any one time and virtual 1-2-3 worksheet kept in your computer's memory.

under the worksheet cursor. Thus, it is called the *current* or *active cell*. In Figure 2-7, cell A1 is the active cell because that is where the worksheet cursor is located.

The Control Panel

As noted, the section at the top of the screen is called the *control panel*. It gives you information about the current active cell, about the entries you are typing, and about any commands you are selecting.

Constructing an electronic spreadsheet with Lotus 1-2-3 is a two-step process. The control panel is like an electronic scratch pad on which you first prepare your instructions. These instructions can be entries typed as text or numbers, or they can be functions or commands that are built into 1-2-3. Whatever they are, the choices you make appear first in the control panel. You may then edit what you have typed or you may change your mind and back up one or more steps with the **[ESC]** key. You may also decide to cancel everything with a **[CTRL]-[BREAK]**. In any case, whatever you type will not *actually* be entered into a cell on the worksheet until you complete the command or issue the final **[ENTER]**.

The control panel is made up of three lines: the status line, the command line, and the prompt line. Each line displays a different type of information.

The Status Line   The top line of the control panel is the *status line* (see Figure 2-7). It gives you information about the status of the current, active cell. This information includes the address of the cell and its actual content. It also includes information about any local formats that have been set and whether the contents of the active cell is protected from accidental change.

The other piece of information displayed on the status line is the current "mode" in which 1-2-3 is operating. The *mode indicator* is prominently displayed at the right end of the status line in reverse video (black letters on a bright field). You have already been introduced to the Wait and Ready modes. 1-2-3 can operate in eight other modes: Help, Menu, Value, Label, Edit, Error, Find, and Point.

Some keys produce different actions when pressed in one mode or another. The **[RIGHT ARROW]** and **[LEFT ARROW]** keys, for example, move different cursors in Edit mode than when in Point or Menu mode.

In Figure 2-7, the worksheet is in Ready mode. When you press the **[HELP]** key, the mode changes to Help, and a help screen appears. If you begin to type text, the mode changes to Label. As you can see, your actions determine in which mode 1-2-3 operates. Remember, you can always cancel everything and return to the Ready mode by typing **[CTRL]-[BREAK]** or by pressing the **[ESC]** key the necessary number of times.

Command Line   You already learned about the middle line of the control panel, the *command line*, when you learned about the Access System menu. When in Menu mode (as with the Access System), the command line displays the currently available command options. When in Label or Value mode, the command line displays the text or value you are typing. In Edit mode, the command line displays the contents of the active cell, ready for editing.

In Value or Label mode, what you type appears on the command line before it is entered into the worksheet. Because of these different uses, the command line is sometimes referred to as the "edit line" or the "entry line."

Whatever it is called, the command line is where your electronic pencil first touches your electronic paper. It is your point of contact with Lotus 1-2-3.

Command Line Cursor The command line has two types of cursors to indicate which place on the command line is active. In Menu mode, the command line cursor is a bar of light much like the worksheet cursor. It highlights each command as you use the arrow keys to move it from left to right.

When in Ready, Value, Label, or Edit mode, the command line cursor is a flashing bar of light that is one character wide and in the position of the underline character. Each time you type a character, the character appears on the command line at the cursor position, and the cursor moves one space to the right. Since this cursor locates the position where the next character or entry will take place, it is often called the *entry line cursor*.

The Prompt Line You are also familiar with the *prompt line* from its use in the Access System menu. The prompt line prompts you through a command by displaying useful information about your current choice.

Symphony

Symphony's control panel has a slightly different layout than 1-2-3's, but 1-2-3 users will adapt to it quickly. First, the Symphony control panel contains only two lines instead of 1-2-3's three. In both programs, the top or first line is the status line. It contains information about the current cell and, on the right, the mode indicator. In Symphony, however, this line is shared with the prompt line so that whenever you call up a menu, the information about the current cell is replaced with a prompt.

The second line is the command line in both 1-2-3 and Symphony. Menu choices are displayed on this line.

Finally, in 1-2-3 the third line is the prompt line, while there is no third line in the Symphony control panel. Surprisingly, displaying the prompt line above the the command line makes Symphony's commands markedly easier to use than 1-2-3's.

In addition to the rearrangement of the lines in the control panel, Symphony keeps track of where you are in a command by displaying the command and any subcommands you have selected at the bottom left of the screen.

The Bottom Line: Error Messages and Key Indicators

There is one other line to look at on the 1-2-3 screen. The last line of the screen, the one below the worksheet, is reserved for error messages to the left of the line and for a series of key indicators to the right of the line. In Figure 2-11 the key indicators show that the **[NUM LOCK]**, **[CAP LOCK]**, **[SCROLL LOCK]**, and **[END]** keys have all been engaged. This is very useful information since many computers, most notably the IBM PC, give no indication when one or another of these keys is or is not engaged. You can make annoying mistakes, for example, if you think the arrow keys are active when the **[NUM LOCK]** key is engaged. Instead of moving the worksheet cursor, you will be typing numbers.

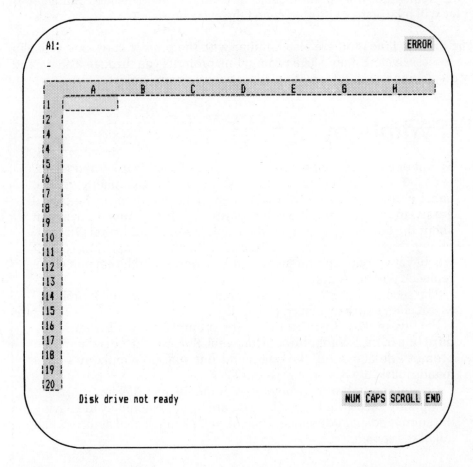

Figure 2-11. 1-2-3 worksheet screen with key indicators and an error message displayed on the bottom line of the screen.

Error messages displayed on the bottom line in Figure 2-11, such as the "Disk drive not ready", are usually self-explanatory. When you receive one, you must press either the **[ENTER]** or the **[ESC]** key to confirm that you have read the error message. You can then take the appropriate action to correct the error. (In this case, make sure the correct diskette is inserted in the drive and the disk drive door is closed.) If you press any other key, you will receive a "beep," and you will remain in Error mode. If you need more information about the specific meaning of an error message, consult the manual.

GETTING AROUND:
THE CURSOR CONTROL KEYS

In the screen tour just completed, you saw that 1-2-3 has three different cursors: two in the control panel (the command line cursor and the entry line cursor) and one in the main body of the worksheet (the worksheet cursor). To use any one of these cursors, you must be able to move it. To move each cursor around its particular area, 1-2-3 provides a rich set of cursor control keys. This section covers the general cursor control commands. Specialized cursor control commands are covered in later sections in the context in which they are used. Note that the exact action of a key such as **[HOME]** or **[END]** often depends on which mode 1-2-3 is in.

Getting Around the Command Line

When in Menu mode, the command line cursor is controlled by the **[RIGHT ARROW]**, **[LEFT ARROW]**, **[HOME]**, and **[END]** keys. The **[RIGHT ARROW]** and **[LEFT ARROW]** keys move the cursor to the right and left, while the **[HOME]** and **[END]** keys move the cursor to the beginning and the end of the command line. If you try to move the cursor beyond the left or right end of the command line with the arrow keys, the cursor will "circle" around and appear at the opposite end of the line.

Getting Around the Entry Line

The **[RIGHT ARROW]**, **[LEFT ARROW]**, **[HOME]**, and **[END]** keys also control the entry line cursor when 1-2-3 is in Value, Label, or Edit mode. The **[HOME]** and **[END]** keys move the entry line cursor to and from the beginning and end of the entry. The arrow keys move the cursor one character to the right or left. You can also use the **[SPACE BAR]** and the **[BKSP]** key to move the cursor one character, but they will *erase* any characters over which they move the cursor.

The **[DEL]** key can be used in Edit mode. It deletes the character at the cursor location. Characters to the right move to the left to fill the space. One character is deleted each time you press the **[DEL]** key.

Getting Around the Worksheet

Moving the worksheet cursor is one of the most common and important functions you perform while using 1-2-3. In Ready mode, you move the worksheet cursor in order to place text, numbers, or a formula into the appropriate cell. In Point mode, you use the worksheet cursor to point to cells to determine the range of operation for a function or for a command such as Copy, Print, or Move.

Lotus 1-2-3 has many different ways to control the worksheet cursor's movement. First, learn to use the primary cursor control keys. You will use these keys most often. Next, learn the context-determined cursor control keys. Context-determined cursor control is unique to 1-2-3, and in many situations it gives you the most flexible, powerful way to move the worksheet cursor. Finally, after you have mastered the primary and context-determined movements, there are some less frequently used cursor control keys to learn to use.

Primary Cursor Control Keys

The most important cursor control keys are the four arrow keys. Each key— **[UP ARROW]**, **[DOWN ARROW]**, **[LEFT ARROW]**, and **[RIGHT ARROW]**—moves the worksheet cursor in the direction indicated.

You will hear a "beep" the call of the "Wild Lotus" if the active cell is at the edge of the worksheet (row 1 or 2,048, column A or IV) and you attempt to move the worksheet cursor off the worksheet. The "beep" tells you that you are trying to do something forbidden by 1-2-3. (Lotus will always "beep" to alert you to any error.)

If the worksheet cursor is at the edge of the screen, but *not* at the edge of the worksheet (cell I40 for example), and you move the worksheet cursor beyond the edge of the screen the screen will *scroll*. Using the analogy of the glass bottomed boat, the screen will slide (scroll) over the worksheet exposing new rows or columns just as the boat glides over the water exposing new parts of the bottom of the bay.

If, for example, the screen is scrolled to the right, columns will be added at the right edge of the screen (the direction the cursor is moving), and they will be deleted from the opposite edge. Scrolling the screen with the arrow keys is one of the most important ways to get particular cells to appear on the screen. If you want cell A35 to appear, simply use the appropriate arrow keys to move the worksheet cursor until row 35 and column A appear on the screen at the same time.

The next primary cursor control key is the **[GOTO]** key. In many situations, you will want to move to a cell far removed from the current cursor location. An example is when the cursor is in cell A1 and you want to move it to cell BK365. Scrolling there with the arrow keys would take 30 or 40 seconds—a *lifetime* in the world of microcomputers! However, you can use the **[GOTO]** function key to move the worksheet cursor directly to BK365. To use it, press **[GOTO]**, type the cell address you wish to go to (BK365, for example), and press **[ENTER]**. The worksheet cursor skips to the designated cell instantly.

The final primary cursor control key is the **[HOME]** key. Pressing the **[HOME]** key moves the worksheet cursor to cell A1. It is like a dedicated **[GOTO]** key where the cell to go to is always A1. This cell is called the "home position" because that is where the worksheet cursor first appears when the 1-2-3 worksheet is loaded into your computer's memory.

Context-Determined Cursor Control Keys

A very impressive set of context-determined cursor controls is provided by 1-2-3. To let the context or structure of your worksheet determine where the cursor will move, first press the **[END]** key, and then press the arrow key for the desired direction.

When using the **[END]** arrow key combination to move the cursor, different things will happen depending on whether *the next cell in the indicated direction is blank or contains an entry.*

If the cell is *blank*, the cursor will move in the indicated direction to the next cell containing an entry. For example, in Table 2-3, when the cursor is on "F. D. Roosevelt" in cell C10 and the **[END] [RIGHT ARROW]** combination is pressed, the cursor moves to the right, across empty cell D10, until the cursor encounters the next cell containing an entry. That cell is E10, and that is where the cursor comes to rest.

On the other hand, if the next cell in the designated direction *contains an entry*, the cursor will move to the last cell before the next blank cell in the column or row. Once again in Table 2-3 on page 40, if the cursor is on C10 and this time the **[END] [DOWN ARROW]** combination is pressed, the cursor will move down to the cell immediately preceding the next blank cell in the down direction. Can you find this cell? It is the one containing "Cleveland," cell C17.

Once you master moving the worksheet cursor with the **[END]** arrow key combination, you will find it an easy, natural way to move the worksheet cursor around an already constructed worksheet.

TABLE 2-3

Context-determined cursor control movements. Typing **[END] [RIGHT ARROW]** moves the cursor across the empty cell D10 to the next cell that contains an entry, E10. Typing **[END] [DOWN ARROW]** moves the cursor to cell C17, the cell before the next empty cell in column C.

	A	B	C	D	E	F
1						
2						
3			PORTRAITS ON U.S. TREASURY BILLS, BONDS,			
4			NOTES, AND SAVINGS BONDS			
5						
6			Savings	Treasury	Treasury	Treasury
7	Denomination		Bonds	Bills	Bonds	Notes
8	==============		===============	===============	============	=========
9	$25		Washington_____		_____	
10	$50		¦F. D. Roosevelt¦————————————→¦Jefferson___ ¦			
11	$75		Truman			
12	$100		Eisenhower		Jackson	
13	$200		Kennedy			
14	$500		Wilson		Washington	
15	$1,000		T. Roosevelt¦	H. McCullock	Lincoln	Lincoln
16	$5,000		McKinley_____ ▼	J. G. Carlisle	Monroe	Monroe
17	$10,000		¦Cleveland_____¦	J. Sherman	Cleveland	Cleveland
18	$50,000			C. Glass		
19	$100,000			A. Gallantin	Grant	Grant
20	$1,000,000			D. Wolcott	T. Roosevelt	T. Roosevelt
21	$100,000,000					Madison
22	$500,000,000					McKinley
23						
24						
25						

The other context-determined cursor control is the **[END] [HOME]** combination. This moves the cursor to the lower right cell of *your* table. This feature is particularly useful in the Print command where you have to specify the range of cells to be printed.

The context-determined cursor movements, like all other cursor controls, can be used *anytime* you need to move the 1-2-3 worksheet cursor. In particular, many of 1-2-3's commands and functions require you to specify the range of cells over which an action such a copying, moving, or adding is to take place. You can make good use of context-determined cursor control in these situations.

Secondary Cursor Control Keys

The **[TAB]**, **[PgUp]**, **[PgDn]**, and **[SCROLL LOCK]** keys can also be used to move the worksheet cursor. The **[TAB]** and the **[SHIFT]-[TAB]** (back tab) keys move the cursor one screen to the right or the left. The **[CTRL]-[RIGHT ARROW]** and **[CTRL]-[LEFT ARROW]** also produce the same cursor movements as **[TAB]** and **[SHIFT]-[TAB]**. These cursor controls are useful for quick horizontal scrolling of the screen. Once you have the right section of the worksheet in view, you can use the arrow keys to move the desired cell.

Symphony

The **[TAB]** and **[SHIFT]-[TAB]** keys *do not* move the Symphony worksheet cursor. The "big right" and "big left" moves are accomplished in Symphony with the **[CTRL]-[RIGHT ARROW]** and **[CTRL]-[LEFT ARROW]** combinations only. Otherwise, 1-2-3 and Symphony have the same cursor control commands.

The **[PgUp]** and **[PgDn]** keys move the screen one page up or one page down. They can be used for quick vertical scrolling of the screen in the same way **[TAB]** and **[SHIFT]-[TAB]** are used to scroll the screen horizontally.

Finally, cursor control can be accomplished with the **[SCROLL LOCK]** key engaged. (You will see a message appear at the bottom of the 1-2-3 screen whenever the **[SCROLL LOCK]** key is active.) However, moving the worksheet cursor with the arrow keys when the **[SCROLL LOCK]** key is engaged takes some getting used to.

When the worksheet cursor is in the middle of the screen and the **[SCROLL LOCK]** key is engaged, the arrow keys cause the *screen* to move in the direction indicated. The worksheet cursor *remains* in its initial cell, but rows or columns (in the case of the right or left arrow keys) are removed from the screen in the indicated direction while rows (or columns) are added at the opposite edge. You can use the **[SCROLL LOCK]** and the arrow keys whenever you want to keep the cursor positioned where it is, but want to see more of the rows or columns immediately off the worksheet.

When the worksheet cursor reaches the edge of the screen, it is "immovable object meets irresistible force" time. Something has to give. The screen can't continue to move while the worksheet cursor remains in one particular cell. What happens is that the cursor remains in position against the edge of the screen, while the worksheet appears to "pass beneath it." (The effect is the *opposite* of what happens when scrolling the screen without the **[SCROLL LOCK]** key engaged.)

HANDS ON:
CREATING YOUR FIRST ELECTRONIC SPREADSHEET

You are now ready to create your first electronic spreadsheet. You have installed DOS and the drivers, you are familiar with the major functions of the keyboard keys, and you have been introduced to the appearance of the 1-2-3 screen. Most importantly, you know how to move the worksheet cursor from one cell to another.

To create the worksheet in Table 2-4, all you need to do is position the worksheet cursor on the appropriate cells and type in the correct information. The trick, of course, is to know what the "correct" information is for each cell.

TABLE 2-4

A day in the life of the average husband illustrated not only that husbands spend, on average, very little time helping out around the house, but how to create a table with 1-2-3 by making Text and Value entries and by using built-in functions and user-defined formulas.

```
      A        B       C       D        E         F        G        H
 1
 2
 3
 4            CHORES: A DAY IN THE LIFE OF THE AVERAGE HUSBAND
 5
 6
 7                                  # OF MINUTES    % DISTRIBUTION
 8
 9    HOUSEWORK                         36              37.5
10    KITCHEN WORK                      12              12.5
11    CARING FOR THE FAMILY             24              25
12    SHOPPING AND HOUSEHOLD
13          PAPERWORK                   24              25
14
15          TOTAL                       96              100
16
```

Source: *American Averages* by Mike Feinsilber and William B. Mead, p. 244, Dolphin Books, Garden City, New Jersey, 1980

To find the correct information, look at Table 2-5. It takes you behind the screens of Table 2-4. At first glance, the entries may appear a bit complicated, but, in fact, they are quite straightforward.

TABLE 2-5

The structure behind the display: What was actually entered into each of the cells of Table 2-4.

	A	B	C	D	E	F	G	H
1								
2								
3								
4		'CHORES: A DAY IN THE LIFE OF THE AVERAGE HUSBAND						
5								
6								
7				'# OF MINUTES		'% DISTRIBUTION		
8								
9	'HOUSEWORK			36		(D9/D15)*100		
10	'KITCHEN WORK			12		(D10/D15)*100		
11	'CARING FOR THE FAMILY			24		(D11/D15)*100		
12	'SHOPPING AND HOUSEHOLD							
13		'PAPERWORK		24		(D13/D15)*100		
14								
15		'TOTAL		@SUM(D9..D13)		(D15/D15)*100		
16								

Source: *American Averages* by Mike Feinsilber and William B. Mead, p. 244, Dolphin Books, Garden City, New Jersey, 1980.

Value Entries and Label Entries

The most important thing to notice about Table 2-5 is that each cell on this, or any other, 1-2-3 worksheet contains either a *value* or a *label*.

Value Entries A value entry is displayed as a number. The program immediately assumes you are making a "value entry" whenever the first character you type is a number **(0-9)**, a left parenthesis **(()**, a plus **(+)** or a minus **(−)** sign. In addition, the "at" symbol **(@)**, the pound sign **(#)**, and the dollar sign **($)** introduce special value entries. When you type any of the above characters at the beginning of an entry, the mode indicator switches from Ready to

Value. Whatever follows is available for worksheet calculations as a number. (If you type something that is mathematical nonsense, you will receive an error message.)

There are three major types of value entries: numbers, built-in functions, and user-defined formulas. Table 2-4 contains examples of each of the three ways to create a value entry. (Refer to Table 2-5 to see exactly what was entered into each cell.)

To begin, the numbers **36, 12, 24**, and **24** in column D were entered directly into the worksheet by typing them on the keyboard. Next, the number 96 in cell D15 was created by typing the built-in function **@SUM(D9..D13)** into the cell. You will learn more about built-in functions in Part B, but for now all you need to know is that the function instructs 1-2-3 to add the contents of cells D9 through D13, inclusive, and to display the *result* in the cell containing the built-in function.

Finally, the numbers in column F (37.5, 12.5, etc.) were calculated by user-defined formulas (see Table 2-5). The formula in cell F9, **(D9/D15)*100**, is a typical user-defined formula. To create this or any other formula, you use cell references in exactly the same way you used X's and Y's to stand for numbers in an algebraic formula. The reference to D9/D15, for example, means "divide the value in cell D9 by the value in cell D15."

You can create as complicated a formula as you require out of arithmetic operators (+, −, /, *, and^which raises a number to a power) and cell references. You can also include built-in functions, such as the @SUM function discussed above, in user-defined formulas.

Be careful not to start a formula with a cell reference alone (e.g. D9/D15) because 1-2-3 will interpret that first letter as announcing a label entry. Use a number, an arithmetic operator (e.g. +D9/D15), or the left parenthesis to signal a value entry. Also, be sure to use parenthesis to let 1-2-3 know the order in which to evaluate the various parts of the formula.

Label Entries If the first character of an entry is not among those which 1-2-3 recognizes as a value entry, Lotus assumes you are entering a "label." The mode indicator changes to Label, and the characters you enter are displayed as text.

Labels are typically used for just that—labeling. The title and the row headings in Table 2-4 are labels. They were typed into their respective cells, and, as you can see, they are displayed as words.

Two things are important to know about labels. The first is what happens when a label is wider than the cell into which it is entered. The second is the technique for getting 1-2-3 to accept as a label something it would normally treat as a value. These two points involve the concepts of *soft cell boundaries* and *forced text entry*.

Whenever you type a label that is longer than the cell into which it is entered, one of two things will happen. If the cell to the right is blank, the label will extend across the boundary of the two cells. Text will continue from cell-to-cell until the entire label has been displayed or until a cell is encountered that is not blank. Because text entered in one cell can cross a cell boundary into adjacent cells, 1-2-3 is said to have *soft cell boundaries.*

The title of Table 2-4 makes good use of soft cell boundaries. It is entered only into cell B4, but it extends all the way across columns C, D, E, F, and into G. The presence of soft cell boundaries in 1-2-3 makes it very easy to enter text into a worksheet.

If something is in the adjacent cell, that entry takes precedence, and the display of text stops. However, if the text in the first cell is many characters long, it may reappear in the next available blank cell. When this happens, the text is difficult to read, and you must change the labels so they make sense.

No matter what the display looks like, the entire text is stored in the cell into which it was entered. All of the text will be displayed whenever the column in which the cell is located is expanded, or when the entries are erased which prevent the text from extending to the right.

The other thing to know about label entries is how to get 1-2-3 to accept something as a label when it would normally be viewed as a value. A telephone number is a good example of something you would want 1-2-3 to display as a label, when everything about the entry suggests a value. If you type 632-4040 into a cell, 1-2-3 will think you want to subtract 4,040 from 632. It will do your bidding and display the number −3,408!

This, of course, is not what you wanted at all. To force 1-2-3 to accept the telephone number as typed and to display it as a label, you must begin by typing one of 1-2-3's *label alignment characters:* ['], ["], or [^]. A label alignment character declares the characters that follow it to be text, and it tells 1-2-3 to align text to the left, right, and center of the cell into which it is entered. The label alignment character is not displayed, but it is part of the entry, and it can be changed by editing.

Lotus normally adds the left alignment character, ['], automatically to any label you type. But when you type any of the three alignment characters as the first character of an entry, you're *explicitly* telling 1-2-3 that you want what follows to be treated as a label, aligned in a particular fashion. If something normally considered a value, such as the telephone number, is entered in this way, it is called a *forced text entry.* You are forcing 1-2-3 to accept as a label an entry it would otherwise consider a value. The character is not displayed, but it is part of the entry, and it can be changed by editing. It also appears on the status line as part of the entry whenever the worksheet cursor is on a label cell.

If you make a mistake and forget to force a text entry (for example, cell D9 of Table 2-4, # OF MINUTES) 1-2-3 will "beep" when you press **[ENTER]**. You began a value entry with the pound sign, but you confused things by then typing text, so Lotus is asking, "What is it? A value entry or a label entry?"

The "beep" alerts you to the confusion. 1-2-3 automatically shifts to Edit mode, and the entry line cursor is positioned on the character where 1-2-3 first became confused. (In this case, in the space right after the pound sign.) You can then take the steps necessary to clear things up. Here, simply press the **[HOME]** key to move the entry line cursor to the beginning of the entry and type **[']** to insert the missing label alignment character. Then finish the entry by pressing the **[ENTER]** key.

Extensions

You can, of course, use 1-2-3 to build much larger, more elegant, and more complicated tables than the one illustrated in Table 2-4. Even with this table, you might want to do more than has been described.

In the following chapters, you will learn to modify the width of individual columns to suit the material they contain. You might want to expand the width of the first column, for example, so that all the row labels are displayed in one column. You will also learn to set different formats. In Table 2-4, you may want the percentages in the right-hand column to be displayed with the same number of places to the right of the decimal. The decimal points would then line up and you would know the accuracy of all the calculations. You may also want percentage signs to appear to the right of each percentage.

Commands to do these and many other tasks are described in the following chapters. In later chapters you will also learn to display this information graphically. (A pie chart showing the toil of the average husband would be particularly appropriate.)

SELF-TEST

QUESTIONS

1. What are the two ways you can choose a command from a 1-2-3 menu?
2. Name the three lines that make up the control panel.
3. Which key do you press to obtain a help screen?
4. Which key do you press if you want to back up one step?
5. Name the three cursors that appear on the 1-2-3 screen.
6. Which key would you press if you wanted to move the worksheet cursor one cell to the right?
7. Which cursor control keys move the screen up and down by one full screen?
8. What mode is 1-2-3 in when you are typing text? Numbers? Using a menu?
9. What are the three different types of value entries?

ANSWERS

1. Type the first letter of the command, or move the command line cursor to the desired command and press **[ENTER]**.
2. From top to bottom: the status line, the command (or entry) line, and the prompt line.
3. The **[HELP]** function key.
4. The **[ESC]** key.
5. The command line cursor, the entry line cursor, and the worksheet cursor.
6. The **[RIGHT ARROW]** key.
7. The **[PgUp]** and **[PgDn]** keys.
8. Label mode. Value mode. Menu mode.
9. Numbers, built-in functions, and user-defined formulas.

PART B

LOTUS 1-2-3'S WORKSHEET CONSTRUCTION COMMANDS

The 1 of 1-2-3 is the worksheet mode. This is the most important of 1-2-3's three modes because everything (spreadsheets, databases, and graphics) takes place within the framework established by the worksheet mode. In this mode, you can create electronic worksheets to do anything you can do with a manual worksheet (budget projections, financial analyses, analytical tables, quarterly reports, etc.), and you can do them quickly and more accurately.

Lotus' electronic worksheet is much like a manual worksheet. It presents a field of cells arranged into rows and columns, and it is a generalized analytical tool for solving a wide range of problems. But because 1-2-3 is an *electronic* worksheet, located in your microcomputer's Random Access Memory (RAM), it has analytical powers far beyond those of a manual spreadsheet.

In the last chapter, you learned to use 1-2-3's cursor control keys to position the active cell. Those commands are necessary *because* 1-2-3 is an electronic spreadsheet. In addition to the cursor control commands, 1-2-3 has a powerful set of "slash" commands and an extensive set of built-in functions.

The slash commands get their name from the fact that you must type a slash, **[/]**, to tell 1-2-3 that you want to issue a command. Once the slash key has been pressed, 1-2-3 enters the Menu mode, ready for you to choose from among the Worksheet, Range, Copy, Move, Print, File, Data, or Graph commands.

The first five commands, Worksheet, Range, Copy, Move, Print, and File are covered in this section. They are the heart of 1-2-3's electronic spreadsheet. The last two commands, Data and Graph, give access to the 2 and 3 of 1-2-3. The Data command is covered in Part C, and the Graph command is covered in Part D.

Just as the electronic nature of 1-2-3 requires slash commands to set display formats, copy or move text and formulas, and save or print worksheets, there are built-in functions for performing routine mathematical operations. These functions are introduced by the at **[@]** symbol and are often called "at functions." At functions can be used to sum or average the values in a group of cells or to find the largest or smallest value in a list of values. They can also be used to calculate the present value of a series of payments, the standard deviation of a set of values, the value of trigonometric functions (sine, log, etc.) and many other statistics. Built-in functions greatly simplify the task of worksheet construction by giving access to the quick, error free calculating power of your microcomputer.

CHAPTER THREE
WORKSHEET COMMANDS

OBJECTIVES

- To become acquainted with 1-2-3's Worksheet commands.
- To master the more frequently used Worksheet commands.

INTRODUCTION

Because 1-2-3 resides in your microcomputer's memory, you have at your disposal a series of commands that can be used to speed the construction of electronic spreadsheets and to increase their usefulness once constructed. These commands are known by the general name of "slash commands" because you must press the [/] key to announce to 1-2-3 that you want to issue a command. When you type a slash, the mode changes to Menu and the slash command menu is displayed in the control panel.

Figure 3-1 on page 52, shows how the 1-2-3 screen looks after you press the slash key. Figure 3-2 on page 53, shows the "command tree" for the slash commands. A command tree is a diagram that gives a quick overview of a command. It begins with the keys you type, and as you progress down the command tree, it shows what happens when you select each option.

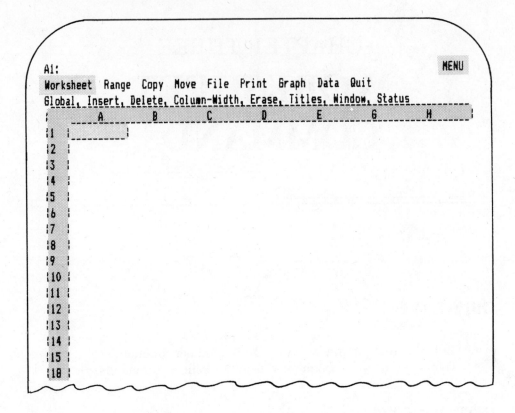

Figure 3-1. When you press **[/]** key, the slash command menu appears in the control panel. The command line cursor is on worksheet, and the prompt line displays the worksheet commands discussed in this chapter.

The choices on the slash command menu (Graph, Table, File, etc.) represent the different things you can do with a 1-2-3 worksheet. If you want to create a graph, you select the Graph command; if you want to save a copy of a worksheet on a diskette, you select the File command. Once in a command, you complete the instructions by selecting options from submenus (and sometimes sub-submenus) and by supplying the information requested by 1-2-3. You build up each and every 1-2-3 command in this logical, step-by-step fashion.

As you know from the discussion in chapter two, if you make a mistake, you can always undo an action by backing up one step with each press of the **[ESC]** key, provided that you haven't issued the last keystroke in a command sequence. If you have, the command has already been executed.

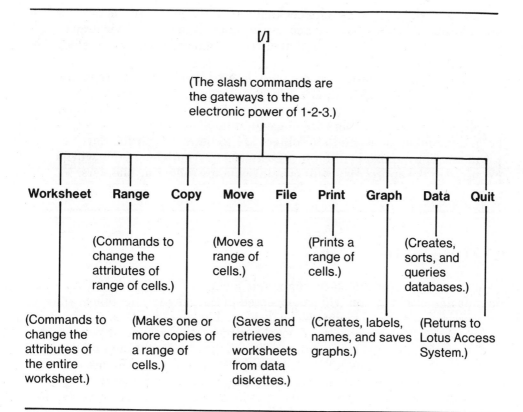

Figure 3-2. Slash command tree.

Symphony

Symphony's command structure is considerably more complicated than 1-2-3's. Most importantly, Symphony always gives you access to *two* different menus at all times. One menu is called "Services" and is accessed through the **[SERVICES]** function key. This menu presents choices such as File and Print that are relevant to all five of Symphony's environments. It is always available, regardless of the environment in which you are working.

The other menu, similar to the Slash Command menu in 1-2-3, is an environment-specific menu. It is accessed through the **[MENU]** function key and it presents choices that are only relevant in the current environment. You can also access this menu in a Sheet environment by pressing the slash key. In that environment, the menu is actually a "slash" command menu.

Lotus 1-2-3's Worksheet commands are distributed between the Services menu and the Sheet environment menu. The Settings command on the Sheet command menu contains many of 1-2-3's Worksheet commands. Others are placed on the Sheet command menu as individual choices, and still others are to be found on the Services menu. The important differences between 1-2-3 and Symphony will be noted at the appropriate points in this and the following chapters.

COMMAND OVERVIEW

The first option on the slash command menu is "Worksheet." The commands under this option will be discussed in this chapter; the other options on the slash command menu will be discussed in later chapters.

The Worksheet commands affect the general appearance of your worksheets on the screen and as printouts. (See Figure 3-3 for the command tree.) Most of the commands (Column-Width, Titles, Window, Status, and the Global Format command) do not affect the actual content of any cell. They just change the way the cell's content is displayed or printed. However, the Insert, Delete, and Erase commands can have a devastating effect on your worksheets, so use them with care.

The Range Commands

It is important to understand the relationship between the Worksheet commands and the second command on the slash command menu, the Range command. Both commands list many of the same options (Format, Label-Prefix, Erase, etc.) but there is a fundamental difference between the Range command and the Worksheet command. The Range command only applies to a *range* of cells, while a Worksheet command applies to *all* of the cells on the worksheet. Each time you use the Range command, you must specify the cell or group of cells to which the command applies. Whenever you use the Worksheet command, the action applies to the *entire* worksheet.

Whenever a Range Format or Range Label-Prefix command has been set for a group of cells, that setting overrides any Worksheet settings. You can set one format at the Worksheet level (Percent, for example) and override it for a

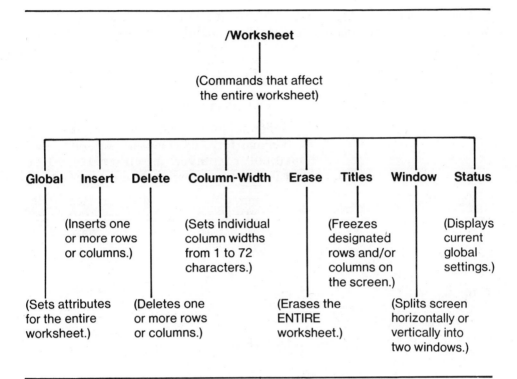

Figure 3-3. The command tree for the Worksheet commands.

particular group of cells with a Range Format command (Currency, for example).

Furthermore, any change you make with the Worksheet command bypass those cells that have been individually formatted. The exception to this rule is the Worksheet Erase command. It erases the entire worksheet and returns all formats, Range as well as Worksheet, to those originally in effect when 1-2-3 was first loaded into your computer.

Default Settings

A default is what happens if you don't do anything. If you don't pay a loan, for example, you are in default. All the Worksheet commands in 1-2-3 have built-in default settings. You could, in fact, construct many electronic worksheets and never use the Worksheet commands, but you'd be missing some of 1-2-3's most powerful and convenient features.

It is important to know what 1-2-3 does if you don't do anything; if you accept the program's default settings. The default settings for 1-2-3 are the following:

Command	Default Setting
Label:	Left aligned in each cell.
Value:	General. Numbers are displayed in either decimal form or scientific notation; e.g., 10,000 displayed as either 10,000 or 1E + 04, depending on the column width.
Recalculation:	Automatic and natural order. Recalculation after every change. Formulas are calculated before formulas that depend on them are calculated.
Column width:	9 characters.
Protection:	Off.
Window:	One.
Titles:	Unlocked.

The Worksheet command lets you change each of these default settings, and it lets you do many other things in addition. It gives you options when constructing an electronic spreadsheet, but if you wish, you can ignore the option and accept the choices 1-2-3 has already made for you.

Using a Command Menu

As noted in the last chapter, you select choices from any 1-2-3 menu in one of two ways. You can type the first letter of the command you want to use, **[w]** for example, to use the Worksheet command from the slash command menu. Alternatively, you can use the **[LEFT ARROW]** and **[RIGHT ARROW]** keys to highlight your desired choice. Once highlighted, you press **[ENTER]** to select that choice.

As you become skilled at using 1-2-3, you will type more and more of your choices. It is much, much faster to type **[/][w][f]** than to type a slash, then position the command line cursor over the Worksheet, then press **[ENTER]**, then position it over Format and press **[ENTER]** again.

The one advantage of using the slower method is that the prompt line in the control panel provides information about each choice. If you are unfamiliar with an option, you might want to view the prompt before selecting it. You can, however, always undo a choice with the **[ESC]** key.

Finally, remember that you can obtain instant, comprehensive help about any command and at any step in the process by pressing the **[HELP]** key. The help screens are interrelated, and after you have received all the help you need, press the **[ESC]** key to return to your previous place in the command. Nothing will have changed—except your understanding—and you can proceed to specify the command.

Symphony

You make selections from a Symphony menu in exactly the same way you make choices from a 1-2-3 menu. The only difference is that Symphony lists, in the lower left corner of the screen, the menu items as you select them.

Using a Command Tree

You have already seen command trees in Figures 3-1 and 3-2. Each command tree shows the options available with a particular command or subcommand. It also provides a brief description of what will happen if you choose a particular option.

On each command tree, those words that will appear on 1-2-3's control panel are highlighted. You can easily distinguish between the actual choices and the explanatory text placed in parenthesis. In addition, the **[ENTER]** keystroke is listed in the command tree whenever it *must* be typed. It is not listed when you have the option of choosing a menu item by typing its first letter or using the **[ENTER]** key to select the item. When constructing worksheets, turn to the appropriate command tree to see all of your options at a glance and to see the consequences of choosing a particular option.

The Most Important Worksheet Commands

You will use some Worksheet commands every time you use 1-2-3; others, you many never use. The most important Worksheet commands are:

Insert

Delete

Column-Width

Erase

Symphony

Symphony recognizes the importance of the Insert, Delete, and Column-Width commands by placing them on the Sheet environment command line as selections in their own right. Since the Erase command is relevant to all environments, it has been placed on the Services menu, where it is called "New."

The Insert and Delete commands are the electronic scissors and electronic glue that eliminate forever the need to cut and paste worksheets. The Worksheet Column-Width command sets individual column widths. Don't confuse this with the Worksheet *Global* Column-Width command which sets the width of *all* the columns at one time.

The Worksheet Erase command erases all the cells of the worksheet and returns the settings to the default settings. You use the Worksheet Erase command when you want to begin constructing a new worksheet.

Note that of all the Worksheet commands, only the Delete and Erase commands perform an action that changes a worksheet in a way that you cannot easily correct. The other commands leave the worksheet's content unchanged, and it is a simple matter to undo the action.

Of the remaining Worksheet commands, the Window and Title commands may be used a little more frequently than the others, but all are used much less frequently than the commands listed above. In fact, you many never have reason to use the Global Default command.

As with other commands, you will soon memorize frequently used keystrokes like [/] [w] [i] [r] which is /Worksheet Insert Row, and you will type them almost without thinking. When you are using unfamiliar commands, the command trees in this book plus the 1-2-3 help screens can provide the support you need to make the correct choices.

THE WORKSHEET GLOBAL COMMAND

The Global command (see Figure 3-4) sets cell attributes for both value cells (Format) and label cells (Label-Prefix). It also sets the universal column width, the method and order of recalculation, the protection of all the cells on the worksheet, and certain default printer and directory settings.

Symphony

Since Symphony has no worksheet command, the options found under 1-2-3's Global Worksheet command are spread throughout Symphony's command structure. The Recalculation, Label-Prefix, Global Column-Width, and the Global Format commands are found under the Sheet environment's Settings command. Format, column-width and the locking of rows and columns on the screen (the Title command) can be set independently for each named window. Other commands, such as Status, are found on the Services command menu.

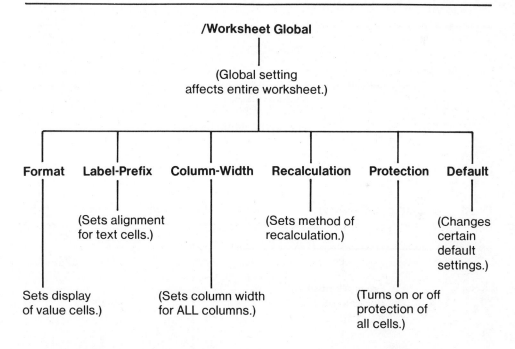

Figure 3-4. Worksheet Global command tree.

As noted above, the 1-2-3's Range command duplicates the Global Format, Label-Prefix, and Protection commands, and because its effect is more focused, you are more likely to use the Range command than the Global command. Also, recall that whenever the same command has been given by both Range and Global, the Range command takes precedent.

If you want to know the options that have been selected for the first five Global commands, you can obtain that information with the Worksheet Status command discussed below.

The Format Command

The Global Format command affects *only the display* of value entries (see Figure 3-5). It doesn't affect the display of label entries and, most importantly, it doesn't change the number, formula, or function entered into a cell.

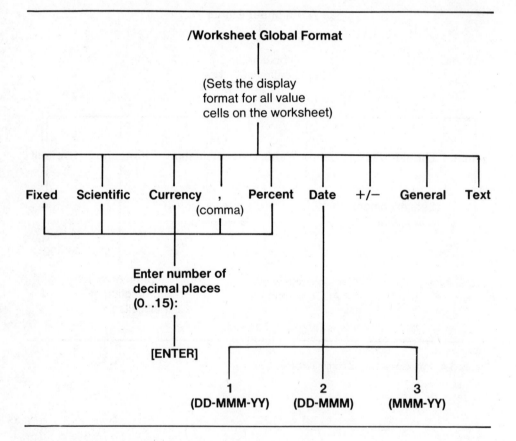

Figure 3-5. Worksheet Global Format command tree.

Table 3-1 shows how one number, 1342.9871, would be displayed under different Global Format commands. The table assumes the column is wide enough to display the number in the designated format. If it weren't, a row of asterisks (* * * * *) would appear in the cell. The asterisks alert you to the fact that a cell contains an entry that can't be displayed under the current combination of column width and format setting.

TABLE 3-1

The number 1342.9871 displayed under different Global Format commands. (Assumes the number of decimal places chosen is two and the column width is wide enough to display the number.)

Format Option	Form	1342.9871
Fixed	±x.xx	1342.99
Scientific	±x.xxE±xx	1.34E+03
Currency	$x,xxx.xx	$1,342.99
, (comma)	Commas and negative numbers in parenthesis	1,342.99
General	xx.xx or xx.xxE±xx	1342.9871 (Very large or very small numbers are displayed in scientific format.)
+/−	Bar graph.	+ + + + + + + + + + (+ or − equal to integer value. 1342.9871 would display as asterisks.)
Percent	x.xx%	134298.71%

Most Global Format commands give you the option of choosing from 0 to 15 decimal places in each display. The default number of decimal places is two. The program will round 1342.9871 to 1342.99 in Fixed display with two decimal places and to 1342.987 with three decimal places. No matter what is displayed, the *actual* number remains in your computer's memory and is used in all calculations. (Numbers are truncated, not rounded, under the General Format.)

The fact that the actual number is used in calculations rather than its rounded form can lead to apparent errors when doing accounting functions.

For example, $0.37 + $0.00 + $0.00 could equal $0.38 if the numbers in the cells were actually $0.369, $0.004 and $0.004. If you need to avoid rounding errors like these, use the the @ROUND function to actually round the numbers in the cells and not just their display.

The Percent command multiplies the number by 100, adds the percent sign, and rounds the number displayed to the desired number of places. The +/− command displays a row of pluses or minuses equal to the integer value of the number. If the integer part is larger than the current column width, a row of asterisks will be displayed. Also, if the +/− format is set, a period (.) will be displayed in blank cells.

To prevent numbers from running together across the screen, 1-2-3 reserves the last character in a value cell as a margin. Thus, value entries must be one character narrower than the cell in which they are displayed. You often find that setting a format adds characters to a value (currency, for example, adds one character for the dollar sign and one for each comma used), and this causes the asterisks to appear. Don't worry. The number is still in memory where it is used in all calculation. It can be displayed by expanding the column width.

The Date Format   The remaining two global formats have special uses. The Date format converts the number in a cell (usually generated with the @DATE or @TODAY function) to a date display such as 10-Jan-84. You are, however, much more likely to use the Range Format Date command than the Global Format Date command since the Global command converts *all* of the values on your worksheet to the date display.

Symphony

In addition to date functions and formats, Symphony keeps tracks of hours, minutes, and seconds. It has functions such as @NOW which replaces @TODAY, and it has formats for displaying the time aspect as well as the date aspect of date/time numbers in several international formats as well as the same "domestic" formats 1-2-3 uses.

The only other difference between Symphony's format options and 1-2-3's has to do with the [,] (comma) format. It has been renamed "Punctuated." Otherwise the format commands are the same in the two programs.

Text Format   The Text format causes the formulas behind each value to be displayed. Use it whenever you want to find out what is really going on behind the scenes.

The Text format is very useful for obtaining a clear picture of the formulas and functions that lie behind a spreadsheet. You can even print the worksheet this way for a record of its structure. If you split the screen into two windows (see the Worksheet Window command), one window can display the formulas while the other displays the results.

Note that when using the Text format, numbers will be displayed in the General format. To return the conventional display, you must reset the format to one of the other options, such as Fixed or General.

The Label-Prefix Command

Just as the Format command controls the display of value cells, the Label-Prefix command controls the display of label cells. (See Figure 3-6 for the command tree.)

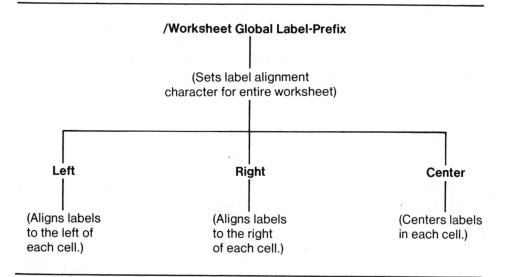

Figure 3-6. Worksheet Global Label-Prefix command tree.

To understand how the Label-Prefix command works you need to understand how 1-2-3 treats label entries. When you type an entry beginning with a letter of the alphabet, 1-2-3 interprets the entry as a label and places a *label alignment character* in front of the entry. This character is either a single quote ('), a double quote ("), or a caret (^). It is automatically made part of the entry. Thus, when the label alignment character is the caret (^) and you type the word "entry", 1-2-3 changes it to " ^ entry."

The label alignment character tells 1-2-3 where to display a label in a cell. The single quote means "align to the left edge of the cell," the double quote means "align to the right", and the caret means "center" the label in the cell.

Right-aligned labels reserve the right-most character in the cell as a margin. Labels that are as wide or wider than the cell are displayed as if they were left aligned, regardless of the actual label alignment character.

The Global Label-Prefix command lets you choose which of the three label alignment characters will be automatically assigned to labels. The default character is the single quote, so left is the default label alignment.

Changing the Label-Prefix It is very important to note that the Global Label-Prefix command *will not* change the label alignment character of text *already* entered into the worksheet. Previously entered text continues to have whatever label alignment character it was given when it was entered. Changing the Global Label-Prefix only affects text entered after the change. It has *no* effect on labels already on a worksheet.

There are three ways to change the label alignment character for a label already entered into a worksheet. If you are changing the alignment character for several cells, use the Range Label-Prefix command. If you are changing the character for a single cell, either retype the entry (assuming the current Global Label-Prefix is the one you want) or use the **[EDIT]** function key to edit the entry by inserting the desired character.

The Column-Width Command

The Global Column-Width command sets the width for all columns on the worksheet at one time. The default width is 9 characters, and you can set the column width to any value from 1 to 72 characters. (See Figure 3-7.)

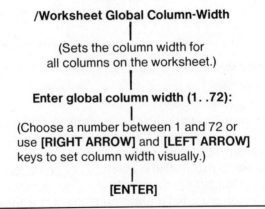

/Worksheet Global Column-Width
|
(Sets the column width for
all columns on the worksheet.)
|
Enter global column width (1..72):
|
(Choose a number between 1 and 72 or
use **[RIGHT ARROW]** and **[LEFT ARROW]**
keys to set column width visually.)
|
[ENTER]

Figure 3-7. Worksheet Global Column-Width command tree.

The width can be set visually by using the **[RIGHT ARROW]** and **[LEFT ARROW]** keys to expand or contract the columns. The arrow keys are very easy to use, and they let you see exactly what the effect of a given column width is on your worksheet. However, if you do know how wide you want the columns, you can type in the number of characters.

With narrow columns, you can display more columns on the screen and print more on each sheet of paper. However, as noted previously, if a column is too narrow to display an entry, a row of asterisks will appear.

Finally, the Worksheet Global Column-Width command *will not* change any column widths that have been set with the Worksheet Column-Width command. The Worksheet Column-Width command, sets column widths individually. You will use it much more frequently than the Global Column-Width command discussed here.

The Recalculation Command

There is really only one frequently used option on the Global Recalculation command. (See Figure 3-8 on next page.) That option is to turn off the automatic recalculation of the 1-2-3 worksheet.

You will use this option to turn off automatic recalculation whenever you are constructing a new worksheet or whenever the worksheet you are using is large and requires several entries to update. If you don't turn off automatic recalculation, 1-2-3 recalculates the worksheet after each entry (or when ever you use the Copy, Edit, File, or Move commands), even when the result of a recalculation is incomplete or in error.

Whenever recalculation is off and you change an entry that requires recalculation, 1-2-3 recognizes this and displays the highlighted word "CALC" on the bottom line of the screen. It is there to remind you that a change has been made and that the worksheet must be recalculated. To recalculate the worksheet, just press the **[CALC]** function key. You can, of course, wait until the worksheet is completed or the updating finished before pressing the **[CALC]** key.

Order of Recalculation Lotus 1-2-3's default method of calculating a worksheet is to respect the "natural order" that underlies its structure. Lotus first calculates those cells on which other cells depend, regardless of the location of the cells on the worksheet.

This method eliminates the problem of "forward references" that often occurs in electronic spreadsheet programs without natural order recalculation. Worksheets with forward references may take several recalculations to arrive at the correct answer. The recalculations are necessary because cells depend upon cells which themselves depend upon cells forward in the order of recalculation.

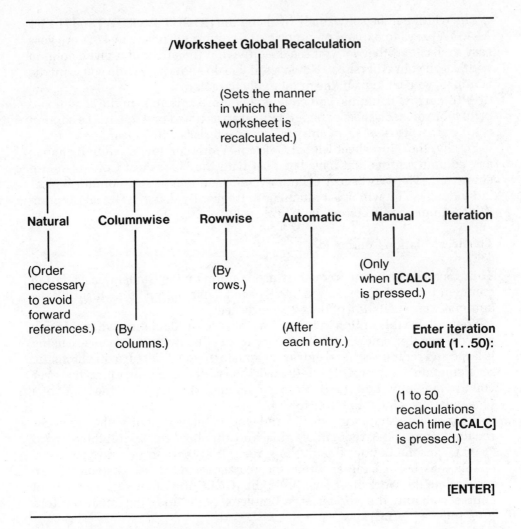

Figure 3-8. Worksheet Global Recalculation command tree.

You also have the option of choosing Column or Row recalculation and Iteration where you choose how many times (1 to 50) the worksheet is recalculated with each press of the **[CALC]** key. These options are often used with worksheets that contain circular references (where a cell refers to itself either directly or indirectly). Chances are you won't need this option unless you are an engineer and your worksheet calculations stabilize only after a number of successive recalculations.

The Protection Command

The Global Protection command activates (or "Enables") protection (see Figure 3-9). This prevents *any* action (*except* Global Erase) from changing the contents of the protected cell. Once a cell is protected, you can't erase it with Range Erase or edit it with the **[EDIT]** key. You can't delete a row or column containing a protected cell; nor can you enter new text or values into a protected cell.

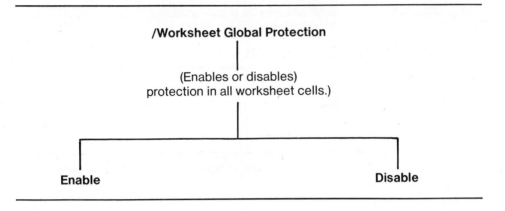

Figure 3-9. Worksheet Global Protection command tree.

You enable protection with the Global Protection command to protect *all* worksheet cells. Then you use the Range Unprotect command to open up or unprotect only those cells you need to change when using the worksheet. These are usually data entry cells. Obviously, protection is one of the last steps in constructing a worksheet.

Protection provides insurance against you or someone else accidentally destroying a worksheet. It is particularly good insurance to have when data is to be entered into your worksheet by someone who is perhaps less careful and less knowledgable than you are.

If you don't use the Global Protection command, you'll never know it's there. When disabled (the default setting), it's as if global protection didn't exist.

The Default Command

The Global Default command is the last Global command. It is one command few user's of 1-2-3 know exists and fewer have reason to use, (see Figure 3-10).

In fact, the 1-2-3 manual places the discussion of the command in the Appendix under Configuring 1-2-3 rather than with the other worksheet commands in the Command Skills section.

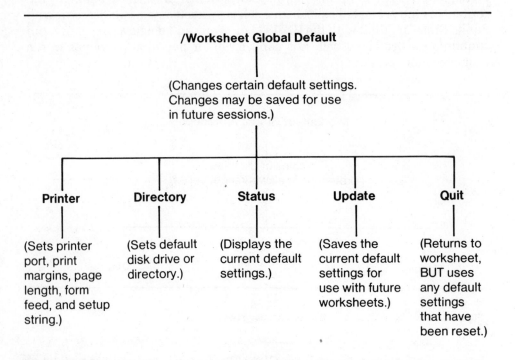

Figure 3-10. Worksheet Global Default command tree.

With that introduction, you might be surprised to find that in certain situations, this command can make your life a great deal easier. Among other things, the Default command lets you reset certain default values in the Print command and to specify which disk drive or directory (on a hard disk) 1-2-3 uses for data storage.

The most important Print command defaults that you can set with the Global Default command have to do with the default margins and page length for printed worksheets. The factory-set default margins are 4 characters on the left and 76 on the right. This assumes you print your worksheets on 8 1/2" wide paper in standard type. If this is what you do, you'll probably never need to use this command.

However, if you always print on a wide printer (15") or if you usually print in compressed type to get more information on a single page (132 characters per line on 8 1/2" paper, 233 on 15" wide paper), then you will have to reset the print margins before you print each worksheet.

Instead of resetting the parameters each time you print, you could use the Global Default command to reset the print margin defaults and the setup string that signals your printer to print in compressed type. Once set, the Update command on the global default menu saves the new default settings on the system diskette. (Remember to remove the write protect tab before using the Update command.)

If you are going to reset the printer defaults or any other defaults that can be reset with the Global Default command, first read the instructions in the Appendix in the manual under "Configuring 1-2-3." The help screens can also give you information about resetting the defaults.

THE INSERT COMMAND

The Insert command is one of those electronic worksheet commands that can bring tears of joy to the eyes of even the grouchiest analyst. This command inserts one or more blank rows or columns into the center of an already constructed worksheet. When the command is used, all other material moves to make room for it, and all references and built-in functions automatically adjust to accommodate the new rows or columns.

Keeping track of everything while making more space is one of those things computers do so well. The result is that you won't have to redo a table because you left out a line item or because someone suggested that more detail needed to be included. No longer will you have to resort to microscopic writing to add an additional column of figures or another row of numbers. (See Figure 3-11 on next page.)

The insert command is very easy to use. All you have to do is type **[/]** **[w][i] [r]** or row insert or **[/] [w] [i] [c]** for column insert.

After you tell 1-2-3 whether you want to insert columns or rows, it asks you to specify where you want them inserted. New rows are inserted *above* the cursor, and new columns are inserted to the *left* of the cursor. If the worksheet cursor is already in the proper position *and* you want to insert only a single row or column, press the **[ENTER]** key and watch 1-2-3 do its stuff.

If the cursor is correctly positioned but you want to insert several rows or columns, use the appropriate arrow key to expand the cursor the desired number of rows or columns. When everything is correct, press **[ENTER]**. Note: the inserted rows will appear above the top edge of the *expanded cursor*. Columns will appear to the left of the *expanded cursor*.

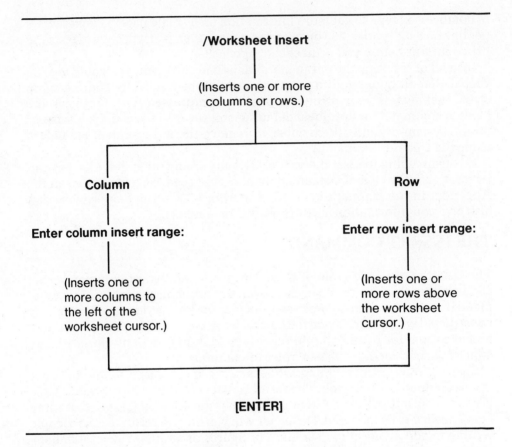

Figure 3-11. Worksheet Insert command tree.

If you want the rows or columns inserted somewhere other than the current cursor location, press the **[ESC]** or **[BKSP]** keys. This will "unstick" the worksheet cursor, and you can then use the cursor control keys to move it around the worksheet. If you want to insert a single row or column, position the cursor correctly (remember rows will be inserted above, columns to the left of the cursor) and press **[ENTER]**. If you want a range of rows or columns, "stick" the cursor back down by typing a period **[.]**. Then use the arrow keys to expand the cursor to the desired size and press **[ENTER]**. The rows or columns will be inserted, and the worksheet cursor will jump back to its original location.

If you found this explanation a bit difficult, don't worry. It is much easier to insert rows or columns into a worksheet than it is to tell someone how to do it.

Worksheet Full While you can't destroy anything when using the Global Insert command, you may get an error message. This happens when the rows or columns you are trying to insert would have the effect of pushing information off the worksheet. This occurs when you have an entry in the last row or the last column of the worksheet.

If you do get a "Worksheet Full" error message, 1-2-3 shifts into Error mode and gets your attention with a "beep." You can't do anything else until you either press **[ENTER]** or **[ESC]** to acknowledge the error. When you do, 1-2-3 will cancel the Insert command and return, to Ready mode.

To correct the error, you must delete a sufficient number of rows (or columns) from the worksheet so that what you are inserting can be accommodated without pushing anything off the edge. You must then go one step farther: you must store and reload the worksheet to deactivate the last row or last column. Otherwise, you will continue to get the "Worksheet Full" error message whenever you try to insert a row (or a column).

Symphony

As noted, Symphony places the Insert and Delete commands on the Sheet environment command menu. When using either of these commands, Symphony gives you the additional option of limiting the operation to the range of cells to which the current window is restricted. Alternatively, you can choose Global and, like the 1-2-3 commands, the operation takes place from one edge of the worksheet to the opposite edge.

The limited Insert and Delete commands prevent the accidental destruction or modification of information outside the restricted range of the current Sheet window.

THE DELETE COMMAND

The Worksheet Delete command (Figure 3-12) is similar in form, but opposite in action, to the Worksheet Insert command. It deletes one or more rows or columns from a worksheet. The prompts for the commands are identical as is the ability to expand the cursor to point to the range of rows or columns to be deleted.

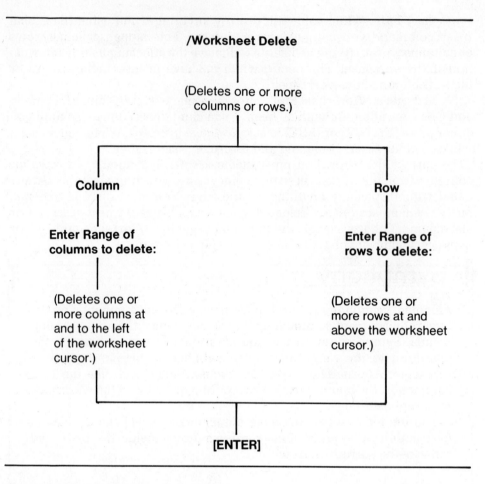

/Worksheet Delete

(Deletes one or more
columns or rows.)

Column

**Enter Range of
columns to delete:**

(Deletes one or
more columns at
and to the left
of the worksheet
cursor.)

Row

**Enter Range of
rows to delete:**

(Deletes one or
more rows at and
above the worksheet
cursor.)

[ENTER]

Figure 3-12. Worksheet Delete command tree.

The major difference between the Insert and Delete commands is that once deleted, a row or column is gone *forever*. Be sure you have correctly specified the rows or columns you want to remove *before* pressing the last **[ENTER]**.

Also remember that the command deletes rows or columns from one edge of the worksheet all the way to the opposite edge of the worksheet. Be careful not to unintentionally delete information that is off the screen, but in the same row or column.

Caution If you delete a row or column that contains a cell referred to by a formula or function elsewhere on the worksheet, the letters "ERR" (for

ERROR) will be displayed in the cell containing the formula or function. Furthermore, the ERR ripples through the worksheet to be displayed in all cells that depend either directly or indirectly on the deleted cell. The same thing happens when the deleted row or column contains a cell that is specified as one of the end points of a range used by any of 1-2-3's built-in functions.

To correct this error, you must correct the cell references in the functions or formulas directly affected by the deleted rows or columns. Sometimes it is hard to identify just which cells are directly affected and which depend indirectly on the deleted rows or columns. In this case, use the Worksheet Global Text command to display all formulas and functions in their respective cells.

Only those cells depending *directly* on a deleted cell will show an ERR in their formula or function. Those cells that depend *indirectly* on a deleted cell will display normal functions or formulas. Once you have identified the formulas depending directly on the deleted cells, you can make the necessary corrections.

THE COLUMN-WIDTH COMMAND

The Column-Width command sets or resets the width of *individual* columns (see Figure 3-13 on next page). This is one of the most frequently used worksheet commands. You will use it with every worksheet you construct because it allows you to tailor each column width to the contents of the column.

The column containing the row labels, for example, can be made wide, while those containing small numbers can be made narrow. You can also insert columns (often just a few characters wide) to separate one column of numbers from another. Often this additional space greatly improves the appearance and clarity of a worksheet.

The Worksheet Column-Width command operates exactly like the Worksheet Global Column-Width command described above, except that only the width of the column containing the worksheet cursor is changed. Be sure to position the worksheet cursor in the correct column *before* entering the command because you cannot move it once in the command.

Using the right and left arrow keys is the best way to change a column's width because you can see the effect the change has on the worksheet. If you already know how wide you want the column to be, you can type in the desired number (1 to 72).

The Reset option resets the column containing the worksheet cursor to the default column width (9 characters) or, if one has been set, to the last column width set by the Global Column-Width command.

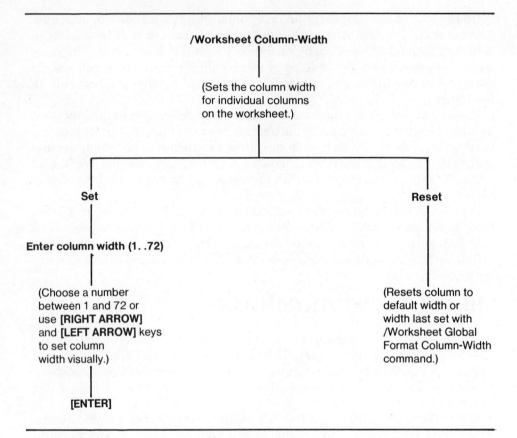

Figure 3-13. Worksheet Column-Width command tree.

Symphony

In Symphony, you set individual column widths by selecting the Width command on a Sheet environment command menu. The global column width is set from the Services menu.

THE ERASE COMMAND

The Worksheet Erase command is another command you are likely to use every time you work with 1-2-3. You use it when you are ready to begin constructing the next worksheet and after you have saved a worksheet to a diskette. You use it whenever you decide that a worksheet you are constructing is beyond repair and you want to start over with a clear slate, (see Figure 3-14).

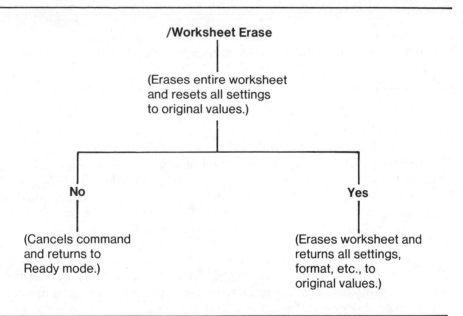

/Worksheet Erase

(Erases entire worksheet
and resets all settings
to original values.)

No

(Cancels command
and returns to
Ready mode.)

Yes

(Erases worksheet and
returns all settings,
format, etc., to
original values.)

Figure 3-14. Worksheet Erase command tree.

The Erase command erases the *entire* worksheet and resets all options (column width, protection, etc.) to their original default setting. The only settings that are not changed by the Erase command are those set with the Worksheet Global Default command.

The Erase command is devastating in its impact. It overrides all other commands including worksheets protected with the Protection Enable command. Consequently, 1-2-3 requires you to confirm your intention to erase a worksheet by either moving the command line cursor to the word "YES" and pressing **[ENTER]** or by typing **[Y]**. This procedure is called a "Sanity Check." It alerts you to the fact that you are about to wipe the worksheet from your computer's memory forever, and it gives you a second chance to save your worksheet with the File command.

You do not need to use the Erase command before using the File Retrieve command to load a worksheet into memory from a data diskette. The File Retrieve command itself automatically erases any worksheet in memory before loading the new one.

Finally, it is important to note that the *Range* Erase command (see Chapter Four) is the command you use when it is the contents of only a few cells, and not the entire worksheet, that you want to send to electronic never-never land.

Symphony

As noted, Symphony's equivalent of 1-2-3's Worksheet Erase command is located on the Services menu and is called "New."

THE TITLE COMMAND

As you know from the last chapter, 1-2-3 has many more cells in the worksheet it keeps in memory than it can display on the screen at any one time. In fact, tables of even modest size (more than 20 rows and 10 or 15 columns) will not display on the screen in their entirety. To compensate for this limitation, 1-2-3 provides two worksheet commands: Title and Window.

The Title command, discussed in this section, "freezes" designated rows or columns on the screen so that other cells can be scrolled past the frozen titles. (See Figure 3-15 for the command tree.) The Window command, discussed in the next section, splits the worksheet into two different windows to display cells at widely different locations.

It is easiest to explain the Title command with an example. Table 3-2 (on page 78) is a table to calculate the balance in a bank account over a 23-year period from 1984 to 2003. It is assumed a deposit of $2,000 is made on the first day of each year and the interest rate over the period is a constant 10%.

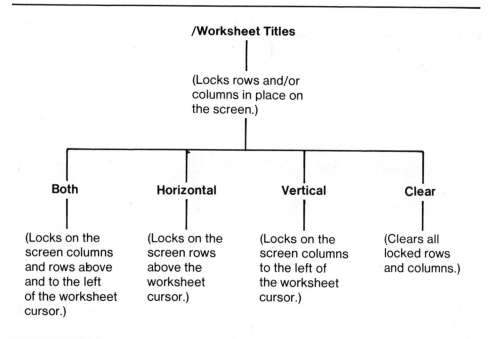

Figure 3-15. The Worksheet Titles command tree.

So much for the assumptions; now to the Title command. As you can see from Table 3-2, the 26 columns that make up the worksheet take up three full screens—too much to view at one time. If you set the Vertical Title command with the worksheet cursor in column C, columns A and B will remain on the screen. You can scroll the yearly information to the left and the right while the row headings remain displayed. (See Figure 3-16 on page 79 where column S is displayed next to column B.)

The Title command is particularly useful if your table has many rows and many columns. You can set the Both option, and the appropriate column headings and row labels will always be on the screen.

Like other worksheet and range commands, any Title command you have set will be stored with the worksheet and will be in force when the worksheet is retrieved with the File command.

TABLE 3-2

This compound interest table stretches over 26 columns and would take three separate screens to display all the information.

	A	B	C	D	E	F	G	H
1	Entry Space							
2								
3	Interest: 10.00%							
4	Deposit: $2,000							
5								
6			1984	1985	1986	1987	1988	1989
7								
8	Balance Forward		$0	$2,200	$4,620	$7,282	$10,210	$13,431
9	Deposits		$2,000	$2,000	$2,000	$2,000	$2,000	$2,000
10	Interest		$200	$420	$662	$928	$1,221	$1,543
11								
12	Total		$2,200	$4,620	$7,282	$10,210	$13,431	$16,974
13								
14								

	I	J	K	L	M	N	O	P
1								
2								
3								
4								
5								
6	1990	1991	1992	1993	1994	1995	1996	1997
7								
8	$16,974	$20,872	$25,159	$29,875	$35,062	$40,769	$47,045	$53,950
9	$2,000	$2,000	$2,000	$2,000	$2,000	$2,000	$2,000	$2,000
10	$1,897	$2,287	$2,716	$3,187	$3,706	$4,277	$4,905	$5,595
11								
12	$20,872	$25,159	$29,875	$35,062	$40,769	$47,045	$53,950	$61,545
13								
14								

	Q	R	S	T	U	V	W	X
1								
2								
3								
4								
5								
6	1998	1999	2000	2001	2002	2003	TOTALS	
7								
8	$61,545	$69,899	$79,089	$89,198	$100,318	$112,550		
9	$2,000	$2,000	$2,000	$2,000	$2,000	$2,000	$40,000	
10	$6,354	$7,190	$8,109	$9,120	$10,232	$11,455	$86,005	
11								
12	$69,899	$79,089	$89,198	$100,318	$112,550	$126,005	$126,005	
13								
14								

```
B3: (P2) 0.1                                                    READY

    ---------------------------------------------------------------
    |      A       B       S       T       U       V    W      X   |
 !1 !       Entry Space
 !2 !
 !3 !Interest:  10.00%
 !4 !Deposit:  $2,000
 !5 !
 !6 !                   2000    2001    2002    2003      TOTALS
 !7 !
 !8 !Balance Forward  $79,089 $89,198 $100,318 $112,550
 !9 !Deposits          $2,000  $2,000   $2,000   $2,000   $40,000
 !10 !Interest         $8,109  $9,120  $10,232  $11,455   $86,005
 !11 !
 !12 !Total           $89,198 $100,318 $112,550 $126,005  $126,005
 !13 !
```

Figure 3-16. Columns A and B have been locked on the screen with the Title command. The rest of the worksheet has been scrolled past the locked titles to reveal the entries in columns S through X.

THE WINDOW COMMAND

The Worksheet Window command is the other way 1-2-3 compensates for the limited number of columns or rows that can be displayed on the screen at one time. (See Figure 3-17 on the next page for the command tree.) The Window command splits the screen into two windows. The split is either horizontal or vertical. Usually one row or column is lost to the new line of column letters (horizontal split) or row numbers (vertical split).

The Window command is often used to view both the beginning of the table where assumptions are often entered, and the end of the table, where totals are calculated. That way, you can quickly do "What If..." analysis. You vary the assumption to see what happens if, for example, the interest rate is 15% or if the deposit is $1,500.

Figure 3-18 on page 81 shows the compound interest table split vertically so that both the Entry Space at the beginning and the Totals at the end can be viewed at the same time.

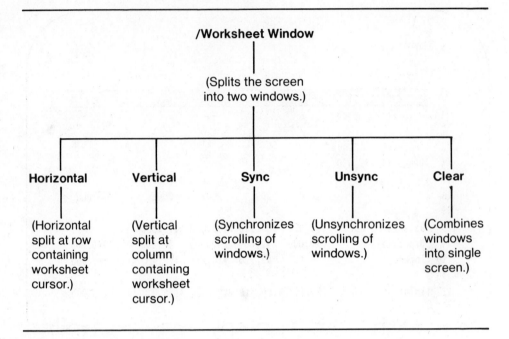

Figure 3-17. The Worksheet Window command tree.

Another reason to split the screen is to display more columns or rows. This is illustrated in Figure 3-19 on page 82 where twice as many columns are displayed by splitting the screen horizontally. Notice that the Title command has also been used to freeze the row titles on the screen in both windows.

The Window command also gives you the option of having the two windows scroll together (synchronized) or scroll independently (unsynchronized). When the split is horizontal, synchronized windows show the same columns in each window. When you scroll the columns in one window, columns in the other window also scroll.

When the split is vertical, the same rows appear in each window. The windows are synchronized when first split. If you want to unsynchronize them, you must do so explicitly with the Worksheet Window command.

Each window of a split screen acts like *independent* copies of the same worksheet. You can view the same cells in both windows, and you can set different formats, label-alignments, and column widths in each window. However, when you merge the windows to unsplit the screen, the settings in the top or left window will be the settings for the entire worksheet.

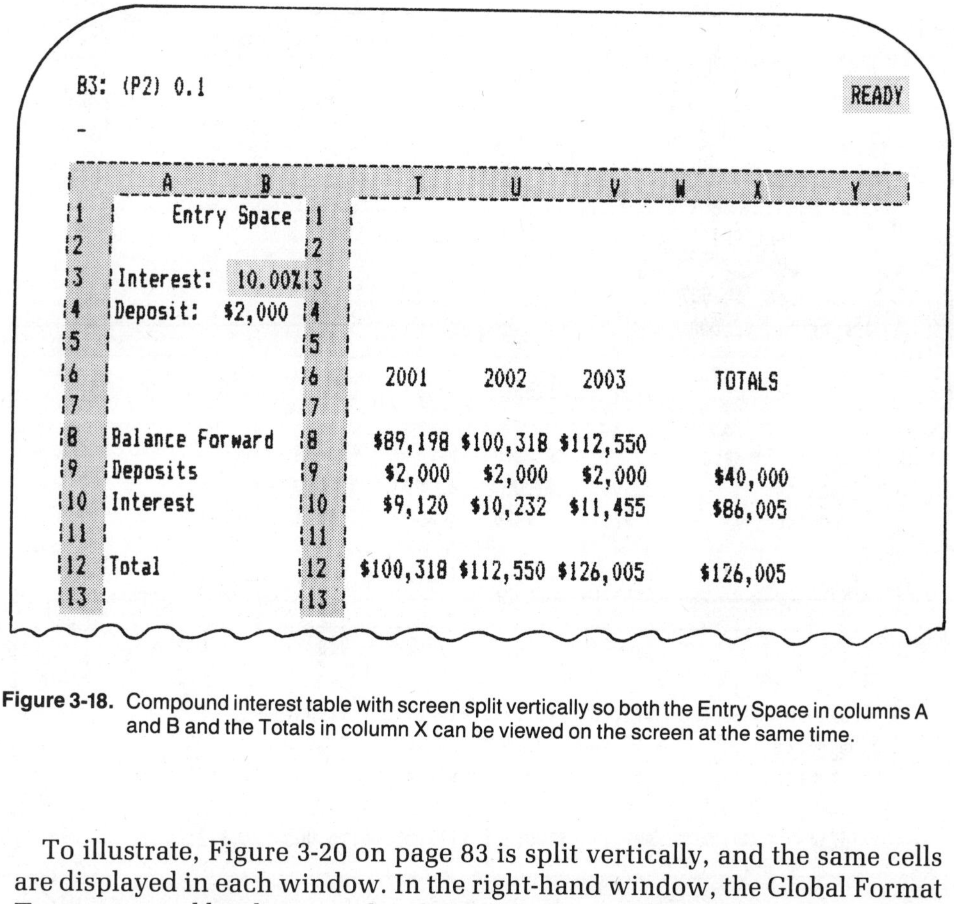

```
B3: (P2) 0.1                                                    READY
  -
      !        A        B                I      U      V     W      X        Y    !
    !1 !       Entry Space  !1 !
    !2 !                    !2 !
    !3 !Interest:   10.00%!3 !
    !4 !Deposit:    $2,000 !4 !
    !5 !                    !5 !
    !6 !                    !6 !   2001    2002    2003         TOTALS
    !7 !                    !7 !
    !8 !Balance Forward     !8 !  $89,198 $100,318 $112,550
    !9 !Deposits            !9 !   $2,000   $2,000   $2,000    $40,000
   !10 !Interest           !10 !   $9,120  $10,232  $11,455    $86,005
   !11 !                   !11 !
   !12 !Total              !12 ! $100,318 $112,550 $126,005   $126,005
   !13 !                   !13 !
```

Figure 3-18. Compound interest table with screen split vertically so both the Entry Space in columns A and B and the Totals in column X can be viewed on the screen at the same time.

To illustrate, Figure 3-20 on page 83 is split vertically, and the same cells are displayed in each window. In the right-hand window, the Global Format Text command has been used to display the formulas behind the numbers in the left-hand window. The columns in the right-hand window have also been expanded so the longer formulas can be displayed.

Only one cell can be active at one time, and when the screen is split, that cell can be in only one window. To move the worksheet cursor from one window to another, 1-2-3 uses the **[WINDOW]** function key. Whenever you press the **[WINDOW]** key, the worksheet cursor skips to the cell it last occupied in the previous window.

THE STATUS COMMAND

The final worksheet command is the Status command (see Figure 3-21 on page 83). This command displays the current global settings for the work-

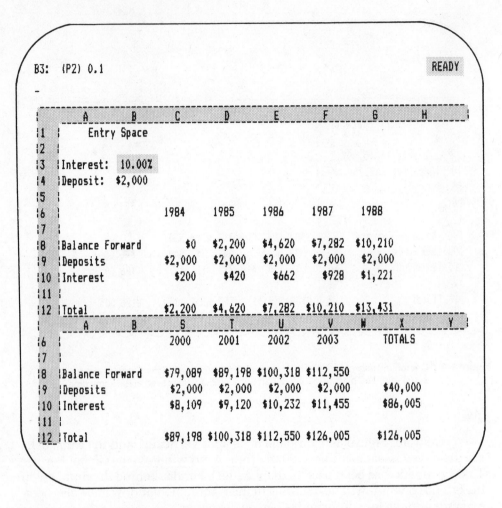

Figure 3-19. Screen split horizontally to display columns at both the beginning and the end of the table.

sheet so you can easily check the values you have set with the worksheet commands. In addition, it tells you how much memory is available for constructing your worksheets.

When you enter the Status command, the control panel at the top of the screen is replaced by the following display:

Recalculation	Format	Label Prefix	Column Width	Avail Memory	Protect
AUTO NATURAL	(G)	,	9	154460	OFF

```
B3: (P2) 0.1                                                        READY
 -
    ┌─────────────────────────────────┬──────────────────────────────┐
    │     A      B      C      D       │        C              D       │
 !1 !        Entry Space              !1 !
 !2 !                                 !2 !
 !3 !Interest:  10.00%                !3 !
 !4 !Deposit:   $2,000                !4 !
 !5 !                                 !5 !
 !6 !              1984    1985       !6 !      1984           1984
 !7 !                                 !7 !
 !8 !Balance Forward    $0   $2,200   !8 !         0   +C12
 !9 !Deposits       $2,000   $2,000   !9 !   +B4          +B4
 !10 !Interest        $200     $420  !10 !  (C9+C10)*B3  (D9+D10)*B3
 !11 !                               !11 !
 !12 !Total         $2,200   $4,620  !12 !  +C11+C10+C9  +D11+D10+D9
 !13 !                               !13 !
```

Figure 3-20. You can set different formats, columns widths, and displays in each window of a split screen. Global Format Text command has been used to display in the right-hand window the formulas behind the numbers in the left-hand window. The column width was also expanded in the right-hand window. Note that the Text command displays numbers in General format (e.g. $0 becomes 0).

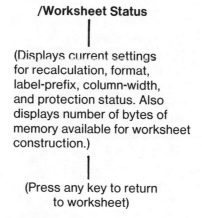

/Worksheet Status

(Displays current settings
for recalculation, format,
label-prefix, column-width,
and protection status. Also
displays number of bytes of
memory available for worksheet
construction.)

(Press any key to return
to worksheet)

Figure 3-21. The Worksheet Status command tree.

You should recognize the default settings for these parameters as they were introduced in the first part of this chapter. When you have finished viewing the display, press any key to return to the Ready mode.

HANDS ON:
USING THE WORKSHEET COMMANDS

You can get a good idea of the power of the 1-2-3 worksheet commands by comparing Tables 3-3 and 3-4. Both tables contain the same information—average weekly and hourly earnings in a number of representative industries—but the "Before" table is crowded and hard to read. The "After" table shows what a few worksheet commands can do to improve a table's appearance.

TABLE 3-3

Table before using worksheet commands to improve its presentation.

	A	B	C	D	E	F	G
1							
2							
3		MAKING MONEY MAKING THINGS					
4			Weekly	Earnings			
5		Industry	Earnings	Per Hour			
6	Steel, Copper, and		430.62	10.25285			
7	Petroleum		377.1	8.38			
8	Automobile		369.27	8.450114			
9	Transportation Equ		320.67	7.689928			
10	Chemicals		292.18	6.989952			
11	Paper		279.48	6.529906			
12	Printing		244.02	6.489893			
13	Leatherworking		231.42	6.1712			
14	Food Processing		231.42	5.8			
15	Electrical Equipme		228.71	5.790126			
16	Lumber		228.71	5.732080			
17	Furniture Manufact		180.96	4.64			
18	Textiles		172.43	4.3			
19	Clothes Manufactur		140.76	3.91			
20							

Source: *American Averages* by Mike Feinsilber and William B. Mead, p. 235, Dolphin Books, New York, New York, 1980.

TABLE 3-4

Table 3-4 after using Worksheet Insert, Delete, Column-Width and Format commands.

	A	B	C	D	E	F
1	MAKING MONEY MAKING THINGS					
2						
3		Weekly		Earnings		
4		Earnings		Per Hour		
5	Industry					
6	Steel, Copper, and Aluminum	$430.62		$10.25		
7	Petroleum	$377.10		$8.38		
8	Automobile	$369.27		$8.45		
9	Transportation Equipment	$320.67		$7.69		
10	Chemicals	$292.18		$6.99		
11	Paper	$279.48		$6.53		
12	Printing	$244.02		$6.49		
13	Leatherworking	$231.42		$6.17		
14	Food Processing	$231.42		$5.80		
15	Electrical Equipment	$228.71		$5.79		
16	Lumber	$228.71		$5.73		
17	Furniture Manufacturing	$180.96		$4.64		
18	Textiles	$172.43		$4.30		
19	Clothes Manufacturing	$140.76		$3.91		
20						

Source: *American Averages* by Mike Feinsilber and William B. Mead, p. 235, Dolphin Books, New York, New York, 1980.

Begin by looking at the Before table, Table 3-3. The information in that table has been correctly entered, but a number of things should be changed.

First, the table elements are too close together. The title, column headings, and body of the table are almost on top of one another. Adding a few blank rows and columns would make the table easier to read.

What about the row labels? What is "Steel, Copper and" what? Something is missing. Indeed, several row labels are truncated because they are too long to be displayed in the 18 characters allotted to columns A and B by the default column width. Column A needs to be expanded.

Finally, the numbers that make up the body of the table are hard to read. The Weekly Earnings figures aren't too bad, but the Earnings Per Hour, which are the result of dividing Weekly Earnings by average number of hours worked per week, have from one to eight digits to the right of the decimal point. It would be much better to display them in standard form, two places to the right of the decimal and a dollar sign to indicate currency.

It takes less than a minute to turn Before into After. (Even Clark Kent takes longer than that in a phone booth.) Begin by inserting rows between the title and the row headings, and between the row headings and the body of the table. These two rows open up the table and make it easier to read, but they also push the last line off the screen. To put the table back on the screen, delete the top two rows. (Remember you can expand the cursor to delete rows 1 and 2 at the same time.)

Next, use the Worksheet Column-Width command to expand column A until all row labels are displayed. Then use the Worksheet Insert command to insert a new column D. This separates the two columns of numbers and their associated labels to make them easier to read. (You could have achieved the same effect by expanding the original column D and right justifying the labels.) Finally, use the Worksheet Global Format command to set the global format to currency. The default choice for number of decimal places, two, is the correct one.

Thanks to the Worksheet commands Insert, Delete, Column-Width, and Format, Table 3-4 now has an easy to understand, professional appearance. The use of these and other Worksheet commands will become second nature to you as you continue to master worksheet construction with 1-2-3.

SELF-TEST

QUESTIONS

1. What character do you type for access to 1-2-3's commands?
2. Which Worksheet command splits the screen into two windows?
3. If both a Range Format command and a Worksheet Global Format command have been set, which will take precedence when there is a conflict?
4. How do you undo a response to a command?
5. How does the Worksheet Global Column-Width command differ from the Worksheet Column-Width command?

ANSWERS

1. The slash [/] character.
2. The Worksheet Window command. (Type [/] [w] [w] to enter the command.)

3. Range commands *always* override Worksheet commands when there is a conflict between the two. However, Worksheet Erase overrides all commands, including Range commands.
4. Press the **[ESC]** key to undo a command, providing you haven't answered the last prompt or pressed **[ENTER]** the final time. If you have done either of these things, the command will be executed immediately.
5. The Worksheet Global Column-Width command sets the widths for *all* 256 columns at the same time. The Worksheet Column-Width command only sets the width of the column containing the worksheet cursor.

CHAPTER FOUR

THE RANGE COMMANDS

OBJECTIVES

- To introduce the Range commands and provide an overview of their functions.
- To learn to use 1-2-3's expanding cursor to specify ranges for use with Range commands and with many other Lotus commands and functions.
- To master the use of the most important Range commands: Format, Label-Prefix, Erase, Name, and Justify.

INTRODUCTION

The Range commands are among the most useful and, thus, most often used, of all Lotus 1-2-3 commands. See Figure 4-1 for the Range command tree.

Several Range commands have the same options and work like Worksheet commands of the same name. You will have little difficulty applying what you learned in chapter three to the Range Format, Label-Prefix, and Erase commands. Other Range commands (Name, Justify, and Input) are unique Range commands. Finally, two Range commands, Protect and Unprotect, are used in conjunction with the Worksheet Protection command.

The major difference between Worksheet commands and Range commands is the scope of action for each command. Worksheet commands work on the *entire* worksheet. Range commands operate on a specified *range* of cells.

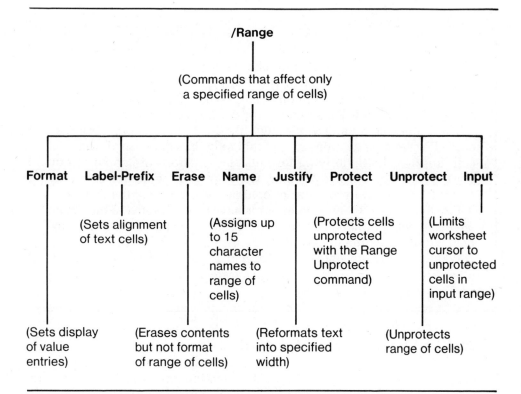

/Range

(Commands that affect only
a specified range of cells)

| Format | Label-Prefix | Erase | Name | Justify | Protect | Unprotect | Input |

(Sets alignment
of text cells)

(Assigns up
to 15
character
names to
range of
cells)

(Protects cells
unprotected
with the Range
Unprotect
command)

(Limits
worksheet
cursor to
unprotected
cells in
input range)

(Sets display
of value
entries)

(Erases contents
but not format
of range of cells)

(Reformats text
into specified
width)

(Unprotects
range of cells)

Figure 4-1. Command tree for all Range commands.

There are other differences. The Worksheet Label-Prefix command doesn't change the alignment (left, right, or center) of labels already entered into the worksheet. It only affects the alignment of labels entered after the command. In contrast, the Range Label-Prefix command only affects the alignment of existing labels. It doesn't affect labels entered after the command has been executed.

Since the Range commands, as well as most other 1-2-3 commands and built-in functions, operate on a range of cells, your first task is to master the techniques for specifying a range. You'll do this in the next section. Later in this chapter you'll explore the Range commands and learn how and when to use them.

Symphony

The Range command on Symphony's Sheet environment command menu includes most of the options of 1-2-3's Range command, but it also includes three options from 1-2-3's Data command, Fill, Distribution, and Table (what Symphony calls "What-If"). In addition, Symphony adds two new Range commands; Values and Transpose.

The Values command works just like 1-2-3's Copy command discussed in the next chapter, except that only the values displayed in a cells and not the underlying formulas or functions are copied from one part of a worksheet to another. The Transpose command converts row information into columns or column information into rows.

Finally, two 1-2-3 Range commands have been elevated to the Sheet environment command menu. They are Range Erase and Range Format, which in Symphony are simply called Erase and Format.

When appropriate, note will be taken in the following description of other differences between the two programs.

HOME, HOME ON THE RANGE...

A *range* of cells must always be a rectangle, but the rectangle can be made in one of four ways. It may be a *single cell*. This is the smallest possible range. It may be part of a *column* or part of a *row*. Finally, a range may be a *block* of cells. See Table 4-1 for an illustration of the four types of ranges.

A 1-2-3 range has only two restrictions. First, as noted, a range must be *rectangular*. It can't have any parts "sticking out" or areas "sticking in." Second, all cells in a range must be next to one another, that is, they must be adjacent or contiguous. You cannot specify a few cells here, skip some cells, and then continue to specify the range in another location. Other than these two restrictions, *a 1-2-3 range can be any rectangle of cells from a single cell to the entire worksheet.*

Specifying a Range

Whenever you need to specify a range for a command, Lotus displays a prompt such as:

Enter range of labels: B3..B3

or

Enter range to format: G25..G25

TABLE 4-1

Lotus recognizes four types of ranges: a single cell, part of a row, part of a column, or a rectangular block of cells.

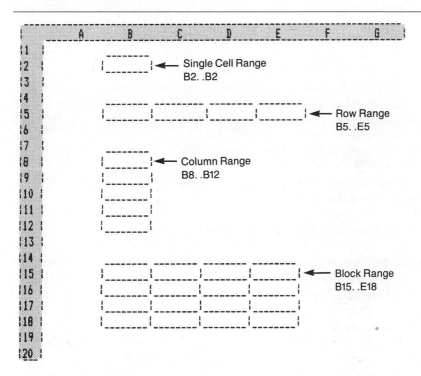

The first part of the prompt is clear enough. It simply asks you to specify a range. The last part is a proposed range.

Lotus ranges are always specified by two cell addresses separated by two dots. The dots are the *range operator*. They separate the first cell address, which is at one corner of the range, from the second cell address, which is at the opposite corner. The range operator is read as "from...to..." as in "the range of cells *from* B3 *to* C4." When both addresses are the same, such as B3..B3 or G25..G25, the range refers to a single cell.

The Range commands always use the current, active cell as the proposed range; B3 above, in the case of labels, and G25, in the case of the format.

Other commands, such as the Database command and the Print command, use as the proposed range the range most recently specified for the command during the current work session. (These ranges are stored with worksheets and are proposed the next time the worksheet is used.) If no range has been specified, the proposed range for all commands is the current, active cell.

The three ways to specify a 1-2-3 range are as follows:

1. Use the worksheet cursor to point to the range.
2. Type the second cell address in the range designation (e.g., B7 in B3..B7).
3. Supply a name previously assigned to a range of cells with the Range Name command.

If you want to use the current active cell as a one cell range, just press **[ENTER]**, and it will be selected.

The easiest way to specify a 1-2-3 range, and the one least likely to result in mistakes, is #1 above; using the worksheet cursor to *point* to the range.

Lotus' Marvelous One-Size-Fits-All Expanding Cursor

Lotus has a powerful feature for specifying ranges. When you are prompted for a range by a command, one corner of the range is usually anchored or *tacked* at the active cell. You are free to use the cursor control commands to stretch the cursor over the range of cells you want to specify. When you do this, 1-2-3 will shift into Point mode. The pointing corner of the range is called the *free* cell. It is the cell you move with the cursor control commands. It is easy to spot because it contains a flashing underline character. As the range expands, *all* the cells in the range are highlighted in reverse video. Thus, it is very easy to see exactly what you have chosen, and errors in selecting ranges are minimized. See Figure 4-2.

As you expand the cursor, the second cell address in the prompt changes. The first remains as the anchor cell, and the second is that of the free or pointing cell at the opposite corner of the range. The address of the free cell changes as you move it around the worksheet with the cursor control commands (see the command line in Figure 4-2).

Table 4-2 on page 94 lists the Lotus cursor control commands. The four arrow keys are most useful when the range you want to specify is small, or when you want to make small adjustments to the size of a range. The **[END]** **[ARROW]** key combination is particularly useful when you want to move the free cell to the end of a row or column. Use it when you want to select all cells containing row labels or all cells in a column for use in a SUM function. Finally, use the **[END]** **[HOME]** combination to select the range from the anchor cell to the end of worksheet.

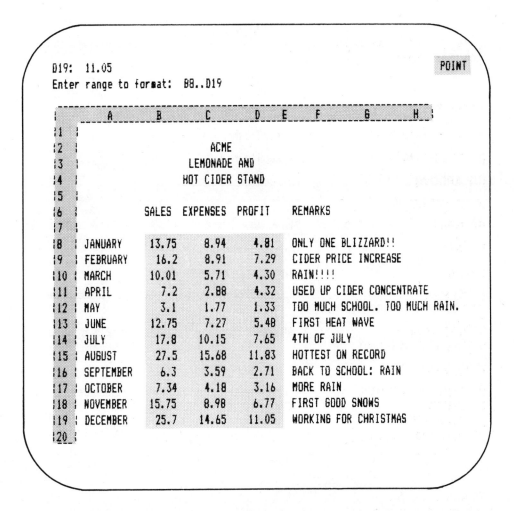

Figure 4-2. Lotus' expanding cursor makes it easy to tell which cells are in a range by displaying them in reverse video. Here, the Range Format Currency command is being issued. The prompt is "Enter range to format:" and the range B8..D19 has been highlighted.

Remember *all* cursor control commands are available for moving the free corner. You can combine commands, and you can adjust the range until you have highlighted exactly the cells you want to include in the range.

When you finish specifying a range, press the **[ENTER]** key and the range is accepted. If you are specifying a range for a Range command, the **[ENTER]** key also causes the command to execute.

TABLE 4-2

Lotus 1-2-3 cursor control commands. (Note, some microcomputers do not have all these keys. See Appendix A.)

Keystroke	Worksheet Cursor Moves . . .
[RIGHT ARROW]	One cell to the right.
[LEFT ARROW]	One cell to the left.
[UP ARROW]	One cell up.
[DOWN ARROW]	One cell down.
[HOME]	To cell A1.
[PgUp]	Up one full screen (20 lines).
[PgDn]	Down one full screen (20 lines).
[TAB] or [CTRL]-[RIGHT ARROW]	Right one full screen (approximately 72 characters).
[SHIFT] [TAB] or [CTRL]-[LEFT ARROW]	Left one full screen (approximately 72 characters).
[END] [HOME]	To last activated cell.
[END] [RIGHT ARROW] [END] [LEFT ARROW] [END] [UP ARROW] [END] [DOWN ARROW]	If next cell is *blank*, stops on last blank cell before next cell containing an entry. If next cell contains an *entry* stop on last entry cell before the next blank cell.

Special Features of the Point Mode

Several 1-2-3 keys have special functions in Point mode. When you enter a Range command, the position of the active cell is usually where you want the anchor cell to be. Thus, 1-2-3 automatically anchors the range to this cell. However, in many situations, particularly with built-in functions, you don't want the active cell to be a corner of the range, and the active cell is not anchored. When you first enter Point mode with a formula or a built-in function, the cursor control command moves the worksheet cursor around the worksheet, but it doesn't stretch it over a range. When you have positioned the active cell where you want it, you tack it down by typing a period [.]. Think of the dot as the point of a tack.

If you don't like where the anchor cell has been tacked, you can untack it any time by pressing the **[ESC]** key. This has two effects: the range shrinks back to the location of the anchor cell, and the anchor cell is untacked. You are still in Point mode, but you are free to move the active cell around the screen with the cursor control commands. When you get to a cell you want to be one corner of the range, anchor the worksheet cursor to it by typing a period **[.]**. Then proceed to use the cursor control keys to expand the cursor to point to the range.

Canceling Proposed Ranges

If you have already specified a range for a command, such as the Print or File commands during a 1-2-3 work session, Lotus proposes that same range the next time you select the command. This proposed range is often a time saver because you are likely to want to use the same range several times.

Sometimes, however, you do not want to use the range proposed by 1-2-3. In those cases, you can cancel a proposed range by pressing the **[BKSP]** key. The proposed range disappears, and the worksheet cursor is positioned over the *active cell*. This is where the worksheet cursor was located immediately before you entered the command. It is likely to be in a different location than the anchor cell of the proposed range. Again, the active cell won't be tacked down, and you are free to move it with the cursor commands. When it is in the right spot, tack it by typing a period and proceed to point to the range.

You can also cancel a proposed range with the **[ESC]** key. If you do, it shifts the range back to the *anchor cell* of the *proposed range*; not, as with the **[BKSP]** key, to the worksheet cursor's location cursor before entering the command. When canceling a proposed range, decide where you want to begin pointing. Use the **[ESC]** key when you want the anchor cell; use the **[BKSP]** key when you want the active cell.

Moving the Anchor Cell

You can move the anchor cell and, consequently, the free cell, by typing a period **[.]** after the cursor has been expanded. Moving the anchor cell repositions the free cell, and once repositioned, you can expand the range in a different direction.

When you type the period, the anchor cell moves to an adjacent corner of the range, and the free cell moves to the opposite corner. The anchor cell usually moves clockwise, though the actual direction depends on how the range was specified.

COMMANDS COMMON TO RANGE AND WORKSHEET

Each of the Range commands has much in common with its worksheet counterpart.

Format

The Range Format command can modify the display of numeric information in the designated range. See Figure 4-3 for the Range Format command tree.

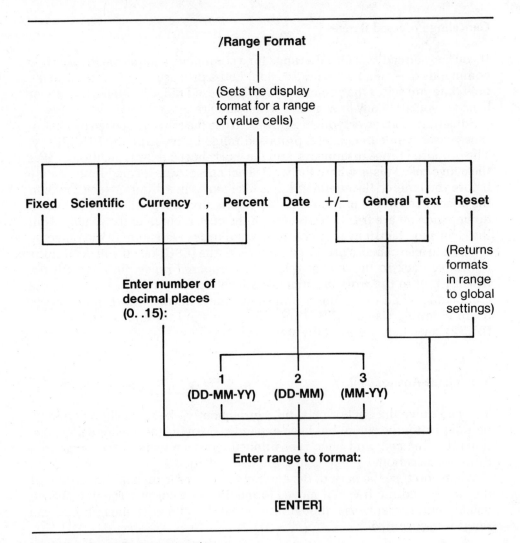

Figure 4-3. Range Format command tree.

The options available under the Range Format command, Table 4-3, are the same as those available under the Worksheet Global Format command. Use the Range Format command to customize the different cells on a worksheet to display their contents in the clearest, most accurate manner: format cells containing dollar amounts with the Currency format; format cells containing percentages with the Percent format. Use the Date format to display cells containing DATE functions in a readable form (e.g., 4-June-85).

TABLE 4-3
Range format command display options. (Same as Worksheet Format display options.)

Format	Description	Examples
General	Trailing zeros suppressed. Initial global display format. Very large and very small numbers are displayed in scientific format.	12.427 −4.24 1.3E+12
Fixed	Fixed number of decimal places (0 − 15).	12 −125.00
Scientific	Exponent scientific notation. Decimals from (0 − 15). Exponent of 10 from −99 to +99.	−4.3E+00 1.2E+01 6.24E−24
Currency	Dollar sign before each value entry. Commas between thousands. Negative numbers in parentheses. Decimal places (0 − 15).	$12.43 ($4.25) $8,999
, (comma)	Same as Currency format except no dollar signs are displayed.	12.43 (4.25) 8,999
+/−	Horizontal pictograph. The number of symbols is the integer part of the value. Symbols: "+" for positive values, "−" for negative, "." for zero.	++++++ ------ ....
Percent	Displays value *times* 100 followed by a percent sign. Decimal places (0 − 15).	1242.7% −4.25%
Text	Formulas are shown as entered; numbers are in General format.	12.427 +C22/4
Date	D1: Day-Month-Year D2: Day-Month D3: Month-Year	15-Mar-84 15-Mar Mar-84

Source: *Lotus 1-2-3 Manual*, Lotus Development Corporation, p. 158, Boston, Mass., 1983.

To use each command, type the first letter of each choice, /**RFF** for Range Format Fixed, for example, or position the command line cursor over your choice and press **[ENTER]**. Then respond to the prompts. In the case of Fixed, Scientific, Currency , (comma) and Percent Format commands, the first prompt asks for the number of decimal places (0 to 15). For all Format commands, the second prompt asks for the range to be formatted. Use one of the techniques discussed in the previous section to specify the range. Then press **[ENTER]**, and the chosen Format command executes for the cells in the range.

Cells formatted with the Range Format command display numbers currently in the cells in the format specified. Furthermore, any numbers subsequently entered into cells in the range will also be displayed under the chosen format.

The status line at the top of the screen displays the Range Format status for the current, active cell. A Fixed format for two decimals would display **(F2)**; a Percent format with zero decimals would display **(P0)**.

One option that appears on the Range Format command menu that doesn't appear on the Worksheet Global Format command menu is *Reset*. If you choose this option, 1-2-3 resets the formats in the specified range to the format set at the global level. Use it whenever you want to return a range of cells to the Global Format settings.

Symphony

As noted in the preceding chapter, Symphony adds international date and time formats to the format options available in 1-2-3. It also renames the comma **[,]** format to the "Punctuated" format. Otherwise, the format commands, both at the Range level and the Worksheet or Settings level, are the same in the two programs.

Label-Prefix

Lotus 1-2-3's Range Label-Prefix command and the Worksheet Global Label-Prefix command work in opposite ways. The Range command changes only the label-prefix of those cells in the range that *already* contain labels. It has no effect on labels later entered into these or other cells in the range. Their alignment will be governed by the label-prefix set at the global level.

Use the Range Label-Prefix command whenever you want to re-align *existing* labels. This is best done after all the labels in a range have been entered. Otherwise, you have to reset the label-prefix several times. Use the Worksheet command to change the alignment of labels yet to be entered. See Figure 4-4 for the command tree.

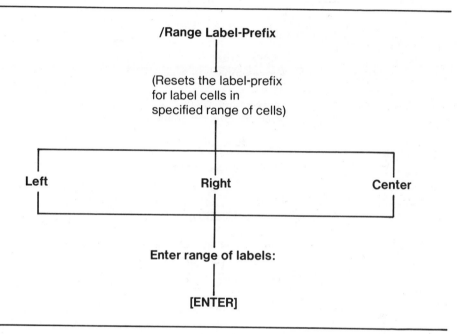

Figure 4-4. Range Label-Prefix command tree.

Erase

The Worksheet Erase and the Range Erase commands work quite differently. Remember, the Worksheet Erase command returns the worksheet to its initial state when first loaded. All formats, including label-alignments, column widths, range names, remembered print ranges, are reset to their default values. You get a clean slate with the Worksheet Erase command.

The Range Erase command is less sweeping in its actions. It erases text or values from only the designated worksheet cells. It does not change the format setting, nor does it change the column width. It does, of course, wipe out the label-alignment character because that is part of each label. Think of the Range Erase command as the eraser on your electronic pencil. Use it to clean up a worksheet (without affecting the location of other cells as the Delete command would) and to remove incorrect or unneeded information.

Beware! As with all 1-2-3 Range commands, 1-2-3 doesn't ask you to confirm your intention to erase a range once you have it specified. Pressing **[ENTER]** after choosing a range executes Range Erase, and the contents of the cells in the range (though not the format settings) are lost forever. See Figure 4-5 for the command tree.

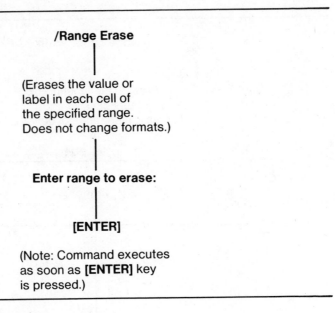

Figure 4-5. Range Erase command tree.

Protect and Unprotect

At first, the operation of the Range Protect command may seem strange. In fact, the Range Protect command is best thought of as an ''Un-Unprotect'' command since its *only* function is to cancel the unprotection status conveyed with the Range Unprotect command. It doesn't even protect a cell *unless* protection has already been enabled with the Worksheet Global Protection Enable command. If protection has been enabled, you can use the Range Protect command to protect any cells that have been unprotected with the Range Unprotect command. See Figure 4-6 for the command tree.

The Range Unprotect command lets you prevent the Global Protection Enable command from locking up all the cells on your worksheet. You can, use it at *any* time before or after using the Global command. Unprotected cells on a worksheet don't need to be next to one another, but you have to enter the Range Unprotect command separately for each non-adjacent group of cells.

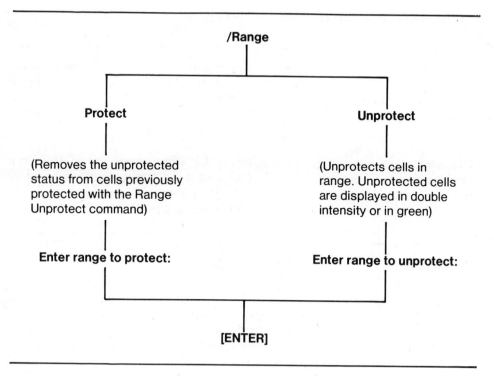

Figure 4-6. Range Protect and Range Unprotect command tree.

Cells you want to unprotect are usually data entry cells in which new information is entered to update a worksheet. In this case, protection prevents the formulas and labels in all but the unprotected cells from being changed accidentally.

Once you unprotect a cell, it is displayed differently from other cells. On monochrome displays capable of displaying in two intensities, unprotected cells are displayed in bright characters. On color displays, unprotected cells are displayed in green. In either case, the status line displays a "U" when the active cell is unprotected.

Finally, you can use the Input command, described later in this chapter, to limit cursor movement to only those cells in a specified range that have been unprotected. This makes the process of updating a protected worksheet even easier.

COMMANDS UNIQUE TO RANGE

Three Range commands do not have counterparts in the Worksheet command: the Name command, used to name a range of cells; the Justify command, used to reformat long text entries into paragraphs; and the Input command, used to create data entry forms.

Name

The most useful of the three commands is the Name command. With it you can assign a name to a range of cells. Once assigned, the name can be used in *any* situation—command, formula, or built-in function—where 1-2-3 allows you to use a range. See Figure 4-7 for the command tree.

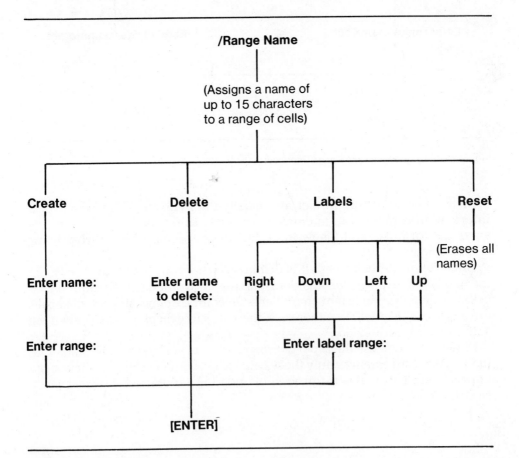

Figure 4-7. Range Name command tree.

Range names are particularly useful in situations where you must specify different ranges for the same command. A good example is the Print command. You will often want to print different parts of a worksheet for different purposes. A summary section might, for example, go to the office manager while a detailed report goes to accounting. You can name the summary range, SUMMARY, and the detailed range DETAIL. When you have to make a printout, you simply specify SUMMARY or DETAIL as the range, and leave the rest to 1-2-3.

If you are creating a worksheet which you or someone else may have to modify, you can assign names to ranges so the summation function, for example, reads SUM(COST) rather than SUM(B4..B8). With names rather than range references, it will be easier for you or someone else to grasp the structure of a worksheet and to correct or modify it.

Assigning Names to a Range Assigning a name to a range is a simple procedure. Begin by typing:

/RNC

This enters the Range Name Create command. You are then prompted to:

Enter name:

You can use up to 15 characters to create your range name. You can use any valid 1-2-3 character, but upper and lower case letters are treated interchangeably. For example, Sales and SALES are the same name to 1-2-3.

The special characters usable in range names include $, &, and % as well as the blank character. However, make it a habit to use either the dash or the underline in place of a blank (e.g., TOTAL_ COST). Avoid blanks because it is easy to misspecify names containing them. Also, don't use a name that is the same as a cell address (e.g., A16). If you specify this in response to a range prompt, 1-2-3 can't tell whether you intend to refer to a single cell or to a range of cells. Lotus resolves this dilemma by assuming you are referring to a single cell rather than to a range name.

The best range names are either logically related to their function, such as the DETAIL and SUMMARY examples above, or they are taken directly from labels on the worksheet. For example, the best name for a group of cells in a row labeled "Labor Cost" is LABOR_COST. This is much better than VARIABLE1 or some other less descriptive name whose meaning you'll soon forget.

After you specify the name, you are prompted to:

Enter range:

Either specify the cell addresses at the beginning and end of the range, or use the cursor control commands to point to the range. Pointing is easier, and you are less likely to make errors. After you specify the range to be named, press **[ENTER]** to complete the command.

Viewing Range Names with the [NAME]Function Key The major problem with range names is that you are likely to forget them, but don't worry. Lotus has a memory an elephant would envy.

Whenever you need to specify a name in response to a slash command prompt, 1-2-3 will be in Point mode. You can then press the **[NAME]** function key and all the names you have assigned on the current worksheet appear on the bottom line of the control panel.

The range names are presented in alphabetical order regardless of the order in which they were created, and only five names fit on a line at one time. You can, however, use the four arrow keys and the **[HOME]** and **[END]** keys to move the command line cursor through all the names. When doing this, the **[UP ARROW]** and **[DOWN ARROW]** keys are particularly helpful. They move you one line up or down in the name list. The **[HOME]** and **[END]** keys move the command line cursor to the first and last names in the list, respectively. See Figure 4-8 for a diagram of how the arrow keys work with a list of names.

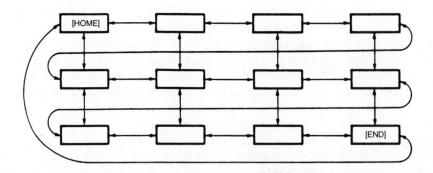

Figure 4-8. Only one row of five names can be displayed at one time on the prompt line in the control panel. The **[RIGHT ARROW]** and **[LEFT ARROW]** keys move the command line cursor horizontally through the list of range names. The **[UP ARROW]** and **[DOWN ARROW]** keys move from one row of five names to the same place in the adjacent row. The **[HOME]** key moves the command line cursor to the first name in the list. The **[END]** key moves it to the last name in the list.

Source: *Lotus 1-2-3 Manual,* Lotus Development Corporation, p. 61, Boston, Mass., 1983.

When you find the name you want, either type it or highlight it with the command line cursor and press **[ENTER]**. The name is entered, and the command executes.

Unfortunately, you *can't* paste names into built-in formulas with the **[NAME]** key. You can, however, type names into formulas and functions where they will work just like any other 1-2-3 range specification.

Viewing Names with Range Name Create If you aren't in Point mode, you can view the assigned range names by entering the Range Name Create command. All current range names are displayed. If the list is more than five names long, use the command line cursor control keys to view the names.

If you want to see the cells to which a range name applies, go one step farther in the Name Create command. Select the name you are interested in and 1-2-3 will highlight the cells assigned to that name. If part of the range is off the screen, type a period **[.]** and the anchor cell moves from corner to corner to display the entire range. When you have finished reviewing the range, press **[ENTER]** to accept it and to exit the command.

When you are finished looking at the range names, you can also press the **[ESC]** key the required number of times or press the **[CTRL]-[BREAK]** combination to cancel the Range Name command.

Symphony

One of the many ways Symphony goes 1-2-3 one better has to do with the viewing of range names. When you press the **[MENU]** function key while viewing names with the Symphony Name command, the screen blanks, and *all* of the range names are displayed. You can then select a name for use by highlighting it with the cursor control keys and then pressing the **[ENTER]** key. If you don't use this feature, Symphony displays names in exactly the same way 1-2-3 does.

Assigning Names with Range Name Label Lotus has a particularly convenient command, the Range Name Label command, that assigns a list of labels to a set of cells. You will often use this command when assigning names to parameters. In Table 4-4 on the next page, for example, the parameters PRINCIPAL, RATE, and WITHDRAWAL can all be assigned as names for the values in cells B5 to B7 by typing:

/RNL

TABLE 4-4

With the Range Name Label command you can name the cells B5 to B7 with the labels in the cells to their right: PRINCIPAL, RATE, and WITHDRAWAL.

```
|              A              B              C              D          |
|1 |
|2 |
|3 |                PARAMETERS
|4 |
|5 |          PRINCIPAL     $1,000.00
|6 |               RATE        10.00%
|7 |         WITHDRAWAL      $100.00
|8 |
|9 |
|10|
|11|                        PERIOD 1       PERIOD 2       PERIOD 3
|12|          Principal     $1,000.00       $990.00        $979.00
|13|         Withdrawal      $100.00        $100.00        $100.00
|14|           Interest       $90.00         $89.00         $87.90
|15|     Balance Forward     $990.00        $979.00        $966.90
|16|
|17| TOTAL INTEREST PAID:     $266.90
|18|
|19|
|20|
```

This enters the Name Label command. You are then given the choice of:

Right   Down   Left   Up

Lotus wants to know where the cells to be labeled are in relationship to the labels. In Table 4-4, the data cells are to the *right* of the labels, so choose "Right." Lotus now asks for the range containing the *labels*, not the range containing the data. In Table 4-4, this is the range A5..A7. Specify the range and press **[ENTER]**, and the three labels are assigned as names to the three data cells.

Using Names in Formulas Lotus' names work best with commands (such as print ranges), but they can also be used in formulas. Table 4-5 shows the formulas behind Table 4-4. The names in the formulas make the formulas easier to understand. Note the use of the name INTEREST_PAID in the @SUM formula. This name combines two words with the underline character.

TABLE 4-5

Range names make the formulas used to construct Table 4-4 easier to understand.

```
             A              B              C              D
 1
 2
 3              PARAMETERS
 4
 5           PRINCIPAL        $1,000.00
 6              RATE             10.00%
 7         WITHDRAWAL          $100.00
 8
 9
10
11                          PERIOD 1              PERIOD 2              PERIOD 3
12         Principal +PRINCIPAL           +B15                  +C15
13        Withdrawal +$WITHDRAWAL         +$WITHDRAWAL          +$WITHDRAWAL
14          Interest +$RATE*(B12-$WITHDRAWAL) +$RATE*(C12-$WITHDRAWAL) +$RATE*(D12-$WITHDRAWAL)
15    Balance Forward (B12-$WITHDRAWAL)+B14 (C12-$WITHDRAWAL)+C14 (D12-$WITHDRAWAL)+D14
16
17 TOTAL INTEREST PAID: @SUM(INTEREST_PAID)
18
19
20
```

Eliminating Names If you want to remove a previously assigned name, use the Name Delete command. The command line displays all the names, and you can choose any name to delete from the list by either pointing to it with the command line cursor or by typing it in.

To eliminate *all* the names on a worksheet, use the Name Reset command. Be careful, however. Lotus erases all the names the *moment* you select the Reset option by either typing the first letter of the command **[R]**, or by positioning the command line cursor over it and pressing **[ENTER]**. You don't get a chance to reconsider your choice, so before using the Reset option, be sure you really want to erase *all* the range names.

When you eliminate a range name, Lotus automatically substitutes the appropriate worksheet cell references into any functions, formulas, or remembered ranges that used the range name. Table 4-6 shows the functions behind Table 4-4 after the Name Reset command has been used.

TABLE 4-6

When a range name is deleted, cell addresses replace the name in all formulas, functions, and remembered names. This table shows the formulas behind Table 4-4 after the Range Reset command is issued.

```
|           A              B            C            D        |
|1 |
|2 |
|3 |            PARAMETERS
|4 |
|5 |        PRINCIPAL    $1,000.00
|6 |            RATE       10.00%
|2 |      WITHDRAWAL     $100.00
|8 |
|9 |
|10|
|11|                    PERIOD 1     PERIOD 2     PERIOD 3
|12|      Principal +B5          +B15        +C15
|13|     Withdrawal +B7          +B7         +B7
|14|        Interest +B6*(B12-B7)  +B6*(C12-B7)  +B6*(D12-B7)
|15|  Balance Forward (B12-B7)+B14  (C12-B7)+C14  (D12-B7)+D14
|16|
|17| TOTAL INTEREST PAID: @SUM(B14..D14)
|18|
|19|
|20|
```

Lotus performs a similar function when you name a range of cells that has already been used in a function, formula, or as a remembered range for graph, print command, or database function. In this case, Lotus substitutes the range name for the cell references.

If you assign a new name to a previously named range, the new name is substituted for the old range name. However, the old range name is still on the range name list, and you can still use the old name. But every time you do, it is converted to the new name.

If you assign an already assigned name to a new range of cells, the new cells are used in any formula, function, or command that previously used the range name.

Limitations There are two reasons Range names are not particularly easy to use with user-defined formulas or with built-in functions. First, you cannot use the **[NAME]** function key to specify cell references for formulas and functions. This is a great drawback because you must *type* each name into each formula. You can't even view the names you have assigned, so the possibility of making mistakes is greatly increased.

Second, when the Copy command is used to copy information from one cell to other cells, range names are treated as *relative* cell references even though you might intuitively think the move would always refer to the same location. The Copy command is discussed in detail in the next chapter but, for now, all you need to know is that relative cell references in formulas adjust from cell to cell as they are copied, so they refer to cells *relative* to the cell containing the copy of the formula.

However, you usually want named ranges to refer to *specific* cells on a worksheet (the PRINCIPAL, RATE, and WITHDRAWAL cells in Table 4-4, for example). This would be an *absolute* cell reference, so that when the formula was copied from cell-to-cell, the reference would remain unchanged.

To get a range name to act as an absolute cell reference, you must precede the name with a dollar sign **[$]**. A dollar sign is how 1-2-3 designates absolute cell references. Unfortunately, you can't specify the dollar sign as part of the name when you create it. If you do, the dollar sign is treated as any other character. It won't designate the name as an absolute cell reference.

Regardless of these shortcomings, named ranges are particularly useful in situations where you need to specify different ranges for the same command over and over. Use a range name whenever it is easier to assign the name than to point to the range with the expanding cursor.

Justify

The Range Justify command formats long labels into paragraphs. With this command, you can enter text, up to 240 characters in a single cell, and then reformat it into a width that looks best on the screen or the printed page. See Figure 4-9 on the next page for the command tree.

Symphony

Symphony doesn't have a Justify command. Instead, one of its environments, "Doc" for "Document," provides standard word processing features that are much more powerful than 1-2-3's Justify command. Text, however, is still stored as left-justified long labels, and it can be edited as can any other long label when in a Sheet environment.

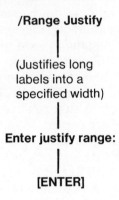

/Range Justify

(Justifies long
labels into a
specified width)

Enter justify range:

[ENTER]

Figure 4-9. Range Justify command tree.

To use the Justify command, type text as long labels in a *single* column *one cell wide*. Lotus begins justifying text at the first cell in the column and continues until it reaches the first non-label cell. In practice, this is usually a blank cell, although it can be a value cell.

To understand how the Justify command works, look at Table 4-7 which displays the first part of Abraham Lincoln's Gettysburg Address. It would have been easy for Lincoln to get his ideas down quickly by letting Lotus' soft cell boundaries display characters to the right of each cell in column B. Once the text has been composed, it would look better on the screen and be easier to read if it were justified over four or five columns. To do this, position the worksheet cursor on *the first text cell* in the column and type:

/RJ

This enters the Range Justify command. Lotus prompts:

Enter justify range:

There are two ways to specify the range to justify. Learn both, because each produces a different effect.

Single Row As noted, the cursor should be positioned on the first cell containing text; cell B4 in Table 4-7. If it isn't, press either the **[ESC]** key or the **[BKSP]** key, and reposition the worksheet cursor over the appropriate cell. Anchor it there by typing a period **[.]**, and then use the **[RIGHT**

TABLE 4-7

The text for the first few lines of the Gettysburg Address are entered as long labels in cells B4 through B7 in Part A. In Part B this text has been justified over columns B to E.

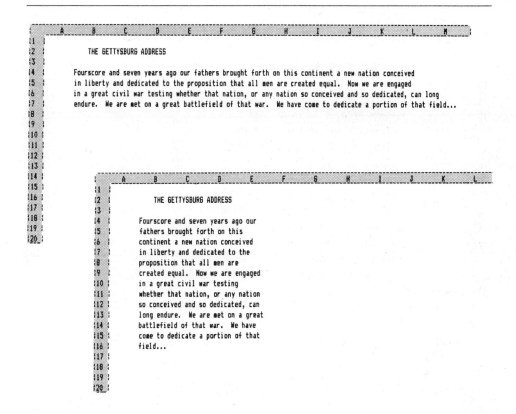

ARROW] key to expand the cursor over the desired number of columns.

When you are finished, press **[ENTER]**, and 1-2-3 justifies the text into the specified width. As it does, 1-2-3 writes down the screen for as many rows as it takes to display *all* the text. If necessary, it moves entries *in column B* down the worksheet to make room for the justified text. Only specify the range as a single row when you are sure there is sufficient space for the text down the screen at its new width.

In Table 4-8, a table of civil war casualties appears below the cells containing text. When the text is justified down the screen in response to a single row justify range, the text writes over the first part of the table. None of the contents of the cells in the table are destroyed, but the table is confusing.

TABLE 4-8

When the range for the Justify command is specified as a single row of cells, 1-2-3 justifies all of the text.

```
    A       B     C      D        E       F        G       H

 1
 2            THE GETTYSBURG ADDRESS
 3
 4           Fourscore and seven years ago our
 5           fathers brought forth on this
 6           continent a new nation conceived
 7           in liberty and dedicated to the
 8           proposition that all men are
 9           created equal.  Now we are engaged
10           in a great civil war testing
11           whether that nation, or any nation
12           so conceived and so dediCIVIL WAR CASUALTIES
13           long endure.  We are met on a
14           great battlef Battletha   OtherWe   Wounds
15           have come to  Deaths a  Deathsof not Mortal   Total
16  UNION FORthat field...
17     1861-1865            140,414   224,097   281,881   646,392
18
19  CONFEDERATE FORCES
20     1863-1866             74,524    59,297      ---    133,821
21
22
23
24
25
```

Source, casualties: *The World Almanac and Book of Facts 1983,* Newspaper Enterprise Association, Inc., p. 337, New York, New York, 1983.

Multiple Row You can prevent the intermixing of different parts of your worksheet by specifying a *block* of cells in response to the "Enter range to justify" prompt. The width of the block determines the width of the justified text, just as it did before. But now the number of *rows* in the block determines the number of rows into which text can be justified. This way, you can prevent justified text from moving material that is below it.

If the area specified is too small to contain all the justified text in the specified width, Lotus gives the error message:

Justify range is full or line too long

That's "Ok." When you respond to the error message by pressing **[ENTER]** or **[ESC]**, as much text as possible is justified and the last few lines remain unjustified. See Table 4-9 for an example.

TABLE 4-9

When you specify the justify range as a block of cells, 1-2-3 limits justification to the number of rows in the block. If that isn't enough room to justify the text, the last few lines of text remain unjustified.

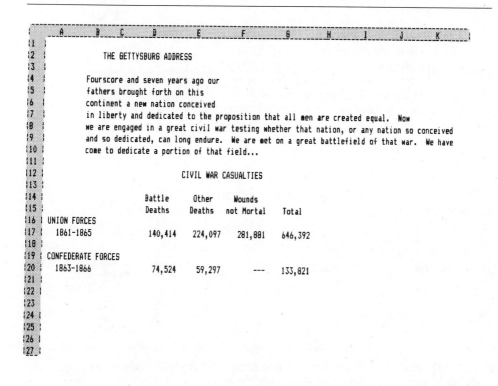

Source, casualties: *The World Almanac and Book of Facts 1983,* Newspaper Enterprise Association, Inc., p. 337, New York, New York, 1983.

If the justified text won't fit, insert some rows and repeat the Justify command. Usually only one or two trial and error adjustments are required to arrive at a correctly justified block of text. See Table 4-10.

TABLE 4-10

You can use the Worksheet Insert Row command in conjunction with the Justify command to be sure justified text and the other material on the worksheet fit together properly.

```
        A       B    C     D        E         F        G        H
 1 
 2                 THE GETTYSBURG ADDRESS
 3 
 4              Fourscore and seven years ago our fathers
 5              brought forth on this continent a new nation
 6              conceived in liberty and dedicated to the
 7              proposition that all men are created equal.
 8              Now we are engaged in a great civil war
 9              testing whether that nation, or any nation so
10              conceived and so dedicated, can long endure.
11              We are met on a great battlefield of that
12              war.  We have come to dedicate a portion of
13              that field...
14 
15                         CIVIL WAR CASUALTIES
16 
17                      Battle     Other    Wounds
18                      Deaths     Deaths   not Mortal   Total
19 UNION FORCES
20     1861-1865        140,414   224,097   281,881   646,392
21 
22 CONFEDERATE FORCES
23     1863-1866         74,524    59,297      ---     133,821
24 
25 
26 
27 
```

Source, casualties: *The World Almanac and Book of Facts 1983,* Newspaper Enterprise Association, Inc., p. 337, New York, New York, 1983.

The forgoing example showed long lines of text being justified into a narrower column of cells, but the Range Justify command also justifies shorter lines into longer ones. The same procedure is used, except the range to justify is wider than the text. Again, you can prevent cells below the text cells from moving in response to the Justify command by specifying a block of cells rather than a single row.

You can use Lotus' soft cell boundaries and Range Justify command to place extended comments on your worksheets. You can also use the Headers and Footers option of the Print command to combine text and tables into a short report.

Beyond this, release 1A of Lotus 1-2-3 doesn't contain other word processing features. Still you can use the Justify command in conjunction with soft cell boundaries and the **[EDIT]** key for short writing tasks.

Input

The last Range command is the Input command. It's a specialized command that limits the worksheet cursor's movement to those cells in the Input command range that have been unprotected with the Range Unprotect command. Remember, unprotected cells are displayed in double strength (bright) characters on most monochrome monitors and in green on color monitors. See Figure 4-10 for the command tree.

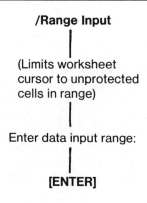

/Range Input

|

(Limits worksheet
cursor to unprotected
cells in range)

|

Enter data input range:

|

[ENTER]

Figure 4-10. Range Input command tree. (Note: At least one cell in the input range must be unprotected with the Range Unprotect command.)

The Input command is most often used to create data entry forms where the operator (usually someone inexperienced in the use of electronic spreadsheets) is prevented from moving the cursor to any cell other than unprotected, data entry cells. In conjunction with the Global Protect Enable command, the Input command provides protection for the worksheet's structure while allowing for easy data entry.

To use the command, type:

/RI

You are prompted:

Enter data input range:

By now you know you can respond to this prompt either by typing a cell address, by pointing to the range, or by supplying a range name. Since you are likely to use the Input command repeatedly, using a previously assigned range name is the most convenient option. You can then use the **[NAME]** function key to enter the name in response to the prompt.

Once the range has been supplied, 1-2-3 does several things. It places the worksheet cursor on the first unprotected cell in the input range. It also repositions the table so the upper left corner of the input range is in the upper left of the screen. This displays the largest possible amount of the input range. If you don't want to have the information above and to the left of the input range moved off the screen, include it in the input range. The size of the range doesn't affect the data entry cells; it just affects where 1-2-3 positions them on the screen.

Finally, 1-2-3 limits the worksheet cursor's movement to unprotected cells in the input range. The four arrow keys and the **[HOME]** and **[END]** keys are active. The other cursor control keys are disabled. The **[RIGHT ARROW]** key skips the worksheet cursor to the right to the next unprotected cell. If there is none in the first row of the input range, 1-2-3 searches down the rows until the next unprotected cell is found. The other arrow keys operate in a similar fashion. The **[HOME]** key moves the cursor to the first unprotected cell in the input range. The **[END]** key moves it to the last unprotected cell in the range.

The input range must have at least one unprotected cell, otherwise you receive the error message:

No unprotected cells in range

Also, the cursor does not move to unprotected cells that are not in the designated range.

To end the Input command, press either the **[ESC]** key or, if you have not pressed any other key, the **[ENTER]** key. If you have already pressed a key, pressing either the **[ESC]** key or two successive presses of the **[ENTER]** key exits the command.

The most convenient way to use the command is to name the input range and then pick the range name off the name list with the aid of the **[NAME]** function key. This speeds entry into the Input command and minimizes the knowledge required of a data entry clerk. You can make the Input command easiest to use if the input range name is the *only* named range on the worksheet. Then it can be selected by simply typing **[NAME]** and **[ENTER]** in response to the "input range name" prompt.

HANDS ON: USING THE RANGE COMMANDS

The Range commands are powerful tools for editing an electronic spreadsheet and for making it clearer and easier to understand. The Before part of Table 4-11 (on page 118) shows a hypothetical invoice in which long labels disappear, date functions appear as date numbers, and the text at the bottom extends far beyond the right edge of the invoice.

In the After part of the table, column widths are expanded. Integer and Currency formats are set where appropriate. The headings under the description are right-justified, and the text is formatted with the Range Justify command. Rows are inserted to open up the table in order to make it easier to understand, and the date numbers are converted to readable dates (in the Day-Month-Year format).

Table 4-11 illustrates several special things. The address at the top of the invoice (Rust, Rot, And Wreckage, etc.) is centered by inserting spaces *before* the text. The center option of the Label-Prefix command won't center the long labels because they extend beyond a single cell boundary. (Recall that long labels are always left-justified.) To insert the blanks, simply use the **[EDIT]** function key, position the edit line cursor in the appropriate space, and press the **[SPACE BAR]**. The **[DEL]** key can be used to remove spaces if you insert too many. You may have to edit the same label several times before it is correctly positioned.

More will be said about 1-2-3's built-in functions in chapter eight, but now you should know that the @TODAY function, entered into B8, reads the date entered into your system. Remember, you are prompted for the date whenever you load 1-2-3. The Payment Due date is simply today's date plus 30; payment is due in thirty days. Since 1-2-3 keeps track of dates as numbers, this operation is easy to perform. The Range Format Date command then displays the date numbers in an understandable format.

TABLE 4-11

The Range commands and the Worksheet Column-Width command can make the difference between a worksheet that is almost impossible to decipher and one that is clear and easy to understand.

In the Before worksheet date functions display numbers in cells B8 and B9 and many of the long labels do not appear because the columns are too narrow to display them.

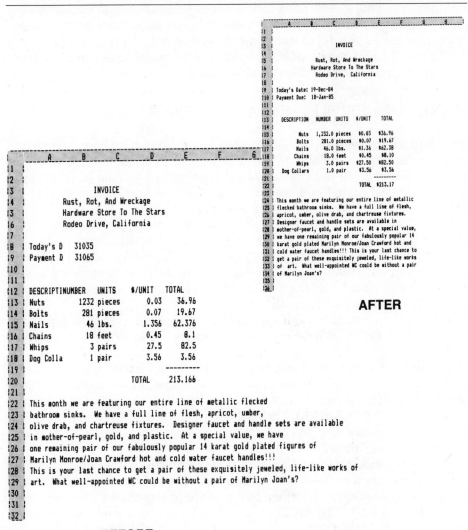

AFTER

BEFORE

The Before and After parts of Table 4-11 dramatically illustrate the power of the Worksheet and Range commands to improve a spreadsheet's appearance. You would, however, be misled if you thought you should wait until construction was completed to apply the commands. In practice, the Range and Worksheet commands are used as you build the worksheet. If you enter a formula or type a label and discover, for example, that the column width is too narrow, Press a few keys and it is changed. Then you enter some more labels and decide to align them to the right rather than the left. A few keystrokes and the labels are where you want them.

There is constant interaction between the formulas, functions, and labels you enter to construct the worksheet and the Worksheet and Range commands you use to improve the worksheet's appearance. Working back and forth between construction and appearance is an easy, natural way to create electronic spreadsheets.

The Range commands discussed in this chapter and the Worksheet commands discussed in the last chapter make up the bulk of the special electronic tools 1-2-3 has for constructing spreadsheets. As you construct more spreadsheets, commands such as the Worksheet Column-Width, Insert, and Delete commands, and the Range Format, Label-Prefix, and Erase commands will become second nature to you. You will type from memory /**WC** whenever you want to set a column width. You won't even look at the control panel. But when it comes to the less-used commands; Name, Range, or Justify, for example, 1-2-3 stands ready with full word descriptions and prompts. Should you become stuck at any point, press the **[HELP]** function key, and an entire screen of information relevant to your current position in a command will appear.

SELF-TEST

QUESTIONS

1. Which command should you use to change the label-prefix character of labels already entered into a worksheet?
2. Explain three ways to specify a range for use with one of the Range commands?
3. What are the major differences between the Worksheet Erase and the Range Erase commands?
4. Give the two ways to specify the column width for justifying text with the Range Justify command.
5. What key do you press to untack the anchor cell?
6. What happens when you press the period key when the cursor has been expanded in Point mode?

ANSWERS

1. The Range Label-Prefix command. This command affects only those labels already entered into a worksheet.
2. You can (1) point at the range with the cursor control keys, (2) type in the cell addresses for the beginning and end of the range, or (3) use a range name.
3. The Worksheet Erase command erases the entire worksheet and resets all settings to their default values. The Range Erase command only operates on a designated range of cells. Furthermore, it only erases the contents of the cells while leaving the format settings and the column-width settings unchanged.
4. You can specify either a row or a block. If you specify a row, 1-2-3 justifies all the text into that width, even if it means moving entries in cells down the worksheet. If you specify a block, the text does not extend beyond the block, and entries below the block are not affected. If there isn't enough space to justify the text, the last few lines remain unjustified.
5. You can always untack the anchor cell by pressing the **[ESC]** key.
6. Each time you press the period key, the anchor cell moves to an adjacent cell so you can use the cursor control keys to expand the range in another direction.

CHAPTER FIVE
THE COPY, MOVE, AND QUIT COMMANDS

OBJECTIVES

- To learn to use the Copy command to construct electronic worksheets quickly and efficiently.
- To learn to use the Move command to construct and modify electronic worksheets.
- To end a Lotus 1-2-3 work session with the Quit command.

INTRODUCTION

Chapters Three and Four introduced you to most of the Lotus 1-2-3 commands for constructing and modifying electronic spreadsheets. The Format commands, Label-Prefix commands, the Insert, Delete, and Erase commands, and the Column-Width command will be used with every electronic spreadsheet you construct. However, the commands discussed in this chapter are, if anything, more important and more frequently used than the commands introduced in the last two chapters. They are productivity commands which magnify your ability to quickly create and modify spreadsheets.

The Copy command copies text and values, as well as label-prefix characters and display formats, from a source range to a target range. With it you can quickly spread formulas and functions across a table to finish a worksheet or to prepare multi-period projections.

The Move command moves the contents of cells from one location on the worksheet to another. With it you can easily modify an existing worksheet's structure.

The Quit command, like the Copy and Move commands, is on the slash command menu. Thus, it can be executed with a minimum of keystrokes. You use the Quit command to end a 1-2-3 work session and to exit to the Lotus Access System. Recall from Chapter Two that the Access System performs file management tasks on data diskettes, imports files created by other programs such as VisiCalc and dBASE II, and from it you exit to your computer's operating system or to the PrintGraph program to print 1-2-3 graphs.

Symphony

The Copy command and the Move command work in exactly the same ways in both Symphony and 1-2-3. The only difference is a slight change in the wording of the prompts for each command.

Also, as noted, Symphony has a Range command, that copies only the values displayed in the source range into the cells in the target range. Finally, you leave a Symphony work session by selecting Exit from the Services menu rather than Quit from the Slash command menu.

THE COPY COMMAND

The Copy command is the most important of the three commands discussed in this chapter. It may be the most important worksheet construction command 1-2-3 offers. By copying text, numbers, formulas, functions and their formats, you can quickly construct a worksheet, spread formulas across columns and rows, and complete other routine, time-consuming, tedious tasks. Figure 5-1 shows how a few keystrokes and the Copy command can spread the contents of one cell across an entire worksheet.

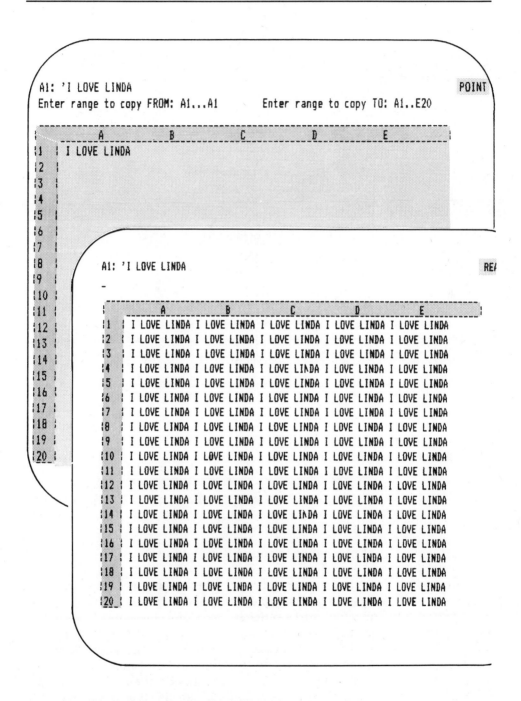

Figure 5-1. With the Copy command you can take your simple message (Part A) and, with a few keystrokes, shout it to the world (Part B).

FROM: and TO:

A quick look at the command tree for the Copy command, Figure 5-2, shows this to be a simple command to use.

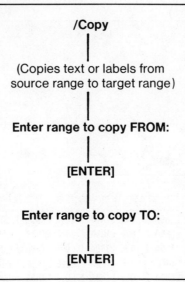

/Copy

(Copies text or labels from
source range to target range)

Enter range to copy FROM:

[ENTER]

Enter range to copy TO:

[ENTER]

Figure 5-2. Copy command tree.

To begin the command, type:

/C

You are prompted to:

Enter range to copy FROM: A1..A1

The prompt is followed by a proposed range which is the current, active cell. If the active cell is A1, as in the example, the proposed range is A1..A1.

Lotus wants to know the source range for the Copy command. The source range is the cell or group of cells you are going to copy. It may be *any* valid 1-2-3 range: a single cell, a row, a column, or a block of cells. As always, when Lotus prompts for a range, it is ready to switch to Point mode so you can supply the range by pointing. As you do, the worksheet cursor expands to highlight the source range in reverse video. You can also type the correct cell addresses, supply a range name, or accept the proposed range by pressing the **[ENTER]** key.

Once the source range has been specified, press:

[ENTER]

The worksheet cursor returns to the active cell, and 1-2-3 prompts:

Enter range to copy TO: A1..A1

Now Lotus wants the target range. This is the range where the copied information will appear. Once again, the proposed range is the current, active cell. Supply the range by pointing with the cursor, by typing cell addresses, or by supplying a range name.

The "TO" prompt appears on the right side of the command line, while the "FROM" prompt remains on the left side (see Figure 5-2). You can see both the source and target ranges at the same time. If you need to, you can use the **[ESC]** key to return to the source range. When you have finished specifying the target range, press:

[ENTER]

and 1-2-3 immediately executes, the Copy command.

The Relationship Between Source and Target Ranges

Lotus accepts *any* range of cells as the target range. There is, however, a specific relationship between the shape of the source range and the *interpretation* 1-2-3 gives to the target range.

If the .Source Range is a . . .	Lotus Interprets the Target Range to be. . .
single cell	whatever is specified (cell, column, row, or block)
a row of cells	a column (left in a block)
a column of cells	a row (top in a block)
a block of cells	a single cell (the upper left cell in a row, column, or block)

Regardless of the target range's shape, 1-2-3 interprets it as shown above. Thus, when the source range is a block, for example, you can specify either a row, column, or block as the target range. The program ignores everything in the target range except the single cell in the upper left corner of the range.

The result of a Copy command varies depending on the shape of the source and target ranges. Tables 5-1 through 5-4 show what happens when each of the four different types of source ranges are copied into the various target ranges. Each source range produces a particular type of copy:

TABLE 5-1

When the source range is a single cell, the target range may be any range: a single cell, a row, a column, or a block.

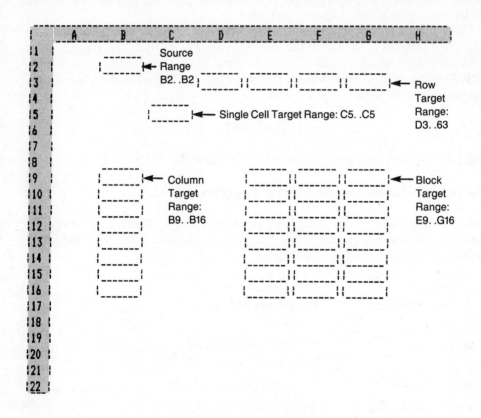

TABLE 5-2

When the source range is a row, the resulting range is either a row (when the target range is a single cell or a row) or a block (when the target range is a column or a block).

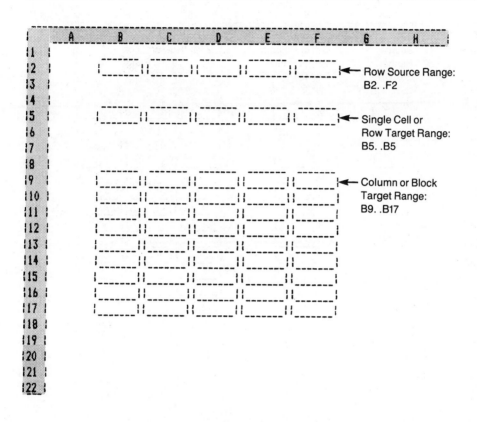

TABLE 5-3

When the source range is a column, the resulting range is either a column (when the target range is a single cell or a column) or a block (when the target range is a row or a block).

	A	B	C	D	E	F	G	H
1		Source		Cell or Column			Row or Block	
2		Range:		Target Range:			Target Range:	
3		B5..B17		D5..D5			F5..H4	
4								

TABLE 5-4

When the source range is a block, the resulting range is always a block regardless of whether the target range is a cell, row, column, or block.

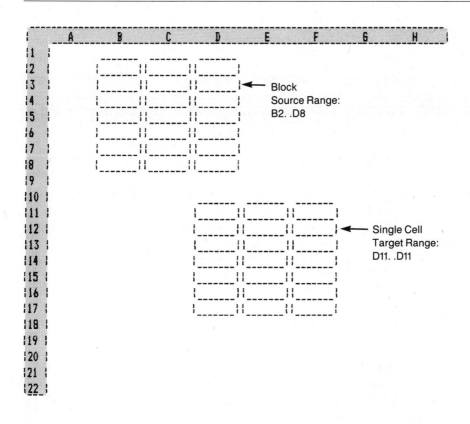

Block
Source Range:
B2. .D8

Single Cell
Target Range:
D11. .D11

- When the source range is a cell, the copy is a cell, a row, a column, or a block (Table 5-1).
- When the source range is a row, the copy is a row or a block (Table 5-2).
- When the source range is a column, the copy is a column or a block (Table 5-3).
- When the source range is a block, the copy can only be a block (Table 5-4).

Study Tables 5-1 through 5-4 until you are familiar with the relationship between source ranges and target ranges. But don't worry. In practice, the relationship is an easy, natural one. In any case, Lotus always makes a consistent determination of the target range, regardless of the shape you specify.

Two additional points about the Copy command. First, any cells in the target range already containing text or values will have their contents *replaced* by material from the source range. If the source range has blank cells, they will blank corresponding cells in the target range. So be careful when specifying the target range, or you may accidentally erase important information.

Second, you can use the Copy command on a worksheet that you have protected with the Worksheet Protect Enable command. However, you receive an error message if any cells in the target range are protected. If you receive this error message, respond by pressing either the **[ESC]** or the **[ENTER]** key. Lotus then copies into any unprotected cells in the target range. Protected cells are, of course, unaffected.

Relative and Absolute Cell References

One truly miraculous thing about Lotus 1-2-3 is that it keeps track of the cell references in formulas as you use the Copy or Move commands. This means you can create a formula in one place on the worksheet and when copied to a new location, it refers to the correct cells.

You have already seen how cell references are used to define active cells and ranges of cells in the various slash commands (including the Copy command). Cell references can also be used to create formulas. For example, the simple formula +B1/B4 says, "Take the value in cell B1, divide it by the value in cell B4, and display the result." Cell references can be used to create functions in much the same same way X's and Y's are used in algebra.

An example illustrates how the Copy command keeps track of cell references when it copies functions from the source range to the target range. Table 5-5 contains a very simple worksheet with a very simple function. The function, in cell B4, is simply +A1.

TABLE 5-5
In this simple worksheet, the reference in cell B4 is +A1.

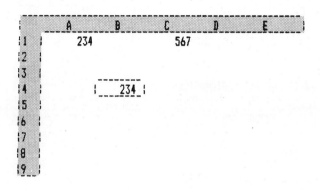

The function says, "Get the value from cell A1 and display it in this cell." This is clear enough, but for a real understanding of the process, you need to know how 1-2-3 "thinks" about the +A1 entered into cell B4: it *doesn't* keep track of cell A1 at all. What Lotus does is to keep track of cell references *relative* to the cell into which they are entered. Thus, 1-2-3 records something like, "Get the value three rows up and one column to the left of the current cell." This, of course, is just another way of identifying cell A1 *relative* to cell B4. Because the location of A1 is defined relative to B4, it is said to be a *relative cell reference*.

Now if B4 were the source range for a Copy command and D4 were the target range, the cell reference would be adjusted relative to the cell in which it is entered. In this case, the contents of C1, 567, would be displayed in D4 because C1 is "three rows up and one column to the left of the current cell." In fact, if B4 were copied to any cell on the worksheet, it would display the contents, if any, of the cell "three rows up and one column to the left of the current cell."

Table 5-6 shows relative cell addresses in action. The figure shows the number of cars produced by American automobile manufacturers. A formula, @SUM(B9..B14), has been entered into cell B16. It adds the 1980 output of the various manufacturers and displays the total. The cell references in this formula are relative.

The bottom part of Table 5-6 shows what happens after the formula in B16 has been copied into cells C16 and D16. The totals for these columns are displayed, and by examining the formulas, you can see that the cell references have adjusted so the correct range of cells is added in each column.

TABLE 5-6

The formula in cell B15 contains relative cell references. When it is copied into cells C15 and D15, the references automatically adjust.

```
        A              B         C         D        E
 1
 2
 3                 WHO MAKES THE MOST AUTOMOBILES
 4
 5                        PRODUCTION
 6                                           1982
 7      Company            1980      1981   7 months
 8
 9   American Motors     164,725   109,319    39,927
10    Chrysler Corp.     638,974   748,774   353,053
11    Ford Motor Co.   1,306,948 1,320,197   671,231
12 General Motors Corp. 4,064,556 3,904,083 1,963,263
13 Checker Motors Corp.    3,197     3,010     2,000
14 Volkswagen of America 197,106   167,755    60,160
15
                       --------- --------- ---------
16          Total:    :6,375,506::6,253,138::3,089,634:
17                       /|\       /|\       /|\
18                        |         |         |
19                     B16 --->  /COPY --> C16 and D16
20                        |         |         |
21                   @SUM(B9..B14) @SUM(C9..C14) @SUM(D9..D14)
```

Source: *The World Almanac and Book of Facts 1983,* Newspaper Enterprise Association, Inc., p. 157, New York, New York, 1983.

In the back of your mind, you may have some questions: "Do all cell references have to be relative? What if I don't want a cell reference to adjust?" Good questions. In many situations, you do *not* want a cell reference to adjust. In the last chapter, Table 4-4, an Entry space was used for the parameters Principal, Rate, and Withdrawal. You would certainly want each reference to one of these parameters to be the same in each formula where it was used. Another example is a percentage distribution where you want the total to remain the same from formula to formula.

In both examples, you want the reference to a cell to remain *unchanged* regardless of where the formula is copied. What you want is an *absolute cell reference.* You can have one by simply inserting dollar signs **[$]** into the cell reference before the letter and the number. Thus the relative reference to cell A1 is "A1," and the absolute reference to the cell is "$A$1." The dollar signs can be typed in, edited in with the **[EDIT]** function key, or inserted when creating the function in Point mode with the **ABS]** function key.

To illustrate the use of absolute cell references, Table 5-7 (on page 134) takes Table 5-6 a step farther. The raw production figures in Table 5-6 are fine. However, a percentage distribution would make it easier to see the relative outputs of different manufacturers and to see what was happening to market share over the period.

The formulas to calculate the percentage share of American Motors in row 20 of Table 5-7 contain an absolute cell reference to the total production in the appropriate year. The reference to total production must, of course, remain unchanged as the formulas are copied down the column to complete the table. The other part of the formula, production by specific manufacturers, must change from row to row. It does because it is entered into the formula in row 20 without dollar signs.

The table is completed when the Copy command copies the three formulas in cells B20, C20, and D20 down the columns. Note that when you do this, you also copy a formula into row 26, which you'd like to leave blank. Don't worry. Do the Copy command and when you are finished, erase the cells in row 24. Also notice that the row labels in the bottom part of the table were copied from the row labels in the top part of the table and didn't have to be entered again.

Finally, recall that named ranges are treated as relative cell addresses. Thus, they are adjusted when copied from one cell to another. If you want a range name to be an absolute reference rather than a relative one, precede the range name with a dollar sign **[$]**. As noted in the preceding chapter, add the dollar sign when you are creating the formula, *not* when you are creating the range name.

In summary, when coping formulas or functions, Lotus adjusts all relative cell references and leaves all absolute cell references unadjusted. You can tell what will happen by simply looking at a formula. Those references without dollar signs will adjust, while those with dollar signs won't.

THE MOVE COMMAND

The Move command has much in common with the Copy command. Like that command, you must specify a source range and a target range. Unlike the Copy command, the source and target ranges are always the same size, so you need specify only a single cell as the target range. (See Figure 5-3 for the command tree.)

TABLE 5-7

The formulas in row 20 calculate the percent of total production accounted for by American Motors. The cell reference to the total production in each period, $B$16, $C$16, $D$16, are absolute cell references. They remain unchanged as the formulas are copied down columns B, C, and D to complete the table.

```
            A              B           C          D          E
 1
 2
 3                    WHO MAKES THE MOST AUTOMOBILES
 4
 5                            PRODUCTION
 6                                             1982
 7          Company           1980       1981   7 months
 8
 9       American Motors     164,725    109,319    39,927
10        Chrysler Corp.     638,974    748,774   353,053
11        Ford Motor Co.   1,306,948  1,320,197   671,231
12   General Motors Corp.  4,064,556  3,904,083 1,963,263
13   Checker Motors Corp.     3,197      3,010     2,000
14   Volkswagen of America   197,106    167,755    60,160
15
16              Total:    6,375,506  6,253,138 3,089,634
17
18                    PERCENT DISTRIBUTION
19                    ---------  ---------  ---------
20      American Motors +B9/$B$16  +C9/$C$16  +D9/$D$16
21        Chrysler Corp.
22        Ford Motor Co.
23   General Motors Corp.  /COPY cells B20, C20 and D20
24   Checker Motors Corp.       down to row 27
25   Volkswagen of America
26
27              Total:      \!/        \!/        \!/
28
29
30
31
```

Source: *The World Almanac and Book of Facts 1983,* Newspaper Enterprise Association, Inc., p. 157, New York, New York, 1983.

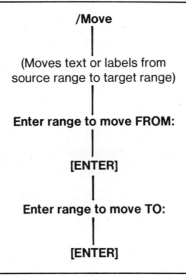

Figure 5-3. Move command tree.

Like the Copy command, the Move command replaces any existing text or labels in the target range with information from the corresponding cells in the source range. You can't move protected cells, and you can't move unprotected cells onto protected cells.

Also, you can't move unprotected cells into a range containing both protected and unprotected cells. If you attempt this move, unprotected cells in the target range are erased. For this reason, always disable protection with the Worksheet Global Protect command before using the Move command.

Unlike the Copy command, the moved information no longer exists in the source cells after the Move command is completed, and relative cell references to cells in the moved range are adjusted to their new location. Relative references to cells outside the moved range, refer to the same cells as they did in their original location.

Furthermore, any formula, function, range name, or remembered range that refers *to* moved cells is adjusted so it refers to these same cells in their new location.

To use the Move command type:

/M

You are prompted for the source range:

Enter range to move FROM: A1..A1

The current active cell is the proposed range (A1 in this case). Accept it with the **[ENTER]** key, or specify another range by pointing, typing cell addresses, or supplying a range name, and then press **[ENTER]**. The worksheet cursor returns to the active cell, and the TO prompt is displayed:

Enter range to move TO: A1..A1

Supply the target range, press **[ENTER]**, and the move is completed. Whatever the shape of the target range, 1-2-3 interprets it as a single cell, the upper left-most cell in the range.

In Table 5-8, the Move command has been used to rearrange the layout of the table on automobile production. It is a simple matter to enter the Move command, designate the source range as the cells containing the percentage distribution and the target range as the cells to the right of the production figures. The title, Percent Distribution, is moved up two rows to make space for the column headings which are copied over from the first three columns. An additional row is inserted below the Production, and Percent Distribution titles, and several blank spaces are placed before the text "Percent Distribution" in cell F4. These spaces improve the table's appearance by centering the label. You can always insert leading spaces to adjust a label's position. Finally, use either Worksheet Delete Row command or the Range Erase command to remove the row labels from the bottom part of the table.

As you can see, the Move command in conjunction with the Copy, Insert, Delete, and Erase commands gives you a powerful set of tools for constructing and changing electronic spreadsheets. These tools are the electronic scissors, paste, pencils, and erasers that take the tedious drudgery out of spreadsheet construction and analysis.

THE QUIT COMMAND

You will use the Quit command exactly once each 1-2-3 work session: to end the session and to return to the Lotus Access System. Like the Copy and Move commands, it is a high-level slash command. You need type only a small number of keystrokes to execute the Quit command, and you have few choices to make along the way. See Figure 5-4 for the command tree.

TABLE 5-8
Table 5-7 rearranged with the Move command.

	A	B	C	D	E	F	G	H
1								
2		WHO MAKES THE MOST AUTOMOBILES						
3								
4			PRODUCTION			PERCENT DISTRIBUTION		
5								
6				1982				1982
7		Company	1980	1981	7 months	1980	1981	7 months
8								
9		American Motors	164,725	109,319	39,927	2.58%	1.75%	1.29%
10		Chrysler Corp.	638,974	748,774	353,053	10.02%	11.97%	11.43%
11		Ford Motor Co.	1,306,948	1,320,197	671,231	20.50%	21.11%	21.73%
12		General Motors Corp.	4,064,556	3,904,083	1,963,263	63.75%	62.43%	63.54%
13		Checker Motors Corp.	3,197	3,010	2,000	0.05%	0.05%	0.06%
14		Volkswagen of America	197,106	167,755	60,160	3.09%	2.68%	1.95%
15								
16		Total:	6,375,506	6,253,138	3,089,634	100.00%	100.00%	100.00%
17								

Source: *The World Almanac and Book of Facts 1983,* Newspaper Enterprise Association, Inc., p. 157, New York, New York, 1983.

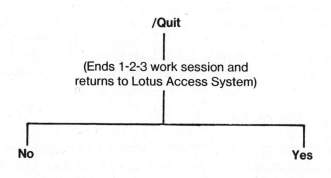

Figure 5-4. Quit command tree.

To use the command, begin by typing:

/Q

The following words are displayed:

No   Yes

The command line cursor is on the word "No," and the command can be canceled by pressing the **[ENTER]** key or by typing the letter **[N]**.

Lotus lets you quit the work session only if you press **[Y]** for yes, or if you move the command line cursor to "Yes" and press **[ENTER]**. If you press any key other than **[ENTER]**, **[Y]**, or **[N]**, Lotus "beeps" an error (on those machines with speakers) and waits for you to find the right key. On other machines, Lotus displays an error message and waits. (You can still use **[ESC]** and **[CTRL]-[BREAK]** to cancel a Quit command.)

Anything in your microcomputer's memory at the time the Quit command is executed will be lost *forever*. Take the opportunity presented by this "sanity check" to be sure that you have saved the current worksheet. If you haven't, you must reaffirm that you don't want to save the worksheet by typing **[Y]**.

HANDS ON: USING THE COPY COMMAND

As noted at the beginning of this chapter, the Copy command is perhaps the most useful and most frequently used of all 1-2-3 commands. With the Copy command you can take a few formulas in a few cells and create an entire worksheet with a few keystrokes.

The command is particularly useful for constructing worksheets that project future performance by means of formulas relating successive periods to a base period. Examples include budgets, sales projections, and business plans. They also include the retirement planning worksheet discussed in this Hands On section.

Constructing an IRA Worksheet

An Individual Retirement Account (IRA) is a tax-free savings program available to most wage earners in the United States. It can be a powerful tool for accumulating a retirement nest egg, and a spreadsheet is a natural way to project the effects of various choices on the savings. This spreadsheet can also be used to analyze any savings program; for college, for a home, or for a vacation.

Table 5-9 contains the starting point for the IRA worksheet. If you are constructing this worksheet, enter the labels (set the Worksheet Global Label-Prefix to Right), and then enter the formulas shown in Part B of the table on page 41. Notice the use of absolute cell references in some of the formulas.

TABLE 5-9A

Individual Retirement Account.

```
|---------------------------------------------------------------------------------|
|             A            B            C            D            E        F       |
|---------------------------------------------------------------------------------|
!1 !
!2 !               INDIVIDUAL RETIREMENT ACCOUNT (IRA) WORKSHEET
!3 !
!4 !      ENTRY SPACE
!5 !
!6 !      Starting Balance:     $0.00
!7 !   Annual Contribution:     $0.00
!8 !         Interest Rate:     0.00%
!9 !
!10 !   SUMMARY SPACE
!11 !
!12 !   Contribution to 65:
!13 !    Balance at Age 59:
!14 !    Balance at Age 65:
!15 !
!16 !
!17 !
!18 !                 Year:     1984         1985
!19 !                  Age:       35           36
!20 !                          ------       ------
!21 !      Balance Forward:     $0.00        $0.00
!22 !  Annual Contribution:     $0.00        $0.00
!23 !       Interest Earned:    $0.00        $0.00
!24 !                          ======       ======
!25 !  Balance at Year End:     $0.00        $0.00
!26 !
!27 !
!28 !
!29 !
!30 !
```

Set the global column-width to 12 characters and the global format to currency. You will also have to set the format for cell B8 to percent, and for the block B18..C19 to fixed, zero decimals.

Certain assumptions must be made. If necessary, you can modify them to fit your circumstances. It is assumed the worksheet is constructed in 1984 and the age of the individual is 35 years.

The assumptions about Starting Balance, annual contribution and interest rate have been entered into an Entry Space rather than as elements in the main body of the table. This makes it easy to do "What If..." analysis. An Entry Space should be a standard part of every worksheet you construct. When the worksheet is finished, you can enter different assumptions to discover what happens to your retirement nest egg.

Since you are not so much interested in the year-to-year details as you are in the amount available at age 59 and at age 65, the worksheet is also constructed with a Summary Space. (The rules allow withdrawals from an IRA account to begin either at age 59 1/2 or at age 65.) The Summary Space and the Entry Space are on the screen at the same time, so you can immediately see the results of a change in one of the assumptions.

Note that the year and the age (rows 18 and 19) are simple counting functions: each cell is one more than the cell to the left. This makes it easy to modify the time span and the age by entering different years and ages into cells B18 and B19. Alternatively, age and starting year could be included in the Entry Space.

The completed worksheet, Table 5-10 on page 142, is created by using the Copy command to copy the contents of cells C18..C25 to the right the required number of columns. When you specify the range to copy to, be sure to use the **[TAB]** key. This stretches the cursor to the right a full screen at a time.

You don't need to calculate the number of columns required. The Copy command is so easy to use that trial and error is the most efficient way to complete the table. Copy a number of columns and let 1-2-3 tell you if you have made enough copies. If you have too many, use the Range Erase command. If you have too few, make some more copies.

When you have completed the main body of the table, locate the cell references for the information in the Summary Space. The worksheet is now finished.

Using the IRA Worksheet

Table 5-11 shows the worksheet in action. It is a simple matter to discover what happens if you double your annual contribution, begin with a certain balance, or are able to earn a higher or lower interest rate. What would take hours with a pencil, paper, and calculator can be performed instantaneously with 1-2-3.

TABLE 5-9B

Formulas for worksheet in Table 5-9A.

```
              A                    B              C          E          F
 1
 2                 INDIVIDUAL RETIREMENT ACCOUNT (IRA) WORKSHEET
 3
 4        ENTRY SPACE
 5
 6       Starting Balance:       $0.00
 7     Annual Contribution:      $0.00
 8         Interest Rate:        0.00%
 9
10        SUMMARY SPACE
11
12     Contribution to 65:
13      Balance at Age 59:
14      Balance at Age 65:
15
16
17
18               Year:          1984          1+B18
19                Age:            35           1+B19
20                              ------         ------
21      Balance Forward:        +B6           +B25
22   Annual Contribution:      +$B$7          +B22
23      Interest Earned:     (+B21+B22)*$B$8  (+C21+C22)*$B$8
24                              ======         ======
25   Balance at Year End:   @SUM(B21..B23)   @SUM(C21..C23)
26
27
28
29
30
```

TABLE 5-10

Table 5-9 after the Copy command has been used to copy the contents of C18..C25 into the range D18..AF18.

	A	B	C	D	E		AD	AE	AF
1									
2		INDIVIDUAL RETIREMENT ACCOUNT (IRA) WORKSHEET							
3									
4	ENTRY SPACE								
5									
6	Starting Balance:	$0.00							
7	Annual Contribution:	$0.00							
8	Interest Rate:	0.00%							
9									
10	SUMMARY SPACE			Formulas for SUMMARY SPACE					
11									
12	Contribution to 65:	$0.00	(-- @SUM(B22..AF22)						
13	Balance at Age 59:	$0.00	(-- +Z25						
14	Balance at Age 65:	$0.00	(-- +AF25						
15									
16									
17									
18	Year:	1984	1985	1986	1987		2012	2013	2014
19	Age:	35	36	37	38		63	64	65
20		------	------	------	------		------	------	------
21	Balance Forward:	$0.00	$0.00	$0.00	$0.00		$0.00	$0.00	$0.00
22	Annual Contribution:	$0.00	$0.00	$0.00	$0.00		$0.00	$0.00	$0.00
23	Interest Earned:	$0.00	$0.00	$0.00	$0.00		$0.00	$0.00	$0.00
24		======	======	======	======		======	======	======
25	Balance at Year End:	$0.00	$0.00	$0.00	$0.00		$0.00	$0.00	$0.00
26									

TABLE 5-11

Completed IRA table with assumptions entered into entry spaces.

	A	B	C	D	E		AD	AE	AF
1									
2		INDIVIDUAL RETIREMENT ACCOUNT (IRA) WORKSHEET							
3									
4	ENTRY SPACE								
5									
6	Starting Balance:	$0.00							
7	Annual Contribution:	$1,000.00							
8	Interest Rate:	10.00%							
9									
10	SUMMARY SPACE								
11									
12	Contribution to 65:	$31,000.00							
13	Balance at Age 59:	$108,181.77							
14	Balance at Age 65:	$200,137.77							
15									
16									
17									
18	Year:	1984	1985	1986	1987		2012	2013	2014
19	Age:	35	36	37	38		63	64	65
20		------	------	------	------		------	------	------
21	Balance Forward:	$0.00	$1,100.00	$2,310.00	$3,641.00		$147,630.93	$163,494.02	$180,943.42
22	Annual Contribution:	$1,000.00	$1,000.00	$1,000.00	$1,000.00		$1,000.00	$1,000.00	$1,000.00
23	Interest Earned:	$100.00	$210.00	$331.00	$464.10		$13,420.99	$14,863.09	$18,194.34
24		======	======	======	======		======	======	======
25	Balance at Year End:	$1,100.00	$2,310.00	$3,641.00	$5,105.10		$147,630.93	$163,494.02	$200,137.77
26									

SELF-TEST

QUESTIONS

1. Explain three ways to specify a range of cells for a Copy or Move command.
2. When using the Move command, do the cell references from the source range change when they are moved to the target range?
3. How would you write the cell address A1 as an absolute cell address?
4. How will 1-2-3 treat the target range if the source range for a Copy command is a block?
5. True or False? When you use the Quit command to terminate a Lotus 1-2-3 work session, you lose the worksheet in memory.

ANSWERS

1. You can type in the beginning and ending cell addresses, you can point to them, or you can specify a named range by either typing it in or by using the **[NAME]** function key to display the assigned names.
2. Yes. They are adjusted to continue to point to the same cell contents that they did previously. If the reference cell was part of the block which was moved, the reference is changed to the cell's new location.
3. Lotus uses the dollar sign to indicated an absolute reference. Thus, an absolute reference to cell A1 would be $A$1.
4. Lotus allows only one-to-one copies of blocks. Consequently, 1-2-3 treats any target range as if it were a single cell, the upper left cell in the target range.
5. True. The Quit command does not make a copy of the current worksheet. Be sure you have saved the current worksheet with the File Save command *before* using the Quit command. If you don't save it, it is lost forever.

CHAPTER SIX
THE FILE COMMAND

OBJECTIVES

- To learn to use the File Command to store and retrieve worksheets.
- To learn to choose good filenames and to organize your library of stored worksheets.
- To learn to store and retrieve parts of worksheets and to combine them with worksheets already in memory.

INTRODUCTION

The need for the File command arises from the fact that 1-2-3 is an *electronic* spreadsheet. The worksheets you create in your microcomputer's memory are temporary. They exist only as long as a steady supply of electricity is available, and they disappear the instant the power is interrupted. Furthermore, only one worksheet can reside in memory at one time, so you must have a place to store worksheets when you aren't using them.

In addition to a complete loss of power, other variations in the electric supply can spell disaster for worksheets in your computer's memory. *Voltage spikes* caused by electrical equipment such as office copiers or elevators and *brown outs*, a slow reduction in the voltage level supplied, have the potential to cause the loss of a worksheet in memory as surely as turning off the power switch.

To avoid losing valuable information and the time you have taken to construct a worksheet, save your worksheets to a diskette or to a file on a hard disk. If you have saved the worksheet and you do lose the contents of your microcomputer's memory, you will still have a copy of the worksheet in the form of a diskette file.

In addition to storing copies of every worksheet you want to use again, make it a habit to store partially constructed worksheets. This guards against power failures as well as any serious mistakes you might make while constructing a worksheet, such as using the Worksheet Erase command at the wrong time. *A good rule of thumb is to store a worksheet whenever you have put in more time and trouble than you'd care to repeat.*

The first three rules of microcomputer use are: (1) Backup! (2) Backup! and (3) Backup! You must also make *backup copies* of your data diskettes with the File Copy command in the Access System. Backup copies of the diskettes are necessary because diskettes do wear out, and they are subject to unexpected failure due to stray magnetism (from metal paper clips, for example). The time required to copy a diskette is tiny compared to the time required to recreate the worksheets when a diskette fails.

Once stored, a worksheet can be recalled and re-used at any time. Stored worksheets become an electronic file cabinet into which you place worksheets and from which you retrieve past worksheets for examining, updating, or using as the bases for new worksheets.

Figure 6-1 on the next page shows the overall command tree for the File command. The first two options, Retrieve and Save, operate on the entire worksheet. You will use these options most often.

Symphony

Since the File command affects all environments, the Symphony File command is located on the Services menu which is displayed when you press the **SERVICES** function key. Except for the addition of two new options, discussed later in this chapter, and the choice to have all files displayed when choosing the List option, the Symphony and 1-2-3 File commands are identical.

The next two options, Combine and Xtract, operate on a range of cells rather than on the worksheet as a whole. They are powerful tools for consolidating information from two or more worksheets into a single worksheet. The Import option takes standard text files such as those created with many word processing programs and translates them into 1-2-3 spreadsheets. The final options, Erase, List, and Directory, are used to manage your library of stored worksheets.

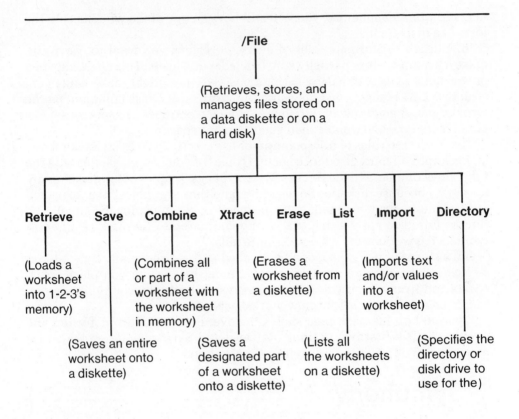

Figure 6-1. File command tree.

FILENAMES

Before you can use the File command on a worksheet you must assign a *filename* to that worksheet. A filename is simply a group of letters, numbers, and, sometimes, other characters. Lotus uses filenames to keep track of stored worksheets; consequently, stored worksheets are often called *files*.

The exact characters that can be used in a filename vary from microcomputer to microcomputer, so check your manual. Filenames for use on the IBM PC, for example, are restricted to letters A-Z and numbers 0-9, and the underline character. Furthermore, a filename can be no longer than eight characters, and it cannot contain spaces or other characters, such as the dollar sign or the percentage sign. You may type letters as either upper or lower case, but 1-2-3 converts all letters to upper case.

Good and Bad Filenames

Within the constraints imposed on you, you must choose filenames that give good information about what the file contains and give some indication of how a file is related to similar files. Informative filenames are important because days or even months may pass between assigning a filename and the next time you want to load the file. If the filename doesn't tell you what the file contains, you may have to waste time loading several different files before you find the one you are looking for.

With a little care and practice, you can master the art of choosing good filenames. Here are some examples:

GOOD FILENAMES	BAD FILENAMES
CH6_TBL1	TABLE1
BUD_PROJ	BUDGET
BUD_ACTL	BUDGET
TRAVL_XP	EXPENSES
SALES_1Q	1ST_QT
TRIAL_BL	TEST

The AUTO123 Filename   If you name a file AUTO123, the file automatically loads when you first enter 1-2-3 from the Access System. If you always begin your work sessions with a particular worksheet, this feature saves a few key strokes.

Symphony

Symphony allows you to specify the name of the file you wish to have automatically loaded. You aren't restricted to the AUTO123 filename.

Filename Extensions

To keep track of the different types of files you can create, Lotus 1-2-3 automatically adds an *extension* to each filename. The extensions are .WKS for worksheet files, .PIC for graph (or "picture") files, and .PRN for print files. Worksheet files contain electronic worksheets. Picture files contain graphs for printing with the PrintGraph utility. Print files are copies of 1-2-3 worksheets stored in a format that can be used by many word processing programs.

Symphony

Symphony assigns a .WRK filename extension to its worksheet files. However, it uses the same extensions as 1-2-3, .PRN and .PIC, for its print and picture files.

You can use print files to incorporate 1-2-3 worksheets into reports. For example, most of the 1-2-3 worksheets in this book were placed into the manuscript by using print files. Print files are not created with the File command. They are created with the Print command discussed in the following chapter.

The complete filename for a typical worksheet file would be **CH6_TBL1.WKS**. There could exist, at the same time on the same diskette, a graph file **CH6_TBL1.PIC** and a print file **CH6_TBL1.PRN**. Even though the main part of the filename is the same, 1-2-3 distinguishes between the worksheet file (.WKS), the graph file (.PIC), and the print file (.PRN). Since you can create picture files and print files only after you have created the worksheet, the same filename with different extensions is a good way to express the relationship of a print or picture file to the underlying worksheet file.

Organizing Your Worksheet Files

It won't take you long to generate a large number of 1-2-3 worksheets, and if you expect your microcomputer to make your organization tasks easier, you may be in for a big surprise. Generating worksheets is easy, but the result can be as hard to use and as messy as many people's hall closet.

You have to organize your worksheets, and the sooner you adopt a system—any system—the sooner you can get the full use of your worksheet library.

Here are some guidelines for organizing worksheets files.

1. *Choose informative filenames.* As already noted, picking informative filenames is the most important step you can take in organizing your worksheet files.
2. *Keep printed copies of each worksheet.* A printed copy of a worksheet tells exactly what the file contains. This, of course, makes it easier to locate a particular worksheet.
3. *Store similar worksheets together on a single diskette or in a single directory on a hard disk.* If, for example, all budget projections are on a diskette labeled "Budget Projections," you won't have to sift through personal

records, expenses accounts, or sales records to find what you are looking for.

4. *Include the exact filename as a line of text on each worksheet.* Thus, the filename appears on each printout you make, and you can easily return to the file to modify, update, it or make additional copies. If you want to omit the filename from a particular printout, erase it with the Range Erase command just before printing.

5. *Set the date and time when you first load 1-2-3.* You can use the File Manager in the Access System to view the time and date when a worksheet was stored. This additional information is useful in distinguishing worksheets.

These suggestions should help you organize your worksheet files. What is more important than specific suggestions is that you recognize the need for organization and adopt a system for keeping track of the files. Otherwise, you will end up denying yourself easy access to your rapidly growing library of electronic spreadsheets.

THE FILE SAVE AND FILE RETRIEVE COMMANDS

The most frequently used options of the File command are the Save option and the Retrieve option. See Figure 6-2 on the next page for the command tree. Both operate on an entire worksheet, and both allow you to pick an existing filename from the prompt line in the control panel.

The File Save Command

If you have a hard disk, you probably have adequate room to store your worksheets. If, on the other hand, you use diskettes, you *must* have a formatted data diskette available before you can save a worksheet. Diskettes are formatted with the Disk Manager section of the Lotus Access System (see Chapter Two).

You *must* perform the formatting procedure while in the Access System and *before* entering the Lotus 1-2-3 worksheet program. You *cannot* format a data diskette just before you save a worksheet. If you don't have a formatted data diskette or if your data diskette is full when you want to save a worksheet, you have only two unpleasant options. Either you can erase one or more worksheets from the data diskette, or you can lose the worksheet in memory when you Quit 1-2-3 to go to the Access System. Either way, you lose at least one worksheet.

Avoid these problems by keeping at least one blank, formatted data diskette in reserve at all times.

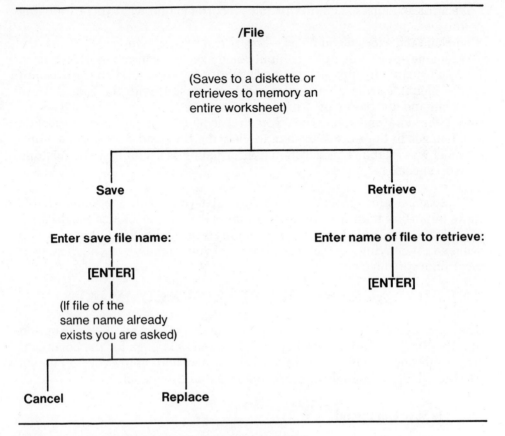

Figure 6-2. The File Save and the File Retrieve command tree.

Assuming you have room on your data diskette and that you want to save the *entire* worksheet (saving parts of worksheets is accomplished with the File Xtract command, discussed later in this chapter), enter the File Save command by typing:

/FS

You are prompted:

Enter save file name:

If you have retrieved a file during a work session, the filename of the last file retrieved appears as the proposed filename (see Figure 6-3). The way

Lotus chooses a proposed filename makes it easy to perform an updating operation: you load a worksheet, update it, and then save the updated version under the same filename.

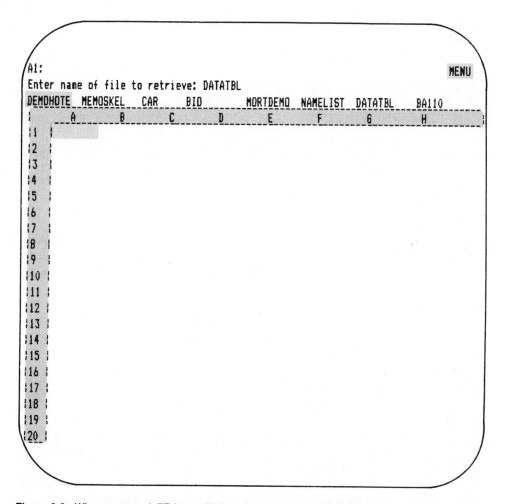

Figure 6-3. When you type \ **FR** Lotus displays the filenames of the worksheets on the current data diskette. The proposed filename is the most recently used filename.

If you want to accept the proposed filename, press **[ENTER]**. Otherwise, type in a new filename or select an existing filename from those listed on the bottom line of the control panel.

If you try to save a worksheet under a filename that already exists, 1-2-3 asks whether you want to cancel the command. Since each filename can be assigned to only one file at a time, saving a worksheet under an existing filename *erases* the worksheet previously stored under that filename. Lotus does not automatically create backup copies of stored worksheets.

To prevent the accidental erasure of stored worksheets, 1-2-3 asks you to confirm your intentions to replace a worksheet. If you want to change the filename and thus save the already stored worksheet, select Cancel. If you want to replace the existing file, as you would if you were updating it, select Replace.

Worksheets stored with the File Save command contain all the information necessary to reconstruct the worksheet *exactly* as it was at the moment the File Save command was executed. In particular, column widths, screen splits, named ranges, proposed ranges, protection status, the location of the worksheet cursor, as well as all Global and Range command format and label alignment choices, are stored.

The File Retrieve Command

Once stored, a worksheet can be reloaded into memory at any time. If you want to load the *entire* worksheet, use the File Retrieve command. See Figure 6-2 for the command tree. If you want to load only *part* of a worksheet, use the File Combine command, discussed in the next section.

To retrieve an entire worksheet from a data diskette, type:

/FR

The filenames of the worksheets on the data diskette appear on the bottom line of the control panel. *Only* files with the filename extension .WKS are displayed since they are the only files that can be loaded into memory with the File Retrieve command.

Select a file to load by either typing its name or by using the cursor control keys to move through the existing filenames until the desired filename is highlighted. Then press **[ENTER]** to select that file.

Be careful. Once you have selected a file for loading, 1-2-3 performs the equivalent of a Worksheet Erase command. This erases any worksheet currently in memory and returns all settings (format, column width, etc.) to their default values. The retrieved worksheet is loaded into memory, and unless the worksheet originally in memory was saved, it is lost forever.

The retrieved worksheet is an exact copy of the worksheet at the moment it was stored with the Save option.

Symphony

All 1-2-3 worksheet files are compatible with Symphony and can be loaded directly into the program. To load a worksheet file created with 1-2-3, type the full filename, including the extension, in response to the Name of File to Retrieve, prompt.

As a default, Symphony displays only .WRK worksheet files when you enter the command. You can, however, have Symphony display all the files on a diskette or in a directory by typing *.* and **[ENTER]** instead of a filename. The asterisks are "wild cards" and mean "accept any characters from the location of the asterisk to the end of the filename or filename extension." Thus *.* means "select all filenames regardless of filename or filename extension." If you wish to see only .WKS files, type *.**WKS**.The question mark **[?]** can also be use as a wild card. It means "any character may occupy the location of the question mark," and you can use it to select a group of similarly named files.

Like the Name command discussed previously, you can press the **[MENU]** key when displaying filenames in the File command, and all of the filenames will be listed on the screen at one time. You can then use the cursor control keys to highlight a desired filename. This feature makes it easy to find a specific filename in a large group of filenames.

THE FILE XTRACT AND FILE COMBINE COMMANDS

While the Save and Retrieve options of the File command act on the entire worksheet, the Xtract and Combine options load or save only designated ranges of cells.

In many situations, you will only want to save part of a worksheet or will only want to load the contents of a few cells from an already saved worksheet. A typical application is a monthly balance sheet where the balance for each line item is forwarded to the following month (which is on another worksheet) so that a Year-To-Date total can be displayed. Other applications include situations where supporting material on separate worksheets is consolidated into summary tables; for example, consolidating regional or product-specific sales reports into overall reports.

The File Xtract Command

With the File Xtract command, you can save part of a worksheet rather than the entire worksheet. You also have a choice of saving only the displayed values or saving the underlying formulas. The command is called the "Xtract" command rather than the "Extract" command because another choice on the File command menu, Erase, begins with the letter "E." See Figure 6-4 for the command tree.

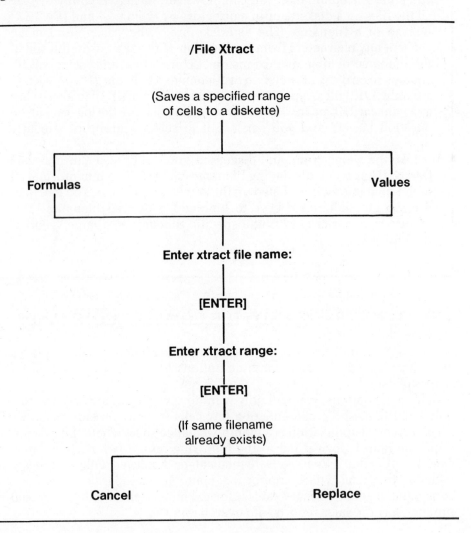

Figure 6-4. The File Xtract command tree.

An important use of the File Xtract command is to convert formulas into displayed values. Lotus has no other easy way to convert a large number of formulas into values. Using the File Xtract and File Combine commands is often the only efficient way to accomplish this conversion.

A worksheet file created with the File Xtract command is very much like one created with the File Save command. They both have the same extensions (.WKS), and they can both be reloaded into memory with either the File Retrieve command or the File Combine command. Furthermore, if you choose a filename for the File Xtract command that already exists, the extracted file replaces the existing file.

Before you enter the File Xtract command, think ahead. You will often want to reload a worksheet created with this command with the File Combine command. If you want to load only part of a worksheet with the File Combine command, you *must* assign a range name to those cells. So, before you use the File Xtract command, use the Range Name command to assign range names to those cells you may want to combine later. A little planning will make your work much easier in the future.

To save part of a worksheet begin by typing:

/FX

The following prompt appears:

Formulas   Values

You are being asked whether you want to save the formulas or to save only the displayed values. If you don't save the formulas, you won't have them for use when the worksheet is reloaded. However, for a formula to operate correctly, it must be loaded into a cell where the references it contains make sense. When combining worksheets, picking the correct location can be tricky. Avoid these problems by choosing to save only the displayed values. Numbers, of course, can be reloaded into any cells on the new worksheet with the File Combine command.

Next, you are asked to:

Enter   Xtract   filename:

If you specify an existing filename, you are given the option of canceling the command or replacing the existing file with the new file.

Finally, you are prompted to:

Enter   Xtract   range:

You can point to the range, give a range name, or type in the cell addresses. The range can even be the entire worksheet. Finally, press **[ENTER]**, and the File Xtract command executes.

The File Combine Command

The File Combine command combines either an entire worksheet file or a named portion of it with the worksheet already in memory. The incoming worksheet supplies only text and values to the cells. The resident worksheet, the one already in memory, controls overall worksheet attributes, such as column width and format settings. See the command tree, Figure 6-5, for of the File Combine command.

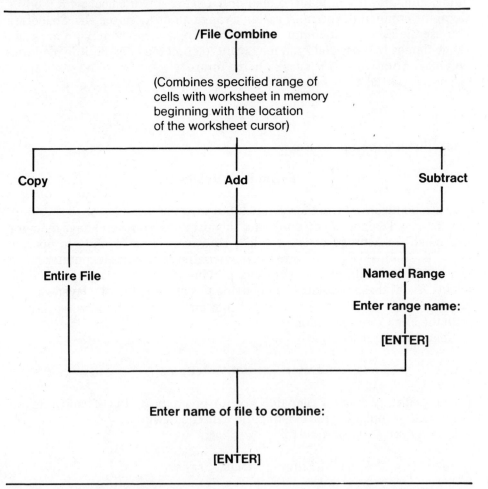

Figure 6-5. The File Combine command tree.

You must correctly position the worksheet cursor *before* entering the File Combine command because the worksheet cursor's location determines where the upper left cell of the incoming range appears.

Once in the command, you are asked whether you want to combine the Entire File or a Named Range. Unfortunately, Lotus doesn't have a way to display the names assigned to ranges in the worksheet to be combined, so you must either assign easy-to-remember names ("combine" for example), or if the combining operation is to be repeated, make a note on the resident worksheet. This note should contain both the filename of the incoming worksheet and the name assigned to the range of cells to be combined (see Table 6-1).

TABLE 6-1

Use notes on worksheets to give you important information about filenames, range names, and the commands to use to update a worksheet.

```
          A            B            C            D           E
 1
 2                          SALES REPORT: ACME INC.
 3                                (000)
 4
 5                      PREVIOUS
 6                      MONTHS'      JUNE'S      Y-T-D
 7         REGION        SALES       SALES       SALES
 8
 9           A                      $1,293
10           B                     $11,052
11           C                     $12,111
12           D                     $21,561
13           E                       $121
14
15
16   To update worksheet use the /Combine      To save worksheet
17   command to load named range UPDATE        use  the /Xtract
18   from the file for the previous month.     command, values only.
19   Be sure to locate the cursor on cell      Use the current month
20   B9 before typing /FC.                      as the filename.
```

Once in the File Combine command, you have the option of having the incoming information copied, added to, or subtracted from the cells of the worksheet already in memory. If you choose the Copy option, the incoming information (values and labels) replaces the resident information. If you choose Add or Subtract, the numeric value of incoming value cells are either added to or subtracted from the contents of the resident cells. Label cells are not loaded. Thus, you can use the File Combine command to convert formulas in the incoming worksheet to displayed values. However, if you want to load labels at the same time, you must save the worksheet with the File Xtract command, Values option.

THE FILE IMPORT COMMAND

The File Import command (see Figure 6-6 for the command tree) is used to import information from standard text files into 1-2-3 worksheets. Standard text files can be created by many word processing programs as well as by specialized computer programming languages such as BASIC and FORTRAN. If you plan to use a word processing program to create your text files, consult that program's manual for the exact details.

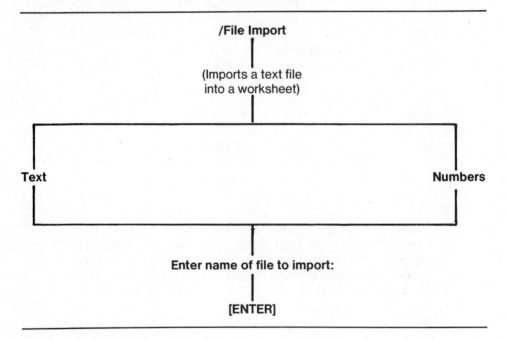

Figure 6-6. File Import command tree.

Note, however, that to be imported, a text file *must* have the standard 1-2-3 print file extension .PRN. A file named TEXT cannot be imported unless you rename it TEXT.PRN. Many word processors let you designate the entire filename when you create the text file. If yours doesn't, you can use the File Manager in the Lotus Access System to rename the file before importing it.

The File Import command is simple to use, but as with the File Combine command, you *must* properly position the worksheet cursor *before* entering the command. The cursor's location determines where imported text appears on the resident worksheet.

To use the File Import command begin by typing:

/FI

The following prompt appears:

Text   Numbers

You are asked to choose whether to import the file as text or numbers. If you choose Text, the file is imported as a column of left-aligned long labels. Each line of text is placed in a separate cell in the column. Blank lines in the text result in blank cells and therefore, blank lines on the worksheet.

If you choose Numbers, each number in the text file is assigned as a value to a separate cell. Any text enclosed in quotes, "text," for example, is placed into a single cell. Any text not in quotes is *ignored* by the File Import command.

Lotus distinguishes separate numbers by the space between them. Thus 123 456 would be considered two separate numbers and they would be placed in separate cells. However, Lotus also treats commas and the mathematical operators as spaces. It would take 123,456 and place 123 in one cell and 456 in a separate cell. If you have 1-2-3 in text, Lotus places the 1 in one cell followed by 2 and 3 in separate cells.

Don't use commas in numbers you want to import, and be careful about other characters in the file you are importing. As always, be sure to save the resident worksheet before attempting a command like the File Import command. That way, if something unexpected occurs, you can start over without having to rebuild the resident worksheet.

After you have chosen whether to import the text file as text or numbers, 1-2-3 prompts:

Enter name of file to import:

Supply the filename, press **[ENTER]**, and the imported material appears on your screen.

THE FILE ERASE, LIST, AND DIRECTORY COMMANDS

The remaining File command options are Erase, List, and Directory. These commands perform straightforward file management tasks.

The File Erase command lets you choose which type of files to erase; worksheets (.WKS), picture files (.PIC), or print files (.PRN). It then displays the filenames for the type you have chosen.

You can select a name off the prompt line, or you can type in the name of the file you want to erase. The last worksheet loaded is supplied as a proposed filename. Thus you can load a worksheet, check to make sure you really want to erase it, then have its filename appear as the proposed response when you enter the File Erase command. See Figure 6-7 for the File Erase command tree.

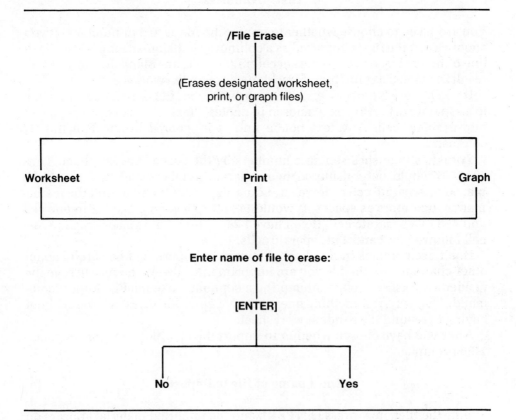

Figure 6-7. The File Erase command tree.

The File List command is a convenient way to view all worksheet, picture, or print filenames on the current data diskette at one time. When you select the type of file to display, the 1-2-3 worksheet screen disappears, and the filenames are listed. The remaining free space on the diskette is also displayed at the top of the screen. This command is a convenient way to find out how much room is left on the current data diskette. When you are ready to return to the worksheet, press any key on the keyboard. See Figure 6-8 for the File List command tree.

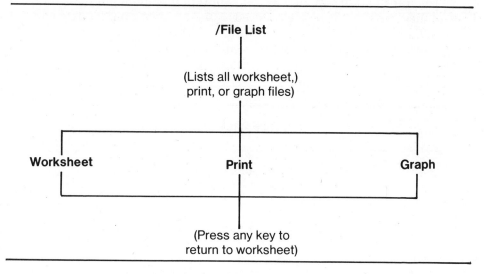

Figure 6-8. The File List command tree.

The last option, Directory, allows you to change the directory currently used as the default directory. This option is important only if you have more than two disk drives or if you store 1-2-3 files in different directories on a hard disk. If you do want to change the current directory, just enter the File Directory command, make your choice, and press **[ENTER]**. See Figure 6-9 on the next page for the File Directory command tree.

Symphony

In addition to the File commands discussed in this chapter, Symphony has two additional File commands: Bytes and Table. Bytes displays the remaining space on the current data diskette. Table loads into the current worksheet (beginning with the current location of the worksheet cursor) a list of files on the current data diskette or in the current directory.

The Table command is an important aid in keeping track of the contents of a data diskette or of a directory on a hard disk. If related files are stored together, you can record all of them on a worksheet for a permanent, readable record. You can also add notes beside each filename to further explain the contents and the relationship between files.

The information supplied by the Table command includes the date and the time the file was last stored. This information is in date and time number form and must be formatted with the Format command before it will display in readable form.

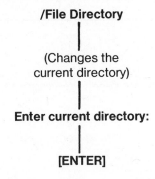

Figure 6-9. File Directory command tree.

HANDS ON: USING THE FILE COMMAND

As noted at the beginning of this chapter, the File Save and the File Retrieve commands are the most important and most frequently used File commands. They are also easy to use, and you should have no trouble mastering the steps necessary to save and load entire worksheets.

In certain situations, however, you will want to save or load only part of a worksheet. For these tasks, use the File Xtract and the File Combine commands. These commands are a bit more complicated to use than the File Retrieve and File Save command; thus, they are the subject of this section.

Constructing the Portfolio Valuation Worksheet

Table 6-2 contains a worksheet you can use to value a portfolio of common stocks. To construct the worksheet, begin by setting the column width to 12 characters (with the Worksheet Global Column-Width command) and set the Global Label-Prefix to Right. Then copy the column headings and other labels into the specified cells.

TABLE 6-2

This worksheet is updated by using the File Xtract command to save the values in columns G and H and then by using the File Combine command to load the extracted file into columns E and F.

	A	B	C	D	E	F	G	H	I	J
1										
2					PORTFOLIO VALUATION WORKSHEET					
3										
4					(To update worksheet save G11..H19					
5	DATE:	24-Jan-84			with /F Xtract and load into E11					
6					with /F Combine.)					
7								Change		
8	Stock	Number of		Purchase		Yesterday's		Today's	from	Overall
9	Symbol	Shares	Price	Purchase	Price	Value	Price	Value	Yesterday	Change
10	----									
11	IBM	100	$120.500	$12,050.00	$117.000	$11,700.00	$116.125	$11,612.50	($87.50)	($437.50)
12	AMD	300	$30.375	$9,112.50	$35.250	$10,575.00	$34.375	$10,312.50	($262.50)	$1,200.00
13	DJ	100	$24.250	$2,425.00	$46.000	$4,600.00	$45.125	$4,512.50	($87.50)	$2,087.50
14	....	....	....	$0.00	....	$0.00	....	$0.00	$0.00	$0.00
15	....	....	....	$0.00	....	$0.00	....	$0.00	$0.00	$0.00
16	....	....	....	$0.00	....	$0.00	....	$0.00	$0.00	$0.00
17	....	....	....	$0.00	....	$0.00	....	$0.00	$0.00	$0.00
18	....	....	....	$0.00	....	$0.00	....	$0.00	$0.00	$0.00
19	....	....	....	$0.00	....	$0.00	....	$0.00	$0.00	$0.00
20	----									
21	TOTALS			$23,587.50		$26,875.00		$26,437.50	($437.50)	$2,850.00
22										

Contents of
Cells in Row 11...

    D11   +B11*C11

    H11   +B11*G11

    I11   +H11-F11

    J11   +H11-D11

Contents of
Cell B5...

    B5   @TODAY (Format: Day-Month-Year)

Contents of
Cells in Row 21...

    D21   @SUM(D10..D20)

    F21   @SUM(F10..F20)

    H21   @SUM(H10..H20)

    I21   @SUM(I10..I20)

    J21   @SUM(J10..J21)

Next create the dashed line in row 10. You could enter 12 dashes as text into cell A10 and then copy the dashes across the row, but there is an easier way. Position the cursor on cell A10 and type: **[\ ]** and **[-]**. The back-slash character **[\ ]** is 1-2-3's *repeating text* symbol. It instructs 1-2-3 to fill the cell with whatever follows; in this case, a row of dashes "————."

You can also use other symbols, such as the equal sign **[=]** to create a row of double dashes, or you can use the plus sign **[+]**, the slash **[/]**, or the period **[.]** to separate parts of a worksheet to make it more readable. After entering **[\ -]** into cell A10, use the Copy command to copy the dashes across row 10.

Now enter the contents of the cells in row 11. Cells containing formulas are listed below Table 6-2. Copy the formulas into the appropriate cells. Now place four dots into the other cells in row 11 by typing "**....** to force a right-justified text entry. The dots indicate those cells that will receive entries when you use the worksheet. The cells containing formulas display 0's.

When you have finished making entries, go back to the cells and set the appropriate display formats with the Range Format command. Format the columns containing individual share prices (columns C, E, and G) as currency with three decimal places. The extra decimal place allows the decimal equivalent of fractional stock prices (1/8, 3/8, etc.) to be displayed. Set the Currency format to two decimal places in the other columns.

To complete the body of the table, use the Copy command to copy row 11 down the required number of rows. Don't forget to use the **[END] [RIGHT ARROW]** combination to select all of row 11 for copying, and remember that the formats as well as the formulas will be copied. There are nine rows in Table 6-2, but you should copy enough rows to accommodate the number of stocks you own plus a few extra rows for additional purchases.

Finish the table by using the back-slash character to create another row of dashes, and then enter the formulas that provide the totals in row 21. The formulas for row 21 are listed below Table 6-2.

Notice that the range used in each @SUM function includes the rows of dashes at the top and bottom of the table. The dashes are text and, as such, are considered to have a value of zero. Thus, including them in the range to be summed does not affect the totals, but it does allow you to delete any rows in the body of the table without deleting one of the end points of a range. As mentioned in the discussion of the Worksheet Delete command, deleting one of the end points causes an error message to display on the screen. The technique just described prevents this from happening.

Finally, enter the @TODAY function into cell B5 and set the date format with the Range Format command so the appropriate form of the date is displayed. Verify your work by entering the values from Table 6-2 and check to see if your worksheet calculates the same values. If it doesn't, correct your errors.

Using the Portfolio Valuation Worksheet

When at least one day passes and you are ready to evaluate your portfolio, you can do so by moving the values from Today's Price and Value to the columns headed Yesterday's Price and Value, and then entering new values into the Today's Price column. Unfortunately, 1-2-3 has no command for simply moving the *displayed values* from one place to another place without *also* moving the underlying formulas. You can, however, achieve the necessary transfer with the File Xtract and File Combine commands.

Begin by positioning the worksheet cursor on cell G11 and type:

/FX

choose the option:

Values

supply the filename:

UPDATE

and then the extract range:

G11...H19

Complete the File Xtract command, and you will have created a file named UPDATE which contains only the values from columns G and H. You are now ready to UPDATE your worksheet.

Begin by moving the worksheet cursor to cell E11. Then type:

/FC

choose the option:

Copy

and the option:

Entire File

and then specify the name of the file to be combined:

UPDATE

Press **[ENTER]**, and the information from the UPDATE file appears in the appropriate cells of columns E and F. Enter today's prices into column G, and the updating procedure is completed.

An Advanced Topic

As you become experienced at constructing electronic spreadsheets, you will often discover several different ways to construct the same worksheet. Table 6-2 illustrates this point.

It would be easier to use the Copy command to copy Today's Price and Value into the Yesterday's Price and Value columns. Unfortunately, if you do that to the formulas in Table 6-2, the adjusted formulas in the Yesterday's Value column are incorrect. The formula in F11, for example, is $+$IV11*E11 instead of the correct formula, $+$B11*E11. Part of the formula is correct (E11), and part is incorrect (IV11).

To prevent the incorrect formula from being copied, you must do something to prevent B11 (the cell containing the number of shares) from adjusting to IV11 (which is blank). You can insert dollar signs ($B$11) to keep the reference absolute.

Now when you copy the formula, $(+$B$11*G11)$ from cell H11, to cell F11, you get the formula $B +$11*E11. This will calculate the correct value for cell F11, but as is often the case, solving one problem creates another.

When you copy the formula in cell H11 down column H, you have an absolute reference to cell B11 in each copy of the formula. That is, the number of shares you own of the stock in row 11 (IBM in Table 6-2) would be used in each formula. That is clearly incorrect.

What you need is a way to let the row change the reference to B11 when the formula is copied down column H, and at the same time, keep the column from changing when the formula is copied into column F. What you need is a *mixed absolute/relative* cell reference. The number of shares is always found in column B, but the number of shares for a particular stock is found in different rows in column B.

Lotus lets you create mixed absolute/relative cell references by placing a dollar sign in front of either the row number or the column letter in a cell reference. In this case, you would want the reference to B11 to be absolute with respect to the column, but relative with respect to the row. Editing-in a dollar sign so the reference reads $B11 accomplishes the desired mix of relative and absolute cell referencing.

Substitute $+$$B11*G11 for $+$$B11*G11, and proceed as described above. You can copy this formula down column H to complete the table, and you can copy the block G11...H19 to E11 to transfer Today's Price and Value to Yesterday's Price and Value whenever you want to update the worksheet.

The moral is that Lotus 1-2-3 provides you with many ways to accomplish the same end. The key to finding the most efficient way to construct a worksheet is to define your objectives clearly and then to be thoroughly familiar with the tools in 1-2-3's tool kit. You will often find that you have solved a problem one way only to discover later that there are other, more elegant, efficient ways to solve the same problem. You can modify the worksheet, and you can keep the solution in mind for the next time a similar problem comes up.

SELF-TEST

QUESTIONS

1. What command do you use to save an entire worksheet as a file on a diskette?
2. Is there any change in the appearance of a worksheet after it is reloaded with the File Retrieve command?
3. What are the main characteristics of a good filename?
4. What filename extension does 1-2-3 assign to worksheet files?
5. Which File command would you use to combine an incoming worksheet with a worksheet in memory?
6. In what two forms can you save a worksheet with the File Xtract command?
7. What filename extensions must a text file have before it can be imported into a 1-2-3 worksheet with the File Import command?

ANSWERS

1. The File Save command is used to save the entire worksheet.
2. No. After a worksheet is reloaded with the File Retrieve command, it will have exactly the appearance it had just before it was saved. The worksheet cursor will be in the same cell, all format settings and column width settings will be the same, remembered ranges will be proposed, and the screen will be split into two windows, if it had been split before saving.
3. A good filename gives as much information as possible about a file's contents, and it gives you information about how this file relates to other, similar files.
4. Lotus assigns the .WKS extension to all 1-2-3 worksheet files.
5. The File Combine command combines incoming and resident worksheets. Don't use the File Retrieve command because this command erases the resident worksheet before loading the incoming worksheet.

6. The two options for the File Xtract command are (1) Formulas, which saves the formulas behind the worksheet, and (2) Values, which saves only the displayed values, not the formulas that generated them.
7. Files imported with the File Import command must have the .PRN filename extension. If a text file doesn't have this extension, you must rename the file with the extension added.

CHAPTER SEVEN
THE PRINT COMMAND

OBJECTIVES

- To master the Lotus 1-2-3 Print command.
- To learn to print a worksheet under the default settings.
- To learn to pause or end the Print command in the middle of printing a worksheet.
- To learn to print worksheets in compressed type.
- To learn to create a print file for later use with a word processing program.
- To learn to use the advanced features of the Print command to place headers, footers, page numbers, and dates on printed worksheets.

INTRODUCTION

The Printer/File Option

The Print command is used to produce two different types of output. (See the command tree, Figure 7-1.) The first type of output is the familiar printed, or *hard copy*, version of a 1-2-3 worksheet. You can print all the worksheet, or you can select a range of cells to print.

The other type of output created with the Print command is a *print file*. A print file is an electronic image of a worksheet stored on a data diskette. This image is exactly like the image sent to the printer by the other part of the Print command which is why creating a print file is sometimes called "printing to the disk."

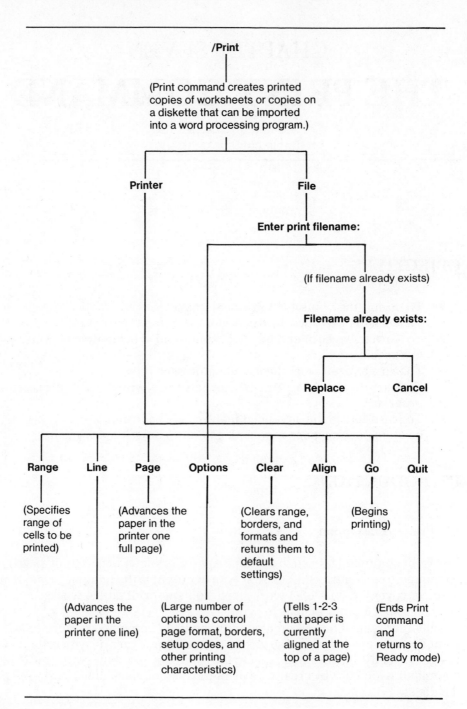

/Print

(Print command creates printed
copies of worksheets or copies on
a diskette that can be imported
into a word processing program.)

Printer   **File**

Enter print filename:

(If filename already exists)

Filename already exists:

Replace   **Cancel**

Range   **Line**   **Page**   **Options**   **Clear**   **Align**   **Go**   **Quit**

(Specifies
range of
cells to be
printed)

(Advances the
paper in the
printer one
full page)

(Clears range,
borders, and
formats and
returns them to
default
settings)

(Begins
printing)

(Advances the
paper in the
printer one line)

(Large number of
options to control
page format, borders,
setup codes, and
other printing
characteristics)

(Tells 1-2-3
that paper is
currently
aligned at the
top of a page)

(Ends Print
command
and
returns to
Ready mode)

Figure 7-1. The Print command tree.

But, a print file is different from a worksheet file created with the File Save command. A print file *cannot* be reloaded as a functioning electronic worksheet into 1-2-3 with the File Retrieve command because a print file doesn't contain any of the information necessary to reconstruct the worksheet. However, you can load it into 1-2-3 as a text file with the File Import command (see Chapter Six).

If you use the File Import command, each row of the table will be entered as a single long label in a single column of cells. To distinguish print files from worksheet files, 1-2-3 assigns the filename extension .PRN to all print files.

While a print file can't be used as a worksheet by 1-2-3, it can be imported into a word processing program where the worksheet can be combined with text to form a report. This feature greatly extends the usefulness of 1-2-3 worksheets. Depending on the particular word processing program, you can improve the appearance of your worksheets by adding titles and text and by using special characters such as underlining, bold facing, and different type fonts.

The steps necessary to import a print file into a word processing program vary from program to program, so consult your word processing program's manual for the exact instructions. You will find them under something like "Importing Text Files," or "Incorporating Electronic Worksheets into Word Processing Documents."

Symphony

In addition to printing worksheets as hard copy and as print files, Symphony can print a range of cells to a different range of cells *on the same worksheet.* In the destination cells, the material will be in the form of long labels regardless of its form in the source cells.

Symphony also has a number of options designed for printing documents. You can, for example, begin printing on any page in a document and end the printing on any page. You can choose to have the document printed with single, double, or triple spacing.

Finally, when you select the Print command from the Services menu, Symphony displays a screen containing the current print settings. This makes reviewing the current print settings quick and easy (see Figure 7-2). Whenever you select Settings and change a setting, the new setting appears in the print setting sheet. You can even create a library of named print setting sheets and call them up when needed.

```
┌─────────────────────────────────────────────────────────────────────────────────
│
│  Start printing using current settings                                     MENU
│  Go  Line-Advance  Page-Advance  Align  Settings  Quit
│  ,---------------------------------------------------------------------------------,
│  ! Page                           Source:                                         !
│  !   Length:      66              Destination:  Printer                           !
│  !   Spacing:     1               Init-String:                                    !
│  !   Number                       Margins          Other                          !
│  !     Print-Number:  1             Left:    4      Space Compression:  No        !
│  !     Start-Page:    1             Right:   76     Attributes:          Yes       !
│  !     End-Page:      999           Top:     2      Format:  As-Displayed          !
│  !   Breaks:     Yes                Bottom:  2      Top-Labels:                    !
│  !   Wait:       No                                 Left-Labels:                   !
│  !   Header:                                                                       !
│  !   Footer:                                                                       !
│  '=======================================================Print Settings:  MAIN="
```

Figure 7-2. Print Command Settings Sheet.

Printing Plain and Printing Fancy

Outside of the Database and Graphics commands, the Print command is certainly the command most people find hardest to master. The reason is that the Print command provides a great many options for printing a worksheet. There is a necessary trade-off between the power of a large number of options and the ease with which a command can be learned and used. The more options, the harder to learn. The fewer options, the easier to use. Furthermore, if you are not familiar with the way 1-2-3 views the printed page, the results you get will often be unexpected.

To help you master the Print command, this chapter is divided into two major parts. The next section describes "Printing Plain." In it you learn to make simple, straightforward printouts under Lotus' default settings for margins and page length. You also learn what happens when your worksheet won't fit on what 1-2-3 considers a standard or "default" page.

The next section is "Printing Fancy." It discusses how to insert headers and footers, how to change the margins and page length settings, how to send special control codes to your printer, and how to use the other printer options available under the Print command. Once you understand how to make a straightforward printout and how 1-2-3 views the default page, the advanced printing options can be used to enhance the professional appearance of your printed worksheets.

PRINTING PLAIN

An Example

Figure 7-3 shows a 1-2-3 screen containing a simple worksheet. The entire worksheet fits on a single screen, and, as you can see from the control panel, the Print command has been entered.

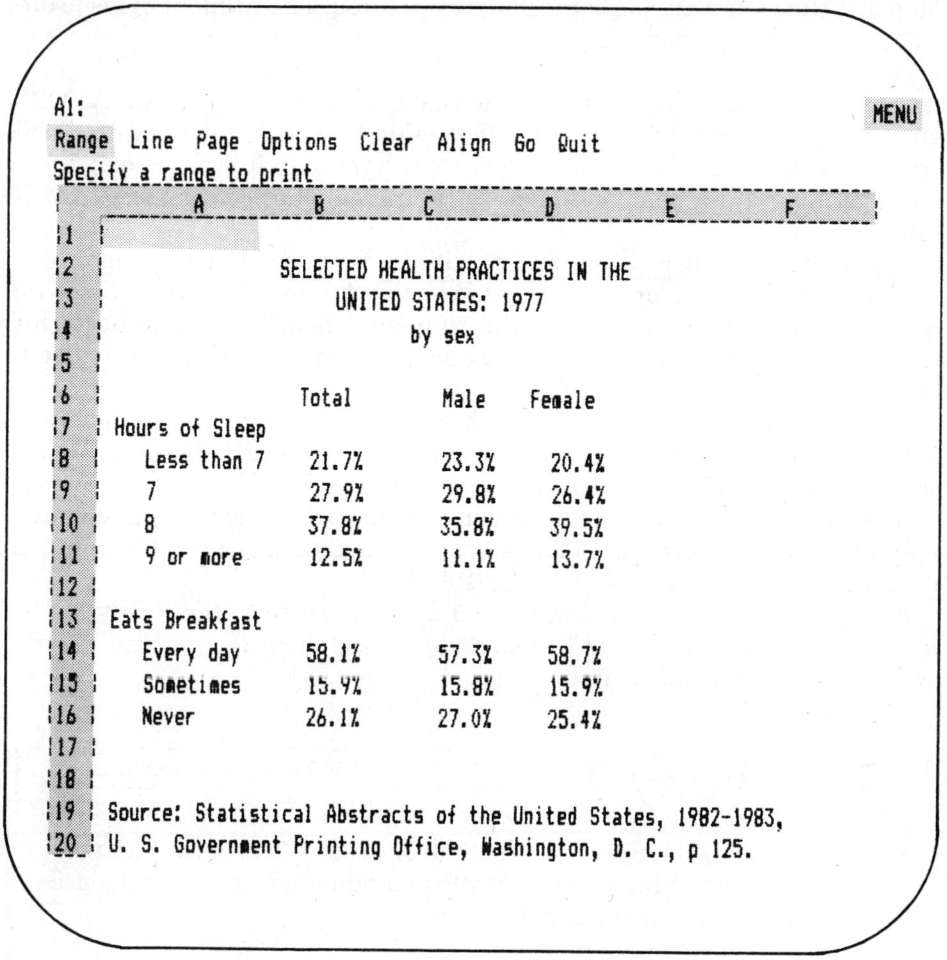

```
A1:                                                              MENU
Range Line Page Options Clear Align Go Quit
Specify a range to print
              A          B          C          D        E        F
 1
 2                       SELECTED HEALTH PRACTICES IN THE
 3                           UNITED STATES: 1977
 4                               by sex
 5
 6                       Total       Male     Female
 7    Hours of Sleep
 8       Less than 7    21.7%       23.3%     20.4%
 9       7              27.9%       29.8%     26.4%
10       8              37.8%       35.8%     39.5%
11       9 or more      12.5%       11.1%     13.7%
12
13    Eats Breakfast
14       Every day      58.1%       57.3%     58.7%
15       Sometimes      15.9%       15.8%     15.9%
16       Never          26.1%       27.0%     25.4%
17
18
19    Source: Statistical Abstracts of the United States, 1982-1983,
20    U. S. Government Printing Office, Washington, D. C., p 125.
```

Figure 7-3. Lotus 1-2-3 in the Print command.

To print this worksheet, go through the following steps (assuming your printer is hooked up and ready to go):

Step 1:   Type **/P** This enters the Print command.
Step 2:   Select **Printer** This indicates you are printing with the printer rather than creating a print file.
Step 3:   Select **Range** This specifies the cells to be printed (A1..D20 in Figure 7-3).
Step 4:   Select **Align** This tells 1-2-3 that the print head of your printer is at the top of the page.
Step 5:   Select **GO** This starts the printing process. The printer begins printing the specified range.

Range   You must *always* specify the range of cells to be printed. As with any other 1-2-3 range, you can specify it either by typing the required cell addresses, by using the cursor control keys to point to it, or by specifying a name by typing the name assigned to the range or by using the **[NAME]** function key.

If you attempt to print a worksheet without first specifying a range, 1-2-3 "beeps" and refuses to proceed. Lotus *doesn't* issue an error message, so you may wonder what is wrong. Check the range specification by pressing **[R]** for range. If no range is specified, specify one and then press **[G]** for Go to begin printing.

As with other ranges, Lotus remembers the last print range you specified and proposes it the next time you need a print range. Furthermore, Lotus saves print ranges with worksheets saved with the File Save and File Xtract commands. (It also saves choices you have made under the Options subcommand.) Once the correct range has been "remembered" by 1-2-3, you can print the worksheet by simply typing **/PPAG**.

After a range has been printed, 1-2-3 doesn't return to the Ready mode. Rather, it remains in the Print command. If you want to, you can specify additional ranges to be printed.

Symphony

Symphony uses the term "Source" in place of 1-2-3's term "Range" because the source for a Symphony Print command can be a database settings sheet as well as a range of cells.

Align The error most frequently made when using the 1-2-3 Print command is not typing **[A]** for Align before selecting Go. Align tells 1-2-3 that the print head of your printer is at the top of a page on line number 1.

When you first load 1-2-3, the program takes the position of the print head *at that time* as the top of a page. Thus 1-2-3 incorrectly assumes the print head is at the top of a page whenever the paper hasn't been properly positioned before you loaded 1-2-3, or whenever you manually change the paper in position in the printer. A manual change occurs whenever you roll a sheet of paper forward so it can be torn off at the perforations.

If the paper isn't properly aligned, or if you don't send the Align command just before printing a worksheet, the result is a page break where it isn't wanted and a missed page break where it is needed. Your worksheets end up with blank lines in the middle of text and with lines printed across the perforations in continuous feed paper. (A "page break" is the space left at the end of the current page and at the top of the following page so printing is properly positioned on the page, and so you do not tear through a line of type when separating continuous feed paper.)

To prevent incorrect page breaks and inadvertent printing across perforations, *always* select the Align command before pressing **[G]** to start printing your worksheet.

The Default Page

Table 7-1 shows how the worksheet in Figure 7-3 looks when the printing process is over. You have printed a worksheet by accepting all of 1-2-3's default settings: top, bottom, left, and right margins, number of lines per page; and type size. To understand and master the Print command, you must look behind the printing process to see exactly what those defaults are.

Lotus assumes that you are making your printouts on standard 8 1/2" by 11" paper. On this page, in standard type, 80 characters can be typed edge-to-edge, and 66 lines can be typed from top to bottom. Lotus' default settings for the margins on this page are:

- Left Margin: at character 4
- Right Margin: at character 76

This results in a line 72 characters long.

- Top Margin and Header: 5 lines
- Bottom Margin and Footer: 5 lines

This results in a page that is 56 lines deep.

TABLE 7-1

Figure 7-2 printed according to 1-2-3's default print settings.

```
             SELECTED HEALTH PRACTICES IN THE
                  UNITED STATES: 1977
                       by Sex

                   Total      Male    Female
     Hours of Sleep
       Less than 7  21.7%     23.3%    20.4%
       7            27.9%     29.8%    26.4%
       8            37.8%     35.8%    39.5%
       9 or more    12.5%     11.1%    13.7%

     Eats Breakfast
       Every day    58.1%     57.3%    58.7%
       Sometimes    15.9%     15.8%    15.9%
       Never        26.1%     27.0%    25.4%


     Source: Statistical Abstracts of the United States, 1982-1983,
     U. S. Government Printing Office, Washington, D. C., p. 125.
```

    See page 179 for a discussion of how the five lines at the top and the bottom of the default page are divided between margins and headers and footers. (Headers and footers are a single line of type placed at the top and the bottom of each printed page.)

    Figure 7-4 contains an illustration of 1-2-3's default page. Notice that the right margin is set relative to the *left* edge of the page. That is, it is set at character 76 which leaves four characters for the right margin. To find the maximum number of characters that can be printed on a line, subtract the setting for the left margin from that for the right margin (e.g., 76 − 4 = 72).

    The default margins are selected by Lotus. However, if they aren't the settings you use most frequently, you can change the defaults. You would certainly want to do this if you make all your printouts on 15" wide computer paper rather than on 8 1/2" wide paper, or if your preferred margins are different from the default settings. See the discussion under the Worksheet Global Default command in chapter three.

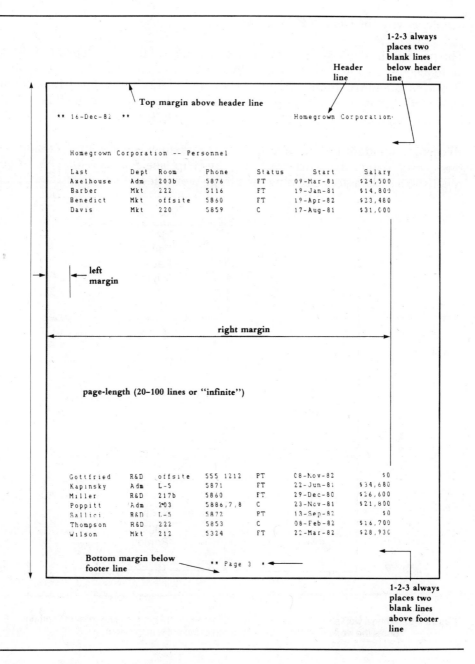

Figure 7-4. Standard Lotus 1-2-3 page with the factory set default values for left, right, top, and bottom margins and page length.

Source: *Lotus 1-2-3 Manual,* Lotus Development Corporation, Boston, Mass., 1983.

Problems with the Default Print Settings

The printout in Table 7-1 works well because *none* of the default print settings are exceeded. None of the lines are longer than 72 characters, and the table contains no more than 56 lines. Had any default print settings been exceeded, Lotus would have printed the worksheet in a predictable, if not entirely satisfactory, way.

Exceeding the Default Line Width   If the worksheet is wider than 72 characters, Lotus prints the worksheet strip-by-strip (see Figure 7-5). This often results in a satisfactory printing for a large worksheet.

First Page Printed	Fourth Page Printed
Second Page Printed	Fifth Page Printed
Third Page Printed	Sixth Page Printed

Figure 7-5. When a worksheet is wider or longer than the current margin or page length settings, 1-2-3 prints the worksheet in "strips" according to the order in this figure.

It sometimes happens, however, that only one or two columns are printed on the last page. It is better to have roughly the same number of columns on each page of a multiple page printout. To accomplish this, adjust the length of the printed line and/or the column width until the results are to your liking.

To get more characters on a page, you can print the worksheet in a smaller type size called *compressed type*. In compressed type, 132 characters can be printed from edge-to-edge on an 8 1/2 " wide page. If your printer can accommodate it, you can use 15 " wide paper. With the wider paper, you can place 132 regular characters or 233 compressed characters edge-to-edge.

Regardless of the method you choose, you must realize that 1-2-3 will *not* print any characters beyond what is set as the right margin. The default margins allow 72 characters on each line. If your worksheet is wider than 72 characters, either accept the printing by strips, or adopt one of the alternatives just described. If you print in strips, you may want to adjust the margin so a reasonable number of columns appear on each page.

How can you tell if your worksheet is wider than 72 characters? The 1-2-3 screen is 72 characters wide (less, with some combinations of column widths), so the rule of thumb is that if *both* the extreme left and right columns can be viewed on the screen at the same time, the worksheet will print within the default margins. If you must scroll the screen to the left and the right to view the first and last columns, then the worksheet is wider than 72 characters, and it won't fit within the default margins.

Long labels present a special problem. A long label is a text label that extends beyond the right boundary of the cell in which it is entered. You will make frequent use of long labels for worksheet titles and sometimes for column headings. If, when the worksheet is printed, a long label extends beyond the right margin, 1-2-3 *truncates* the label at the margin. Furthermore, the rest of the label will *not* continue on the next page of a multiple page printout because the cell actually containing the label is not printed on that page.

If you have used long labels, check to see that all the text appears on your printout. If it doesn't, edit the label, adjust the margins, or make other provisions for printing the text.

Exceeding the Default Page Length   If you specify more that 56 rows in the print range, 1-2-3 prints the additional rows on the next page. The default page parameters reserve a total of ten lines on the page for margins, headers, and footers. There is a two-line margin at the top and a two-line margin at the bottom of each page. Furthermore, *a line is reserved for the header, another for the footer, and two lines are always placed between the header and the footer and the printed table.*

Even if you set the top and bottom margins to zero, you *cannot* eliminate the six lines reserved for the header and the footer. So the longest table that can be printed under the default page length of 66 lines is one with 60 lines.

There are, however, two ways to get more lines on a "page." The first is to select the Unformatted option under the Print command options. When a page is printed unformatted, all settings for headers, footers, top and bottom margins and page length are ignored. Each line is printed one after the other, even if this prints across the perforations of continuous feed paper.

Alternatively, some printers, such as the Epson and Epson-compatible dot-matrix printers, allow you to vary the line spacing. The standard number of lines per page is 66 (6 lines per inch), but these printers can print lines closer together. For example, you can print 88 lines per page, which is 8 lines per vertical inch. To do this, you send a special setup code to the printer. (The setup code required to do this, as well as other setup codes, are described in the following section.)

You must *also* adjust the page length. Even if you tell the printer to print 88 lines per page, 1-2-3 prints *only* 66 lines *unless* you change the page length with the Page-Length command under Options.

Stopping the Printer

Knowing how to stop the printing of a 1-2-3 worksheet is almost as important as knowing what keys to press to get the printing started in the first place. You will want to stop the printer if you see it is printing incorrectly due to the wrong setup code, the wrong margins, or printing the wrong range. You will want to have the printing of a worksheet pause when you need to answer the telephone or talk to someone.

To *stop* the printing of a worksheet, press the **[CTRL]-[SCROLL LOCK]** keys at the same time. On some computers, the **[SCROLL LOCK]** key is also the **[BREAK]** key (see Appendix A). When you press **[CTRL]-[SCROLL LOCK]**, printing stops, the Print command is cleared, and 1-2-3 returns to the Ready mode.

To *pause* the printing process, press **[CTRL]-[NUM LOCK]**. The printer stops, but the Print command continues to be displayed in the control panel. To resume printing, simply press any key and 1-2-3 finishes printing the worksheet.

If you have a "print buffer" or "print spooler" (devices that free up 1-2-3 by holding information for printing), you must consult the buffer or spooler manual for the instructions for pausing or stopping the printing process.

Additional Print Commands

When you type **/PP** the command line reads:

Range   Line   Page   Options   Clear   Align   Go   Quit

The Range, Align, and Go options have already been discussed. The Options option is the subject of the next section, "Printing Fancy." The remaining choices on the Print command menu are Line, Page, Clear, and Quit.

Line and Page   Line and Page advance the paper in the printer to the next line (with each press of **[L]**) or to the top of the next page (with each press of **[P]**). If you use these two commands to advance the paper in your printer, 1-2-3 keeps track of the page breaks.

Clear   When you choose the Clear option, you are presented with four choices:

All   Range   Borders   Formats

If you choose All, all ranges, borders, formats, and *all* other choices made under the Options submenu are reset to their default values. If you choose one of the other three options (Range, Borders, or Formats) only the specified choice is cleared. The Formats option resets to the default values everything except the print range and those columns or rows chosen to border the printout.

Quit   The last choice, Quit, does just that. It ends the Print command and returns 1-2-3 to the Ready mode. You can also return to the Ready mode by pressing the **[CTRL]-[SCROLL LOCK]** combination or by pressing the **[ESC]** key twice. You must use one of these techniques for ending the Print command because, as noted, the command line continues to display the Print command menu after a worksheet has been printed.

PRINTING FANCY

Printing under the default options gives acceptable printouts whenever the worksheet is less than 72 characters wide and less than 56 lines long. In other printing situations, you will probably want to override one or more of the default specifications with margins, page lengths, and type sizes of your own choosing. You may also want to add a header, a footer, the current date, or a page number to your printed worksheets. You can do all these things and more with Options on the Print command. See Figure 7-6 for the command tree.

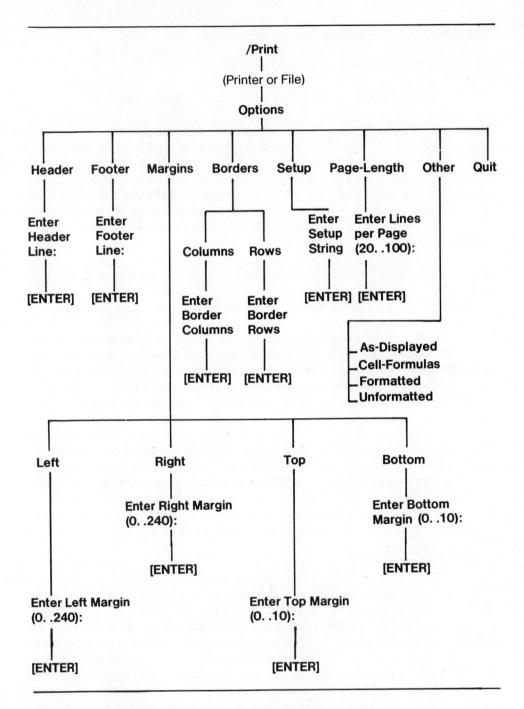

Figure 7-6. Command tree for the Print command, Options.

To select an option when in the Print command menu, press **[O]** for Options. The following menu appears on the command line:

Header Footer Margins Borders Setup Page-Length Other Quit

To make a choice, either type the initial letter or move the command line cursor to the desired word and press **[ENTER]**. Once you make a choice, you are presented with a submenu. After you responded to the submenu prompt by either making a choice or by supplying the requested information (usually followed by **[ENTER]**), you are returned to the Options menu, (*not* the Print command main menu) where you can make additional choices.

When you're ready to print the worksheet, press **[Q]** for Quit or **[ESC]** to move back to the main Print command menu. Printing can begin only with the selection of Go from the Print command main menu.

Page Parameters

The Margins and Page-Length options let you set the left, right, top, and bottom margins as well as the number of lines to be printed on each page.

To print edge-to-edge on 8 1/2" paper, choose 0 for the left margin and 80 for the right. If you are printing in compressed type, be sure to expand the number of characters printed on each line. Otherwise, 1-2-3 leaves about half the page blank after placing the default 72 characters on each line. You also need to expand the number of characters on a line when you are using 15" wide computer paper.

If you never use headers and footers, the maximum number of lines you can print on a standard page is 60 (66 less the 6 reserved lines). To print 60 lines on a page, set the top and bottom margins to 0. Remember, you can change the default margins with the Worksheet Global Default command. Do this if you find the factory-set default margins don't fit most of your printing needs.

The default page length is based on an 11" long page with 6 lines printed to the inch. This is standard, but you have the option of setting the page length to anything from 20 lines per page to 100 lines per page. This lets you print on odd sized paper; checks, mailing labels, form-fed note cards, form-fed envelopes, and so forth. You must also change the page length when you send the control code to print more or fewer lines per page than the standard 66.

Headers and Footers

To specify a header or a footer, choose the appropriate option from the Options menu. Then type in the text. A header and a footer are printed on each page of a multiple page printout. Table 7-2 shows Table 7-1 printed with headers and footers.

TABLE 7-2

Worksheet from Figure 7-1 printed with headers and footers.

```
(HEADER)->   This is a table for Chapter 7                    05-Mar-84
                       SELECTED HEALTH PRACTICES IN THE
                           UNITED STATES: 1977
                                 by Sex

                        Total       Male    Female
             Hours of Sleep
               Less than 7    21.7%     23.3%    20.4%
               7              27.9%     29.8%    26.4%
               8              37.8%     35.8%    39.5%
               9 or more      12.5%     11.1%    13.7%

             Eats Breakfast
               Every day      58.1%     57.3%    58.7%
               Sometimes      15.9%     15.8%    15.9%
               Never          26.1%     27.0%    25.4%

             Source: Statistical Abstracts of the United States, 1982-1983,
             U. S. Government Printing Office, Washington, D. C., p. 125.


(FOOTER)->                         PAGE 1
```

Headers and footers cannot be longer than 240 characters. They must also not be wider than the line defined by the right and left margins. If the header is wider than the line, as many characters as will fit are printed. The remaining characters are truncated. You may have to use trial and error to adjust headers or footers that are wide in relation to the line length you've specified.

The text of a header or a footer can be located in one of three places on the printed page; flush left, centered on the page, or flush right. You use the vertical line character [¦] to position text.

1. Text before the first [¦] prints flush left. For example:

Enter Header Line: This is a draft.

(If the only text in a header or footer is to be flush left, you don't need any vertical lines.)

2. Text after the first [¦]but before the second is centered. For example:

Enter Header Line: :This is a draft.

3. Text after the second [¦]is printed flush right. For example:

Enter Header Line: :This is a draft.

Up to three pieces of text can be used in any header or footer. Simply use the vertical line [;] to separate the parts.

When the last line of a *worksheet* is printed (not the last line of the *page*), the printer stops rather than proceeding to the bottom of the current page. Since the printer doesn't get to the bottom of the page, the footer for that page *will not* be printed. However, if you issue the Page command from the main Print command menu, the page advances and 1-2-3 prints the footer when it reaches the bottom of the page. If you are using a footer, finish printing each worksheet with the Page command to be sure the footer prints on the last page.

Two special characters, the cross-hatch [#] and the at [@] symbol, can be used in 1-2-3 headers and footers. The cross-hatch [#] prints the current page number in place of the cross-hatch. For example, the header "¦Page #" would place "Page 1" in the center of the first page, "Page 2" in the center of the second page, and so on.

The at symbol [@] reads the system calendar in your microcomputer's memory and places the date (presumably today's) on the printout in the location specified by the symbol. For example, a footer entered as "@" would print the system date flush left on the footer line.

The header and footer entered into the Print command that created Table 7-2 were:

Enter Header Line:

This is a table for Chapter 7¦¦@

Enter Footer Line:

¦PAGE #

Borders

The Borders option allows you to specify one or more adjacent columns and/or one or more adjacent rows as borders. The border rows and columns can be located anywhere on the worksheet, but when the worksheet is printed, border columns are printed as the first columns of the corresponding rows, and border rows are printed as the first rows of the corresponding columns. In addition to typing in a row or column range, you can use the cursor control keys to expand the worksheet cursor to designate rows or columns for the Borders option.

If you use the rows containing the column headings, be sure you *don't* also include them in the print range. If you do include them in the print range, you will find *two* sets of column headings on the first page of the printout.

Symphony

Symphony uses the terms "Top-Labels" and "Left-Labels" for the 1-2-3 terms "Column Borders" and "Row Borders," respectively.

The same caution applies to rows designated as column borders. What happens is that 1-2-3 prints the rows or columns designated as borders both in their place in the print range *and* as borders.

You can use the Borders option in a limited fashion to rearrange the location of some of the rows or columns on a worksheet.

Setup Strings

Several references have been made to printing worksheets in compressed type or printing more or less than 66 lines to a page. To accomplish these and other special operations, you must have a printer capable of performing the operation and send the printer the "setup string" or "setup code" it recognizes as the signal to do a particular operation. Lotus printer setup strings are a backslash [\ ] followed by three digits (e.g., \ 015).

Setup strings are sent by means of Setup on the Options menu. The exact code required for a particular brand of printer is unique to that printer. Since setup codes are not standard, consult your printer's manual for the codes it recognizes. See Table 7-3 for the setup strings for the Epson dot-matrix printers. See the appendix of the Lotus 1-2-3 manual for a list of Lotus setup strings that correspond to all of the characters in the common control codes.

Once a setup code has been sent to your printer, the printer is set up to perform in a particular way (print in compressed type, for example). The printer *continues* to print that way (in compressed type) until you either turn the printer off (which resets the printer to its default values), or you send the code that cancels the previous code, or you send a code (such as enlarged type) that replaces the first code. This is true even if you erase the setup code from the Print command, erase the entire worksheet, or load another worksheet. Turning the printer off is often the easiest and most convenient way to clear the printer of setup strings.

TABLE 7-3

Setup strings for Epson dot matrix printers. Note: some setup codes must be preceded by the code for escape, \ 027. Setup strings for other brands of printers may be different. Check your printer manual.

Setup String	Function
Type Fonts	
\ 015	Turns on compressed printing (Doesn't work with emphasized printing)
\ 018	Turns off compressed printing
\ 014	Turns on double width printing (Line 1 of page only)
\ 020	Turns off double width printing
\ 069	Turns on emphasized printing
\ 070	Turns off emphasized printing
\ 071	Turns on double strike mode
\ 072	Turns off double strike mode
\ 052	Turns on italic printing
\ 053	Turns off italic printing
Line Spacing	
\ 048	Sets line spacing to 1/8"
\ 049	Sets line spacing to 7/72"
\ 050	Returns line spacing default 1/6"
\ 051N	Sets line spacing to N/216" where N is a number between 1 and 255.
\ 065N	Sets line spacing to N/72" where N is a number between 1 and 85
Cancel All Special Settings	
\ 064	Resets all special modes to their power up default states

OTHER Option

When you select the Other option on the Options menu, the following submenu appears:

Displayed Formulas Formatted Unformatted

These four options really give you **two** either/or choices.

You can choose to have the worksheet printed either As-Displayed or as Formulas. Choosing As-Displayed results in a normal printout with the information arranged in columns and rows. Formulas, on the other hand, provides a laundry list of the contents of each cell, printed one cell to a line. The list begins with the first cell in row 1 containing an entry. It continues from left to right, down the worksheet, until all cells containing entries have been listed. Blank cells are not printed in the list. (Don't confuse Formulas with the Range and Worksheet Format Text which is used to display the contents—numbers, formulas, or functions—in the worksheet cell into which they have been entered.)

Table 7-4 is a printout of the formulas for the worksheet in Table 7-1. Notice that the entries are decimals. In Table 7-1 they were displayed as percentages under the percentage format. Decimals were entered, so decimals are listed.

Printing the formulas is a way to make a record of the contents of each cell. You can use it to make a hard copy backup of the structure of a worksheet just as you use the File Save command to make an electronic backup copy.

The other either/or choice is Formatted and Unformatted and refers to whether the headers, footers, and page length are to be used to format the printout. When you choose Formatted, the formats are used. As noted earlier in this chapter, when you choose Unformatted, the formats are ignored. No headers or footers are printed and printing continues until every line in the worksheet has been printed. There are no page breaks; the table is printed across the perforations in continuous feed paper.

You will usually want to print your worksheets Formatted, but in several instances, the Unformatted option is better. When you are making a print file, for example, you will often want to eliminate headers, footers, and page breaks because you will add them later to conform to the style of the document into which the text file is being imported.

The Unformatted option also allows you to print the maximum amount of information on a given page. It is the only way, in fact, that you can print from the very top to the very bottom of a page since the Formatted option always reserves a total of six lines for the header and the footer.

TABLE 7-4

When you choose Formulas under the other choice on the Print Options menu, you get a listing of the contents of each cell of the worksheet, beginning with cell A1. Blank cells are ignored in the listing. This listing is for Table 7-1.

```
B2:  "SELECTED HEALTH PRACTICES IN THE
B3:  "        UNITED STATES: 1977
B4:  "                by Sex
B6:  "Total
C6:  "Male
D6:  "Female
A7:  'Hours of Sleep
A8:  '    Less than 7
B8:  0.217
C8:  0.233
D8:  0.204
A9:  '    7
B9:  0.279
C9:  0.298
D9:  0.264
A10: '    8
B10: 0.378
C10: 0.358
D10: 0.395
A11: '    9 or more
B11: 0.125
C11: 0.111
D11: 0.137
A13: "Eats Breakfast
A14: '    Every day
B14: 0.581
C14: 0.573
D14: 0.587
A15: '    Sometimes
B15: 0.159
C15: 0.158
D15: 0.159
A16: '    Never
B16: 0.261
C16: 0.27
D16: 0.254
A19: "Source: Statistical Abstracts of the United States, 1982-1983,
A20: "U. S. Government Printing Office, Washington, D. C., p. 125.
```

The defaults for Other are As-Displayed and Formatted. You need to enter this subcommand only when you want either to print the formulas or to suppress the formatting. The Clear option on the main Print command menu resets the Other to the default values.

THE PRINT FILE COMMAND

As noted in the introduction to this chapter, you can create two different types of output with the 1-2-3 Print command; printed worksheets and print files. Print files can be imported into word processing programs where they can be edited, printed under special formatting, or combined with text in a document.

Creating a Print File

To create a print file, select File after typing /P. Lotus then prompts you for a filename. Supply it, or select one of the current print filenames from the current data diskette. If the filename you select already exists on the current data diskette, 1-2-3 asks whether you want to "Replace" the existing file or "Cancel" the Print command.

If you select Replace, 1-2-3 erases the existing file and proceeds into the Print command. If you select Cancel, 1-2-3 terminates the Print command and returns to Ready mode. To change a filename you have just assigned, a better choice than Cancel is to press the **[ESC]** key. You then back up one stage to the filename prompt where you can enter a new filename. Lotus automatically adds the filename extension .PRN to all print files it creates.

Once you have specified the filename, 1-2-3 moves on to the main Print command menu (see Figure 7-1). From here on, the same options are open to you when creating a print file as when printing a worksheet. The only difference is that the Setup option for sending control codes to the printer doesn't work with a print file.

As always, you *must* specify the range of cells to be printed by selecting the Range option. If you are satisfied with the default page parameters (72 characters per line, 66 lines to a page, 10 lines for top and bottom margins and for headers and footers) select Align and then Go, to create the print file.

As with a printed worksheet, align the worksheet when creating a print file. If you don't, the print file may be created with the same kinds of errors (page breaks in unexpected places) that occur with a printed worksheet when the print head is misaligned relative to the top of the page.

All the subcommands and options of the Print command (except Setup) are available, and it is most important to be aware of the pitfalls as well as the opportunities these choices present. In particular, make sure that one or more of the margin, page length, header or footer choices doesn't cause a result you didn't intend.

You can check to see whether the print file you created is the one you intended by using the File Import command. Remember the File Import command allows you to read into a 1-2-3 worksheet a text file with the extension .PRN. The file is read in as a column of long labels, but you can to whether margins have been exceeded (resulting in printing in strips) or whether page breaks occurred in the wrong places.

Even though you can view a print file with the File Import command, you should also save, as a worksheet file, *any* file from which you create a print file. It is much easier to modify, update, or otherwise edit a 1-2-3 worksheet than it is to change a print file.

The Fancy Print File

As noted, a table printed to a diskette as a print file is subject to the same default settings as a worksheet printed with a printer. In many cases, you will want to suppress the headers, footers, and the page length implied by the default settings. You can easily suppress them by choosing the Unformatted option on the Other choice of the Options submenu. The print file is then printed without page breaks.

However, the default margins are still in effect and control the position of the print file table. In particular, if you want to prevent 1-2-3 from creating the print file in strips when you have more than 72 characters on a line, you must adjust the default margins before creating the print file.

HANDS ON: USING THE PRINT COMMAND

Printing in Compressed Type

If your printer can do it, and most dot-matrix printers can, printing a worksheet in compressed type is an excellent way to get the maximum amount of information onto a single printed page.

Assume for example, you'd like to add more information to Table 7-1, the table on Selected Health Practices in the United States used to illustrate printing under the default page parameters. You might want to show how eating and sleeping vary with income and age as well as with sex. This would make for a more interesting table, but it would also add several columns of information.

Table 7-5 on the next page shows how this expanded table would be printed under the default page parameters. As you can see, there are a number of problems with the way the table has been printed.

First, only part of the heading is printed on the first page, and the heading was truncated because it is made up of long labels that extend beyond the right default margin. Recall that 1-2-3 does not print anything that extends beyond the right margin, and it does not carry the rest of the long label over to the following page because the long label is *only* printed on the page that prints the cell containing the label.

Second, the columns for "55 and over" and the columns relating sleeping and eating to income appear on the second page. They are printed on the second page even though only about half of the available 56 lines on the first page are actually used to print the table. This is because only the first 6 columns of the table can be printed on the first page. To print more would require going beyond the right margin, and this 1-2-3 will not do.

TABLE 7-5

When the expanded Selected Health Practices table is printed under the default settings, the table is printed on two pages, and the last part of the long labels that make up the heading are truncated.

```
THE FOLLOWING COLUMNS ARE PRINTED ON THE FIRST PAGE:


                                                        SELECTED HEALTH
                                                            UNITED STA
                                                          by Age, Sex


                                                  20-34        35-54
                      Total      Male    Female   years        years
    Hours of Sleep
      Less than 7     21.7%     23.3%    20.4%    20.2%        22.4%
      7               27.9%     29.8%    26.4%    28.9%        31.3%
      8               37.8%     35.8%    39.5%    38.2%        37.2%
      9 or more       12.5%     11.1%    13.7%    12.6%         9.0%

    Eats Breakfast
      Every day       58.1%     57.3%    58.7%    41.6%        55.5%
      Sometimes       15.9%     15.8%    15.9%    22.7%        16.2%
      Never           26.1%     27.0%    25.4%    35.8%        28.3%


    Source: Statistical Abstracts of the United States, 1982-1983,
    U. S. Government Printing Office, Washington, D. C., p. 125.


THE FOLLOWING COLUMNS ARE PRINTED ON THE SECOND PAGE:

                   Less
      55 and       than     $5,000-  $15,000-   $25,000
       over       $5,000    $14,999  $24,999   and over

      22.7%       27.0%      21.4%    20.8%      19.3%
      23.2%       20.4%      26.6%    31.7%      33.6%
      38.0%       35.2%      38.8%    37.8%      38.0%
      16.1%       17.3%      13.2%     9.7%       9.2%



      80.1%       64.9%      58.0%    53.3%      56.5%
       7.5%       14.8%      16.0%    17.2%      15.3%
      12.4%       20.3%      26.0%    29.5%      28.1%
```

Finally, it is difficult to make sense out of the information on the second page because there are no row labels. You might be able to guess that as income goes up, the fraction of each income class getting nine or more hours of sleep a night declines rather rapidly. (The early bird does seem to get the worm!) But would you be able to tell that the older you are, the more likely you are never to skip breakfast? The problem is that the row labels are all on the first page. This is because they are entered into the first column and, of course, the first column is only printed on the first page.

You could use the Borders option to designate column 1 as a border column. The row labels would then appear on both pages. If you did this, you'd have to redefine the print range to *exclude* column 1. Otherwise, two sets of row labels would appear on page 1. But there is a better way to solve the problem presented by the default page parameters. You can use compressed type to print the entire table on a single page.

Assuming your printer can print in compressed type, you have to do only two things to have Table 7-5 printed on a single piece of paper. First, you must use Options Setup to specify the proper setup string and second, you must use Options Margins to expand the line width.

As noted, the setup string that instructs a printer to print in compressed type varies from one brand of printer to another. Check your printer manual for the correct setup string for your printer. Choose the Setup choice from the Options menu. The prompt then reads:

Enter setup string:

If you have an Epson printer, type \ **015** and press **[ENTER]**. Any worksheet you print under the control of this setup string is now printed in compressed type.

However, before you give the Go command, you *must* adjust the margins. They are now set at the default values of 4 and 76, so 1-2-3 will print only 72 characters on a line. In compressed type, these 72 characters take up about half the page and leave the rest blank. Since you can print up to 132 characters on an 8 1/2 " wide page, reset the margins to take advantage of the compressed characters. To reset the margins, choose Margins from the Options menu and reset the left and right margins. If you set them to 5 and 127, respectively, you will have defined a line 122 characters long. This is wide enough to print Table 7-5 on a single sheet of paper.

You are now ready to print the worksheet in compressed type. Return to the main Print command menu by pressing the **[ESC]** key or selecting Quit from the Options menu. Now select Align and Go, and the worksheet is printed in compressed type (see Table 7-6 on next page).

Compressed type is very readable, and it is one of the best ways to print large tables. Recall, however, that once you have sent the compressed type setup string to your printer, the printer *continues* to print worksheets in compressed type until you send the setup string (\ 027 \ 064 for the Epson) to return the printer to normal printing. Alternatively, you can turn the printer off and back on again. Either action returns the printer to its default settings which includes printing in standard type. However, the setup string is retained as part of the worksheet.

TABLE 7-6

Printing in compressed type allows you to place many more characters on a line. With compressed type, Table 7-5 prints across a single 8 1/2" wide page.

SELECTED HEALTH PRACTICES IN THE
UNITED STATES: 1977
by Age, Sex, and Income

	Total	Male	Female	20-34 years	35-54 years	55 and over	Less than $5,000	$5,000-$14,999	$15,000-$24,999	$25,000 and over
Hours of Sleep										
Less than 7	21.7%	23.3%	20.4%	20.2%	22.4%	22.7%	27.0%	21.4%	20.8%	19.3%
7	27.9%	29.8%	26.4%	28.9%	31.3%	23.2%	20.4%	26.6%	31.7%	33.6%
8	37.8%	35.8%	39.5%	38.2%	37.2%	38.0%	35.2%	38.8%	37.8%	38.0%
9 or more	12.5%	11.1%	13.7%	12.6%	9.0%	16.1%	17.3%	13.2%	9.7%	9.2%
Eats Breakfast										
Every day	58.1%	57.3%	58.7%	41.6%	55.5%	80.1%	64.9%	58.0%	53.3%	56.5%
Sometimes	15.9%	15.8%	15.9%	22.7%	16.2%	7.5%	14.8%	16.0%	17.2%	15.3%
Never	26.1%	27.0%	25.4%	35.8%	28.3%	12.4%	20.3%	26.0%	29.5%	28.1%

Source: Statistical Abstracts of the United States, 1982-1983,
U. S. Government Printing Office, Washington, D. C., p. 125.

Using the Borders Option

One of the few shortcomings of 1-2-3 is that you can't make a printout that includes the row numbers and the column letters. Without these guides to the location of the cells on the worksheet, it is difficult to tell exactly where you are on a worksheet, or exactly which cell is being referred to by a formula or function.

Table 7-7, for example, reproduces a worksheet from chapter five in which the formulas in the cells have been displayed with the Range Format Text command. The printout of this table is an excellent record of the worksheet's structure, and it can be used to illustrate how the worksheet was created. Unfortunately, it is difficult to tell exactly what cells are referred to in the formulas because the row numbers and column letters aren't included in the printout. The Border Option can be used to supply the row numbers and column letters missing from Table 7-7.

Table 7-8 on page 196 contains the worksheet from Table 7-7, but with the addition of a column of numbers and a column of vertical dashes (columns E and F) and a row of letters (row 29). The dashes in column F make the printout more readable by separating the row numbers from the table. Also, note that the column width of the column containing the dashes is set to a single character so the row numbers appear close to the entries in each row of the table.

TABLE 7-7

You can use the Range Format Text command to display and print the contents of cells in their locations on the worksheet. Unfortunately, it is difficult to trace the cell references in the formulas because the printout contains neither the row numbers nor the column letters that appear on the 1-2-3 screen.

```
                    INDIVIDUAL RETIREMENT PLAN (IRA) WORKSHEET


        ENTRY SPACE

    Starting Balance:           $0.00
  Annual Contribution:          $0.00
        Interest Rate:          0.00%


        SUMMARY


  Contribution to 65:
    Balance at Age 59:
    Balance at Age 65:




                Year:           1984 1+B18
                 Age:             35 1+B19
                                ------         ------
    Balance Forward: +B6                       +B25
  Annual Contribution: +$B$7                   +$B$7
     Interest Earned: (+B21+B22)*$B$8   (+C21+C22)*$B$8
                                ======         ======
Balance at Year End: @SUM(B20..B24)   @SUM(C20..C24)
```

The letters in row 29 are centered in each cell as are the actual column letters along the top border of the screen. Furthermore, no letters are entered into columns E and F, the columns containing the row numbers. Had you wanted the letters E and F to appear in the top border, then the numbers and dashes would have to be entered farther to the right, perhaps in columns H and I.

To designate columns E and F as the border columns and row 29 as the border row, enter the Borders choice on the Options menu. You will be prompted for "Columns" or "Rows."

TABLE 7-8

The entries to be used by the Border Option are the row numbers in column E, the vertical line in column F (which is set to a column width of 1 character), and the letters A through D in row 29.

```
           A                    B              C              D         E     F    G
  1                                                                      1 |
  2                       INDIVIDUAL RETIREMENT PLAN (IRA) WORKSHEET      2 |
  3                                                                      3 |
  4        ENTRY SPACE                                                   4 |
  5                                                                      5 |
  6        Starting Balance:      $0.00                                  6 |
  7     Annual Contribution:      $0.00                                  7 |
  8          Interest Rate:       0.00%                                  8 |
  9                                                                      9 |
 10        SUMMARY                                                      10 |
 11                                                                     11 |
 12     Contribution to 65:                                            12 |
 13      Balance at Age 59:                                            13 |
 14      Balance at Age 65:                                            14 |
 15                                                                     15 |
 16                                                                     16 |
 17                                                                     17 |
 18                   Year:       1984 1+B18                            18 |
 19                    Age:         35 1+B19                            19 |
 20                                ------        ------                 20 |
 21      Balance Forward: +B6                   +B25                    21 |
 22    Annual Contribution: +$B$7               +$B$7                   22 |
 23      Interest Earned: (+B21+B22)*$B$8  (+C21+C22)*$B$8              23 |
 24                                ======        ======                 24 |
 25    Balance at Year End: @SUM(B20..B24)  @SUM(C20..C24)             25 |
 26                                                                     26 |
 27                                                                     27 |
 28
 29         A                    B              C              D
 30
 31
 32
 33
```

When you choose Columns, you are prompted to "Set border columns to appear to the left of each range." In the example, this is columns E and F. You can point to the columns, and you can use the expanding cursor to designate them.

Next choose Rows. You are now prompted to "Set border rows to appear above each range." In the example, this is row 29. You can type in the row number, but it must be in the form of a valid cell address, such as A29. You can also point to the row with the worksheet cursor.

When you have finished designating the borders, choose Quit from the Options menu and then select Align and Go from the main Print command menu to have the worksheet printed. Table 7-9 is the result. The row numbers appear to the left, and the column letters appear at the top. Compare this table to 7-7, and you will see how much easier it is to locate the cells referred to in the formulas in columns B and C.

TABLE 7-9

Worksheet in Table 7-8 printed with borders from columns E and F and row 29.

```
                    A              B              C          D
   1 |
   2 |               INDIVIDUAL RETIREMENT PLAN (IRA) WORKSHEET
   3 |
   4 |      ENTRY SPACE
   5 |
   6 |   Starting Balance:        $0.00
   7 |Annual Contribution:        $0.00
   8 |      Interest Rate:        0.00%
   9 |
  10 |      SUMMARY
  11 |
  12 | Contribution to 65:
  13 |  Balance at Age 59:
  14 |  Balance at Age 65:
  15 |
  16 |
  17 |
  18 |               Year:     1984 1+B18
  19 |                Age:       35 1+B19
  20 |                          ------        ------
  21 |   Balance Forward: +B6            +B25
  22 |Annual Contribution: +$B$7          +$B$7
  23 |    Interest Earned: (+B21+B22)*$B$8  (+C21+C22)*$B$8
  24 |                         ======        ======
  25 |Balance at Year End: @SUM(B20..B24)  @SUM(C20..C24)
  26 |
  27 |
```

When using the Border option, remember that the designated columns are printed next to the rows and the designated rows are printed above the columns. Furthermore, since the borders take up space on the printed page, you may have to readjust the margin settings. A little trial and error printing will soon solve any problems you have.

SELF-TEST

QUESTIONS

1. What two types of output can be created with the Print command?
2. What is the default paper size?
3. What is the default line width?
4. Under the default settings, how many lines does 1-2-3 reserve between the top and bottom of the paper and the top and bottom of the printed table?
5. How do you *start* the printing of a worksheet?
6. How do you *terminate* the printing of the worksheet before the entire worksheet is printed?
7. How do you *pause* the printing of a worksheet so printing can be resumed?
8. What character separates the three parts of a header or footer?
9. What do [#] and [@] mean when used in a header or footer?
10. What filename extension is added to the filename of all print files created with the Print File command?

ANSWERS

1. A printed table and a print file.
2. 8 1/2″ by 11″.
3. 72 characters. The default margins are set at character 4 and at character 76.
4. Lotus reserves five lines at the top and five lines at the bottom of each page for a total of ten lines. Two of the five lines are margins, one is reserved for the header or the footer (whether one is specified or not), and two lines are reserved to separate the header or the footer and the main body of the table.
5. You can begin printing a worksheet only by selecting Go from the Print command menu. (You should also select Align just before selecting Go.)

6. Pressing **[CTRL]-[SCROLL LOCK]** terminates the Print command and returns 1-2-3 to the Ready mode.
7. Pressing **[CTRL]-[NUM LOCK]** stops printing. When you are ready to resume printing the worksheet, press any key.
8. The vertical line character: **[:]**.
9. When used in a header or footer, the cross-hatching **[#]** is replaced by the current page number on a multiple page printout and the at symbol **[@]** is replaced by the current date logged into your microcomputer's system calendar.
10. Lotus always adds .PRN to designate a print file.

CHAPTER EIGHT
CONSTRUCTING LOTUS 1-2-3 WORKSHEETS

OBJECTIVES

- To learn to construct effective worksheets using values, formulas, and 1-2-3's extensive list of built-in functions.
- To master the use of the Data Fill command to produce a list of numbers.
- To construct One- and Two-Way Data Tables to display the results of different assumptions.
- To review the principles of good worksheet construction including the appropriate use of entry spaces, work spaces, and summary spaces.

INTRODUCTION

The preceding chapters introduced all of the slash commands available to construct 1-2-3 worksheets. By now you know the difference between value and text entries and how to make and edit each type of entry. You know how to set formats and label prefix characters, and how to copy and move the contents of cells from one place to another on a worksheet. You know how to use the File command to store and retrieve worksheets and how to use the Print command to print worksheets and to create print files.

The next two parts of this book extend your knowledge of 1-2-3 to advanced features of the program: the Database command and the Graphics command. But before moving on to those commands, several additional topics are required to complete your knowledge of the construction of 1-2-3 worksheets. The first, and most important topic, is Lotus' library of built-in functions.

BUILT-IN FUNCTIONS

Electronic spreadsheets are constructed by defining the contents of rows and columns with labels, by entering values, and by defining the relationships between the cells of the worksheet. The formulas that define the relationships between worksheet cells can be divided into two categories: *built-in functions* and *operators*.

The built-in functions instruct 1-2-3 to perform particular computational tasks such as adding, averaging, or converting numbers to sines or cosines. The operators create formulas by combining numbers, cell references, and built-in functions into mathematical expressions. The operators include addition [+], subtraction [−], multiplication [*], and division [/] Once defined, the value resulting from a formula or a function is displayed in the cell in which it is entered.

After you have constructed a worksheet and defined the relationships, you can leave the task of calculating quick, error-free results to your microcomputer. Thus, you can easily change parameters to see what will happen to the values on the worksheet under a large number of different assumptions.

The ability to quickly and accurately examine alternative assumptions is at the heart of the microcomputer revolution. It is called "What If..." analysis, and it is one of the most important things you can do with electronic spreadsheets. In fact, this technique alone is why an electronic spreadsheet *is* an entirely new mousetrap rather than just a better way to do the same old things.

General Rules

Before discussing the specific built-in functions, you must be aware of the general principles that apply to all built-in functions. To begin with, every 1-2-3 built-in function must begin with the at symbol [@], as in @SUM or @ROUND. If you don't begin with [@], 1-2-3 enters what you type as text.

Next, most built-in functions require at least one *argument* on which to perform their function. Some, such as the @ROUND function require more than one *argument*. It requires two; one to specify what is to be rounded, and a number to indicate the numbered decimal places to round to. The arguments for functions come in many different forms. They can be a number, cell address, range of cells, named range, or a list combining these elements.

When specifying arguments for a built-in function, remember that you can use *all* the cursor control commands to point to cells or a range of cells. The **[END] [ARROW]** key combinations are particularly useful for specifying a range of cells as the argument for a function.

Remember also that when you are specifying a range of cells, the address of the first and last cell in the range *must* be separated by 1-2-3's range operator: two dots (..). In Point mode, the period **[.]** you type to tack the anchor cell automatically supplies the two dots. The free cell is then ready to stretch the cursor over the desired range. When you are typing the cell addresses instead of pointing to them, you must supply the first dot.

Also, if you are using two or more cell references or ranges as arguments for a single built-in function, you *must* separate the individual parts of the argument with commas. For example, @SUM(D18,G56,B1..B10) is an @SUM function that adds the values in cells D18 and G56 to the sum of the values in the range of cells B1 through B10.

If you make a mistake when entering a function, 1-2-3 "beeps," changes to Edit mode, and waits for you to correct your mistake. A very common mistake is to press the **[ENTER]** key before typing the final parenthesis (e.g. @SUM(A1..A10 **[ENTER]**.)

You can edit any formula in any cell. Just move the worksheet cursor to that cell, press the **[EDIT]** function key, and type in the changes. You can even change a formula into text by editing one of the label alignment characters into the appropriate place.

Finally, as in algebra, you can use parentheses to determine the order in which to perform several operations in a formula. For example, use parentheses to tell 1-2-3 whether you want a formula to be evaluated as $(1+2)/3^2$, $1+(2/3)^2$, or as $1+2/(3^2)$. If you use parentheses to give clear instructions to 1-2-3, you won't be surprised by an answer.

When using parentheses, make sure every left parentheses is closed with a corresponding right parentheses. If you do leave an open parentheses, 1-2-3 will refuse to accept your formula until each pair of parenthesis is complete.

The built-in functions and operators which follow are easy to appreciate and understand when they are divided into seven categories: (1) Arithmetic Operators, (2) Statistical Functions, (3) Logical Functions and Logical Operators, (4) Date Functions, (5) Financial Functions, (6) Arithmetic and Trigonometric Functions, and (7) Special Functions.

Symphony

Symphony adds additional built-in functions to the functions discussed in this chapter. Some, such as @NOW deal with Symphony's expanded date abilities, others such as @CELL and @CELLPOINTER are entirely new functions which return different aspects of a cell such as a cell's address, column width, or numeric format. Except when noted, the built-in functions discussed in this chapter work the same in both 1-2-3 and Symphony.

In addition to an expanded list of built-in functions, Symphony adds the ability to use references to cells containing labels in much the same way 1-2-3 uses references to cells containing values. For example, if cell A1 contains the words "This is a label cell," any cell containing the formula + **A1** would display the same text. This feature opens up great possibilities for "smart" worksheets that responds with verbal messages. In addition to simple references to label cells, Symphony allows you to combine the contents of two or more label cells, and it has a large number of @ functions (called "string functions") for performing operations on label cells.

Arithmetic Operators

The simplest operators are those that perform basic arithmetic operations (see Table 8-1). (Recall: Value entries must begin with one of the following characters: [+], [−], [(], [@], or [#].)

TABLE 8-1

Arithmetic operators.

Function	Description
+	Addition.
−	Subtraction.
*	Multiplication.
/	Division.
^	Exponentiation.

You can use the operators to add, subtract, multiply, divide, or raise to a power any 1-2-3 value. The value may be a number, a cell reference containing a value, or a built-in function. The arithmetic operators can be used to combine numbers, cell references, and built-in functions to form mathematical formulas—exactly like the operators are used to define these relationships on a sheet of paper. The only difference is that 1-2-3 performs the calculations defined by the operators instantly and without error.

Here are some examples of the arithmetic operators in action:

FUNCTION	OPERATORS
5+7	+
B12*C35	*
A45^.7	^
@SUM(A1..A8)/25	/
((B2−C8)+(N267*G37))^Y18	−,+,*,^

Only the result of a formula (12, in the case of 5+7) is displayed in the cell containing the formula. The formula itself is only displayed under the Worksheet or Range Format Text command, or in the status line when the worksheet cursor is on the cell.

The operators are the work horses of worksheet construction. The only limitation on the expressions you can create are your courage and the number of characters that can be entered into a single 1-2-3 cell, 240.

In the case of a long or complicated formula, however, it is best to break the formula into smaller parts and then to combine the parts. If you do this, it is much easier to find and correct any errors that may be made as you enter the formula.

Statistical Functions

Statistical functions perform straightforward operations such as summing, counting, averaging, and finding the largest and smallest number in a list. Table 8-2 lists 1-2-3's statistical functions; Table 8-3 shows some of them in action. The formulas are shown to the right of the cells into which they are entered.

Among other statistics, the functions in Table 8-3 calculate the maximum and minimum average salaries paid to National Football League players in 1979. The last item calculated is the wage bill for an average NFL team (exclusive of substitutes and special team members). The formula that does this is the sum of three numbers (11*F16, 11*F19, and C16) rather than the sum over a range of cells.

TABLE 8-2

Statistical functions. A "list" may be a cell, a range, a block, a formula, a range name, or a combination of these separated by commas.

Function	Description
@COUNT (list)	Number of arguments.
@SUM (list)	Sum of values.
@AVG (list)	Average value.
@MIN (list)	Minimum value.
@MAX (list)	Maximum value.
@STD (list)	Standard deviation.
@VAR (list)	Variance.

TABLE 8-3

Statistical functions in action.

```
        A              B           C          D         E           F         G         H
 1
 2      AVERAGE SALARIES IN THE NATIONAL FOOTBALL LEAGUE
 3                 BY POSITION, 1979
 4
 5
 6                          AVERAGE
 7      POSITION            SALARY                    STATISTICS            FORMULA
 8
 9      Quarterback         $113,932                    COUNT:         8 <-- @COUNT(C9..C16)
10      Running Back        $74,194                   MAXIMUM:  $113,932 <-- @MAX(C9..C16)
11      Defensive Lineman   $75,246                   MINIMUM:   $53,030 <-- @MIN(C9..C16)
12      Offensive Lineman   $66,584                   AVERAGE:   $71,234 <-- @MAX(C9..C16)
13      Receiver            $64,631        STANDARD DEVIATION:   $17,532 <-- @STD(C9..C16)
14      Linebacker          $63,377
15      Defensive back      $58,874        AVERAGE OFFENSIVE
16      Kicker              $53,030        PLAYER'S SALARY:      $72,786 <-- @SUM(C9,3*C10,6*C12,C13)/11
17
18                                         AVERAGE DEFENSIVE
19                                         PLAYER'S SALARY:      $68,623 <-- @SUM(6*C11,2*C14,3*C15)/11
20
21                                         WAGE BILL FOR AN
22                                         AVERAGE NFL TEAM:  $1,608,531 <-- @SUM(11*F16,11*F19,C16)
23
24
25
26
```

Source: *American Averages* by Mike Feinsilber and William B. Mead, p. 364, Dolphin Books, New York, New York, 1980.

Logical Functions and Logical Operators

The logical functions and logical operators are listed in Table 8-4. The logical operators, such as "greater than" [>] and "equal to or greater than" [> =], are easy to understand when you realize that all they do is make *comparisons*. They are used to create expressions like (A1>B1) which poses the question "Is the value in cell A1 *greater than* the value in cell B1?" The answer to this question must either be *true* or *false*. If it is true (i.e., A1 *is* greater than B1), then 1-2-3 displays a 1 in the cell. If it is false (i.e., A1 is *not* greater than B1), then 1-2-3 displays a 0 in the cell.

TABLE 8-4

Logical functions and logical operators.

Functions and Operators	Description
Logical Functions (1-2-3 considers any non-zero value to be TRUE. Only 0 itself is FALSE).	
@FALSE	Value is 0 (FALSE).
@TRUE	Value is 1 (TRUE).
@IF(cond,x,y)	x if cond is TRUE (non-zero); y if cond is FALSE (zero).
@ISNA(x)	Value is 1 (TRUE) if x = NA.
@ISERR(x)	Value is 1 (TRUE) if x = ERR.
Logical Operators	
<	Less than.
< =	Less than or equal to.
>	Greater than.
> =	Greater than or equal to.
< >	Not equal.
# NOT #	Logical *not* (not A nor B, etc.).
# AND #	Logical *and* (A and B and C, etc.).
# OR #	Logical *or* (A or B or C, etc.).

Logical operators are useful in their own right, but they are most powerful when combined with @IF functions. The @IF function is a function that chooses between two alternatives, depending on whether the first part of the @IF function is, or is not, equal to zero. A logical comparison can be used as the first part of the @IF function where the comparison evaluates to 1 if true and 0 if false.

Note that each part in the following example is set off from the other parts by a comma.

Part 1	Part 2	Part 3
@IF(A1 < > 0,	B1/A1,	0)
Logical comparison	Choose Part 2 if the logical comparison is TRUE	Choose Part 3 if the logical comparison is FALSE

The logical comparison, Part 1, asks, "Is the value in A1 different from zero?" If the answer is true (A < >10 evaluates to 1), the @IF function executes Part 2. It divides A1 into B1 and displays the result. If the logical comparison in Part 1 is false, the @IF function executes Part 3. Instead of attempting division by zero, which is an error and which causes the letters ERR to appear in the cell, the @IF function enters a 0 into the cell.

To summarize: Part 1 of an @IF function is evaluated as true when its value *is not* zero and as false when its value *is* zero.

The value in the first part of the @IF function may be generated in several ways. The most straightforward is to use a logical comparison entered into the @IF function (as in the example). Alternatively, a reference to another cell containing a logical comparison can be used. Finally, the first part can be a formula or expression involving cell references and numbers which may or may not involve any logical operators.

Note that you can combine @IF functions with other built-in functions, and you can nest @IF functions within one another to create a function with more than two branches.

Here is an example:

Part 1	Part 2	Part 3
@IF(A1 < > 0,	(@IF(D25 = 10,@SUM(B2..K2),0),	@AVE(B2..K2))

This example contains as its Part 2 another @IF function which in turn contains an @SUM function. Part 2 is executed whenever Part 1 is true. Part 3, which contains the function @AVE (to find the average for a range of cells) is executed whenever Part 1 is false. (Note the use of parenthesis to set off each part of the @IF function.) By combining built-in functions and by nesting @IF functions, you can create "smart" worksheets that do one thing in one situation and something different in another.

Date Functions

The date functions are listed in Table 8-5. The @DATE function assign numbers to particular dates. Then the Date format of either the Worksheet or Range Format commands (see chapters three and four) is used to display the date in one of three readable forms: Day-Month-Year, Day-Month, or Month-Year. Note: the date must be entered into the @DATE function in the Year-Month-Day form.

TABLE 8-5

Date functions. The @DATE function generates the absolute number by which 1-2-3 identifies particular days. Absolute numbers are translated to date form with Worksheet or Range Date format commands.

Function	Description
@DATE (yr,mth,day)	Date number of specified date.
@DAY (date number	Day (1..31) of specified date.
@MONTH (date number)	Month (1..12) of specified date.
@YEAR (date number)	Year (00.199) of specified date.
@TODAY	Today's number.

The @DAY, @MONTH, and @YEAR functions take a date number and return the number corresponding to the particular unit of time (e.g., 1 to 31 for @DAY). All the date numbers can be used in formulas, such as @DATE(84,2,25)-@DATE(81,7,20), and they can all be used to do financial calculations where the exact number of days between dates can be important for figuring holding periods for capital assets or in calculating rates of return.

Symphony

Symphony keeps track of hours, minutes, and seconds, as well as days, months, and years. To manage these units, Symphony has @HOUR, @MINUTE, @SECOND, @TIME, and @NOW functions. The last function, @NOW, returns the serial number generated by the current date and time and replaces 1-2-3's @TODAY function.

Financial Functions

Lotus' financial functions, Table 8-6, provide simple, efficient ways to calcu-late such specialized numbers as the internal rate of return, the net present value of a stream of payments, or the payment due on a mortgage of a given principal for a given number of periods, and at a given interest rate. The financial functions are a great aid to anyone who evaluates real estate investments or who deals with other problems involving cash flows over a number of periods.

TABLE 8-6

Financial functions.

Function	Description
@IRR (guess,range)	Internal rate of return.
@NPV (x,range)	Net present value at discount rate of x over range.
@FV (payment,interest,n)	Future value of n payments at a specified interest rate.
@PV (payment,interest,n)	Present value of an ordinary annuity of n pay-ments at a specified interest rate.
@PMT (principal,interest,n)	Mortgage payments per period for n periods of a given principal at a given interest.

Mathematical and Trigonometric Functions

The mathematical and trigonometric functions, Table 8-7, calculate values such as sines and cosines and logarithms to various bases. Other functions supply the value of pi (@PI), round a number to a given number of decimal places (@ROUND), take the absolute value of a number (@ABS), and generate a random number between 0 and 1 (@RAND).

You may be unfamiliar with the @MOD(x,y) function. This function returns the integer value of the remainder of the division of x by y (e.g., @MOD(10,3) is 1). Knowing the remainder is important when dividing lots into equal parts, such as during a stock split or when distributing parts, machine time, or clients among work stations, products, or account execu-tives. If you need a function to do a special task, check the mathematical and trigonometric functions. You are likely to find just what you need there.

TABLE 8-7

Mathematical and trigonometric functions. (Angles in radians).

Function	Description
@ABS(x)	Absolute value of x.
@ACOS(x)	Arc cosine.
@ASIN(x)	Arc sine.
@ATAN(x)	2-quadrant arc tangent.
@ATAN2(x,y)	4-quadrant arc tangent of y/x.
@COS(x)	Cosine.
@EXP(x)	Exponential (e to the x power).
@INT(x)	Integer part.
@LN(x)	Log base e.
@LOG(x)	Log base 10.
@MOD(x,y)	x mod y.
@PI	3.141592653589794.
@RAND	Random number between 0 and 1.
@ROUND(x,n)	Round number x to n decimal places ($+n$ to the right of decimal, $-n$ to the left).
@SIN(x)	Sine.
@SORT(x)	Square root.
@TAN(x)	Tangent.

Special Functions

The special functions, Table 8-8, are a "grab bag" of functions that don't fit neatly into any other category. The most important of these are the two lookup functions: @HLOOKUP and @VLOOKUP. They are used in conjunction with lookup tables.

Lookup tables can be used in any worksheet requiring different values based on the levels of other values. When required, tax tables, commission tables, and discount tables can be included as lookup tables in worksheets.

The following example describes the three parts of any lookup function. You must supply information about each when using the function.

	Part 1	Part 2	Part 3
@VLOOKUP(	B19,	B8..C13,	1)

TABLE 8-8

Special functions.

Function	Description
@NA	NA (not available).
@ERR	ERR (error).
@CHOOSE (x,v0,v1,...,vN)	Selects the xth value from the list v0, v1,...vN.
@HLOOKUP (x,range,offset)	Horizontal lookup table. Looks up x in range, returns value from row specified by offset.
@VLOOKUP (x,range,offset)	Vertical lookup table. Looks up x in range, returns value from column specified by offset.

1. **Search Value:** Part 1 of the lookup function is the value to be looked up. It is called the *search value*, and it is usually supplied by a reference to a cell (B19 in the example).
2. **Range:** Part 2 of the lookup function is the *range*. It is the block of cells containing *both* the cells to be searched (called the *search range*) and the cells containing the values to be returned. In the example, the range is the block given by B8..C13. The search range is always the left-most column (for @VLOOKUP) or top-most row (for @HLOOKUP) of the range. The values in the search range *must* be arranged from smallest to largest, and they must *not* contain any duplicate values.
3. **Offset:** Part 3 of the lookup function is the *offset*. This number tells the lookup function where to find the value it is looking for *relative* to the top row or left column. In the example, the offset is 1, and the lookup function returns a value from the column that is 1 column to the right of the search range.

Here is how the lookup function works. It begins with the top-most (or left-most) cell in the search range and **searches the range until the largest value is found that is less than or equal to the search value**. Then the corresponding value in the column (or row) given by the offset is displayed in the cell containing the lookup function.

The function displays ERR whenever the search value is smaller than the smallest value in the search range. The function also displays the largest value in the search range for *all* search values greater than the largest value in the search range.

Table 8-9 contains an example of a vertical lookup table. To test your understanding of the lookup functions, cover the looked-up values with a sheet of paper and, from the search values, predict the value that should be returned by the lookup function. In a couple of trials, you should have the concept down.

TABLE 8-9

Vertical lookup table.

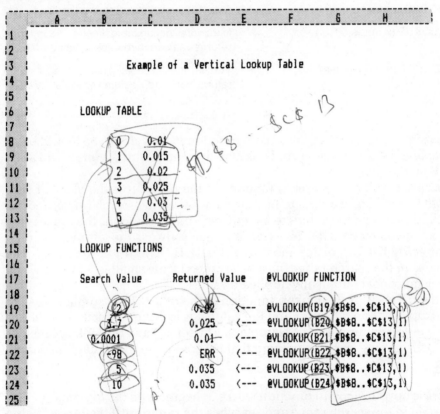

A final point: after you create a lookup table, *test it*. Do this by entering a lookup function into a cell near the table. Be sure you can see both the returned value and the lookup table. Then look up several values and verify that the value returned is the value you expected to be returned. Be sure to choose values larger and smaller than the largest and smallest value in the lookup range. That way you will know what is returned when an out-of-range value is looked up. You can then decide how to handle that occurrence in your worksheet.

RELATIVE AND ABSOLUTE CELL REFERENCES

Relative and absolute cell references have already been discussed at several points, most notably in conjunction with the Copy command in chapter five. This section summarizes this important topic, and adds some additional material about the use of the **[ABS]** function key and mixed absolute/relative cell references.

Relative Cell References

As you know, 1-2-3 formulas and functions make extensive use of references to cell addresses and to named ranges. Unless you explicitly designated it otherwise, a reference to a cell or named range is treated as *relative* to the cell in which the formula or function is entered.

What makes relative cell references important is that whenever you use the Copy command, relative cell references are adjusted to refer to cells in the same position *relative* to the cell or cells into which the formula or function is copied.

Table 8-10 uses the formula +B4/2 to illustrate what happens when the Copy command is applied to a formula containing a relative cell reference. The formula is entered into cell D4. When the Copy command is used to copy the formula from D4 into the range D5..D7, the reference to the cell "in this row, but two columns to the left" adjusts the actual cell reference used in each formula. In the original cell, D4, the reference is to B4, but in successive cells the references are to B5, B6, and B7.

TABLE 8-10

The formula in cell D4 (+B4/2) contains a relative cell reference to cell B4. As you can see, when this formula is copied into the range D5..D7, the reference to cell B4 adjusts.

	A	B	C	D	E	F	G	
1	RELATIVE CELL REFERENCES							
2					Formulas in Column E			
3								
4		100		50	<--- +B4/2			
5		200		100	<--- +B5/2			
6		300		150	<--- +B6/2			
7		400		200	<--- +B7/2			
8								
9								

It turns out that most of the cell references used when constructing 1-2-3 worksheets are relative cell references, so 1-2-3 uses them as its default reference.

Absolute Cell References

In many situations, however, you do not want a reference to a cell address to adjust when the Copy command is used. Perhaps the most important instance is when a formula contains a reference to a parameter in a cell in an entry space. That information is in one cell only, and all copies of the formula should contain that reference. In this case what is needed is an *absolute cell reference*, one that doesn't change when the formula containing the reference is copied to other cells. For example, consider Table 8-11.

TABLE 8-11

The formula in cell D4 (+ B4/$B$9) contains an absolute cell reference to cell B9. When this formula is copied into the range D5..D7, the reference to $B$9 does not adjust.

```
          A        B        C        D        E        F
 1    ABSOLUTE CELL REFERENCES
 2
 3
 4             100              10.0%  <---    +B4/$B$9
 5             200              20.0%  <---    +B5/$B$9
 6             300              30.0%  <---    +B6/$B$9
 7             400              40.0%  <---    +B7/$B$9
 8            =========
 9            1000
10
11
12
13
```

Table 8-11 uses the information from the previous table, Table 8-10, to calculate a percentage distribution.

The formula in cell D4 is + B4/$B$9. The first reference, B4, is to the value of the first element. The second reference, $B$9, refers to the cell containing the total, cell B9. To correctly calculate the percentage distribution, the reference to B9 *must* stay the same when the formula in D4 is copied into cells D5, D6, and D7.

By looking at the formulas in column D, you can see that this is exactly what has happened.

1-2-3 uses the dollar sign to designate an absolute cell reference. The use of dollar signs in front of both the column letter *and* the row number in Table 8-11 indicates an absolute reference to a particular *cell*.

If the dollar sign had appeared before the letter but not before the number (e.g., $B9), the reference would have been an absolute reference to column B. The reference to row 9 would be treated as relative, and it would adjust whenever the cell reference was copied vertically. Likewise, B$9 would be an absolute reference to row 9, but a relative reference to column B. Reference that are part relative and part absolute are called *mixed references*.

Creating Absolute Cell References

The **[ABS]Key** There are two ways to enter the dollar signs that designate a cell reference as absolute. The first is to use the **[ABS]** function key. You can, however, use it only when pointing to cells when creating a formula or specifying a range. After you have pointed to a cell reference you want to designate as absolute, say B9 in Table 8-11, just press the **[ABS]** key and the reference changes from B9 to $B$9. You can then continue pointing to finish the formula, and you can continue to use the **[ABS]** key when needed.

What if you make a mistake or want only the row number or the column letter designated as absolute? Simple, just press the **[ABS]** function key more than once, and with each press of the key, the position of the dollar signs change. The order is absolute cell, absolute row, absolute column, and an additional push of the **[ABS]** key returns the cell reference to relative. In the case of B9, the reference would change as follows:

B9   **$B$9**   **B$9**   **$B9**   **B9**

The **[$] Symbol** The second way to get dollar signs into cell addresses is to place them there directly. Do this by typing dollar signs into the appropriate places as you type the cell address. You *must* do this when a formula has already been entered into a worksheet and you want to change a cell reference from relative to absolute. In that case, use the **[EDIT]** function key to enter the Edit mode, and then proceed to edit in the dollar signs required to designate a particular row, column, or cell as absolute.

No matter what method you use to designate references as absolute, remember: **the dollar sign is the key**. Whenever you see a dollar sign in a cell reference, you know the reference will not adjust when the formula containing the reference is copied to other cells. When there are no dollar signs, you know the reference will adjust.

Ranges and Named Ranges

Two additional points are important when using absolute cell references. First, when used with the Copy command all *named ranges* are treated as *relative cell references*. See Table 8-12 for a simple example of what happens when a formula containing a named range is copied. As you can see from the table, the named range is replaced in the copies by the appropriate *relative* cell references.

TABLE 8-12

Range A4 to A6 is named "TEST." The operation is to copy the formula in cell C5, @SUM (TEST) down column C into the range C5..C9.

```
      A        B        C        D        E        F
 1
 2   EXAMPLE OF COPYING A FORMULA CONTAINING A NAMED RANGE
 3
 4      1                   6 <-- @SUM(TEST)
 5      2                   5 <-- @SUM(A5..A7)
 6      3                   3 <-- @SUM(A6..A8)
 7                          0 <-- @SUM(A7..A9)
 8                          0 <-- @SUM(A8..A10)
 9                          0 <-- @SUM(A9..A11)
10
11
12
```

You can designate a named range as absolute, but *only* by explicitly typing in the **[$]** or by using the **[EDIT]** key to edit a dollar sign into the formula in front of the range name. You *cannot* use the **[ABS]** key when creating the named range to designate the range as absolute. But once the dollar sign is edited in, as in @SUM($TEST), the copied formulas will contain an absolute reference to the named range.

The second point has to do with the cell addresses that designate a range as absolute. If you use the **[ABS]** key, both the beginning and the ending cell address are designated as absolute. For example, @SUM($A$5..$A$15 results from pressing the **[ABS]** key when pointing to cell A15. Furthermore, successive presses of the key change *both* cell references in the same way. For example, the next press produces @SUM(A$5..A$15. If you want something other than uniformity, such as the first reference absolute and the last relative, you *can't* use the **[ABS]** key. Instead, you must edit in the appropriate dollar signs.

THE DATA FILL AND DATA TABLE COMMANDS

Two options of the Database command, Data Fill and Data Table, are most useful when constructing and using regular electronic worksheets. Since some users of 1-2-3 may not need the Database command and, therefore, may skip the Database chapter, these two options, are discussed in this chapter.

Symphony

As noted in a previous chapter, Symphony treats the Data Fill and the Data Table command as part of its Range command. In that command, the Data Table command has been renamed the "What If" command; otherwise the two commands function in Symphony in the same ways they function in 1-2-3.

The Data Fill Command

Lotus 1-2-3's Data Fill command simply fills a range of cells with an increasing or decreasing series of numbers. You specify the *range*, the *starting value*, the *step* increase (or decrease), and the *ending value*. It's not really important to specify the exact ending value as long as it is larger (or smaller if the step is negative) than the largest (or smallest) value to be generated in the range specified. See Figure 8-1 on the next page for the Data Fill command tree.

Table 8-13 on the next page shows several examples of the Data Fill command. Note that you can specify negative as well as positive steps, but if you do, be sure to change the default ending value to one that's smaller than the smallest number in the range. The range can be a block of cells as well as a row or a column. The Data Fill command replaces the contents of any cell in the range with the appropriate data fill number, so be sure not to accidentally write over existing entries.

The Data Fill command has a large number of uses. Whenever you want to use years (1984, 1895, etc.) as column headings, for example, simply enter the Data Fill command, specify the range to be filled, specify the starting year as the starting number, and accept the default step of 1. Press **[ENTER]**, and the

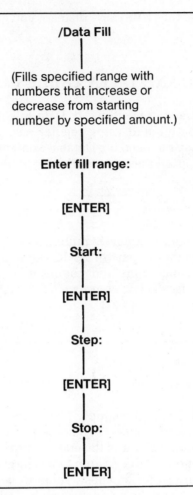

Figure 8-1. Data Fill command tree.

columns are labeled with successive years. If you have a list and want to number the entries, use the Data Fill command. As you will see in the next section, the Data Fill command also speeds the construction of Data Tables.

The Data Table Command

A very common operation with a worksheet is to vary the level of one or two assumptions or parameters underlying the worksheet to observe what this does to the levels of key variables.

TABLE 8-13

Data fill command in action.

	A	B	C	D	E	F	G	H
1								
2			EXAMPLES OF THE DATA FILL COMMAND					
3								
4	0	<-- Start: 0						
5	1	Step: 1						
6	2	Stop: 2048						
7	3	Range: A4..A17						
8	4							
9	5	50	150	250	350	450	<-- Start: 50	
10	6						Step: 100	
11	7						Stop: 450	
12	8						Range: B9..F9	
13	9							
14	10	1	-4	-9	-14	-19	<-- Start: 1	
15	11	0.5	-4.5	-9.5	-14.5	-19.5	Step: -.5	
16	12	0	-5	-10	-15	-20	Stop: -50	
17	13	-0.5	-5.5	-10.5	-15.5	-20.5	Range: B14..F23	
18		-1	-6	-11	-16	-21		
19		-1.5	-6.5	-11.5	-16.5	-21.5		
20		-2	-7	-12	-17	-22		
21		-2.5	-7.5	-12.5	-17.5	-22.5		
22		-3	-8	-13	-18	-23		
23		-3.5	-8.5	-13.5	-18.5	-23.5		
24								

However, the ability to quickly calculate a large number of alternative assumptions generates its own problems. The most serious is the problem of keeping track of the results of multiple rounds of "What If..." analysis. Luckily, 1-2-3 has a special feature that keeps track of the results of multiple recalculations when each recalculation is performed with a different level of a key variable. The tools that do this are the One- and Two-Way Data Tables.

One-Way Data Table

Assume you have constructed the worksheet in Table 8-14 (from the Hands On section of chapter five). Now you would like to know what happens to the amount of savings available for retirement at ages 59 and 65 and the total amount of interest earned at age 65 when the interest rate paid over the period varies from 7% to 12%. It would be a simple matter to include other statistics (total contributions, balance at any particular year, etc.), but these three items are sufficient to illustrate the steps involved in constructing a One-Way Data Table.

TABLE 8-14

Retirement worksheet from Chapter Five.

	A	B	C	D	E	F	G
1							
2							
3	ENTRY SPACE						
4							
5	Starting Balance:	$0.00					
6	Annual Contribution:	$1,000.00					
7	Interest Rate:	10.00%					
8							
9	SUMMARY SPACE						
10							
11	Contribution to 65:	$31,000.00					
12	Balance at Age 59:	$108,181.77					
13	Balance at Age 65:	$200,137.77					
14							
15	WORK SPACE						
16							
17	Year:	1984	1985	1986	1987	1988	1989
18	Age:	35	36	37	38	39	40
19		------	------	------	------	------	------
20	Balance Forward:	$0.00	$1,100.00	$2,310.00	$3,641.00	$5,105.10	$6,715.61
21	Annual Contribution:	$1,000.00	$1,000.00	$1,000.00	$1,000.00	$1,000.00	$1,000.00
22	Interest Earned:	$100.00	$210.00	$331.00	$464.10	$610.51	$771.56
23		======	======	======	======	======	======
24	Balance at Year End:	$1,100.00	$2,310.00	$3,641.00	$5,105.10	$6,715.61	$8,487.17
25							
26							

An important thing to know about constructing a data table is that *all* column headings, formulas, and values must be entered *before* entering the Database Data Table command. Once in the command, you simply define the range of cells that contain the table and designate the cell (in the case of a One-Way Data Table) or the two cells (in the case of a Two-Way Data Table) that will be used as input cells. To repeat, the data table itself *must* be constructed before entering the Data Table command.

Table 8-15 is on the same electronic worksheet as the cells shown in Table 8-14. It shows the outline of a One-Way Data Table. There are three parts to the table.

TABLE 8-15

Outline of One-Way Data Table.

```
|           A              B           C           D        |
:27 :
:28 :
:29 :
:30 :   ONE-WAY DATA TABLE
:31 :
:32 :                                                INTEREST
:33 :             INTEREST  BALANCE AT  BALANCE AT    EARNED
:34 :                 RATE     AGE 59      AGE 65   TO AGE 65
:35 : :_____:+B12_____:+B13_____:@SUM{B22..A:
:36 : :_____7.00%:_____: :_____: :_____:
:37 : :_____7.50%:_____: :_____: :_____:
:38 : :_____8.00%:_____: :_____: :_____:
:39 : :_____8.50%:_____: :_____: :_____:
:40 : :_____9.00%:_____: :_____: :_____:
:41 : :_____9.50%:_____: :_____: :_____:
:42 : :_____10.00%:_____: :_____: :_____:
:43 : :_____10.50%:_____: :_____: :_____:
:44 : :_____11.00%:_____: :_____: :_____:
:45 : :_____11.50%:_____: :_____: :_____:
:46 : :_____12.00%:_____: :_____: :_____:
:47 :
:48 :
:49 :
```

1. The cells in the *first column* contain the values that are substituted into the worksheet. In this case they are 7 to 12 percent. The Data Fill command is an easy way to enter these values; the starting value is .07, the step is .005.
2. The *first cell* of the first row must be left blank.
3. Successive cells in the *first row* contain the formulas that are evaluated in each column. Column headings are *not* part of the range of the data table, but they are important for understanding the table.

 After you have entered the values in the first column, the formulas in the first row, and the labels, you are ready to enter the Database Data Table command. (See the Data Table command tree, Figure 8-2.)

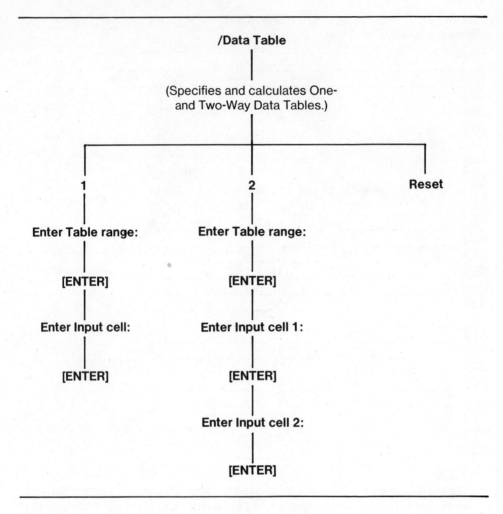

Figure 8-2. Data Table command tree.

To do this type:

/DT

You now must make a choice:

1   2   Reset

[1] is for a One-Way Data Table, [2] is for a Two-Way Data Table, and **Reset** clears the settings.

Since you are specifying a One-Way Data Table, choose [1]. You are asked to:

Enter Table range:

The table range is the *block* of cells beginning with the blank cell in the upper left corner and extending down to the cell at the intersection of the row containing the last value and the column containing the last formula. In Table 8-15, the range would be A35..D46. Note that the column headings are *not* included in the table range. Don't forget that you can use the cursor control keys to point to the table range.

After you have finished specifying the table range, press the **[ENTER]** key. You are asked to:

Enter Input cell:

The input cell is the cell on the worksheet where 1-2-3 enters successive values from the first column of the data table. You want to vary the interest rate in the example, so the input cell is the cell, B7, in the entry space labeled "Interest Rate," (see Table 8-14). Again, you can use the cursor control keys to point to the input cell.

When you have moved the worksheet cursor to the cell (or typed in its address), press **[ENTER]**. Lotus immediately goes into Wait mode. The mode indicator flashes, and 1-2-3 recalculates the worksheet the required number of times. After a few seconds, the results appear in the appropriate cells of the data table (see Table 8-16 on the next page).

Note that the first row of Table 8-16 contains the values ($108,182, etc.) calculated by the formulas for the parameters *actually entered into the work-sheet*. To eliminate any possible confusion, you can can erase these values just before printing the table, or you can erase the parameters from the worksheet cells. The blank cells will cause the formulas in the first row to calculate and display zeros.

To summarize: you must lay out the data table *before* entering the Data Table command. Begin by entering the input values into the appropriate cells in the first column. Then enter the formulas into the appropriate cells in the first row. Be sure to leave the first cell of the first row blank. Finally, supply column headings and other notes to describe the results. Then enter the Data Table command. Choose [1] for a One-Way or [2] for a Two-Way Data Table, specify the table range, and the input cell or cells, and 1-2-3 does the rest.

TABLE 8-16

Completed One-Way Data Table.

	A	B	C	D
29				
30	ONE-WAY DATA TABLE			
31				
32				INTEREST
33	INTEREST	BALANCE AT	BALANCE AT	EARNED
34	RATE	AGE 59	AGE 65	TO AGE 65
35		$108,182	$200,138	$169,138
36	7.00%	$67,676	$109,218	$78,218
37	7.50%	$73,076	$120,566	$89,566
38	8.00%	$78,954	$133,214	$102,214
39	8.50%	$85,355	$147,314	$116,314
40	9.00%	$92,324	$163,037	$132,037
41	9.50%	$99,914	$180,574	$149,574
42	10.00%	$108,182	$200,138	$169,138
43	10.50%	$117,188	$221,966	$190,966
44	11.00%	$126,999	$246,324	$215,324
45	11.50%	$137,688	$273,507	$242,507
46	12.00%	$149,334	$303,848	$272,848
47				
48				

Two-Way Data Table

While the One-Way Data Table just described lets you know how sensitive your worksheet is to variations in a single variable (the interest rate in the example), at times you'd like to know what will happen when two parameters change. This is a good way to discover which parameter has the greater effect on a goal or which combination of two parameters allows you to achieve a critical result.

See Table 8-17 for the outline of a Two-Way Data Table. Like the One-Way Data Table just discussed, this table is based on the retirement worksheet, Table 8-14. The table examines the effect of two variables on the amount available for retirement at age 65. The two variables are the interest rate and the annual contribution. The interest rate again varies from 7% to 12%, while the annual contribution varies from $500 to $2,000.

TABLE 8-17

Outline of Two-Way Data Table.

```
|         A            |    B    |    C      |    D      |    E     |
|49 |
|50 |
|51 |  TWO-WAY DATA TABLE
|52 |
|53 |                          BALANCE AT AGE 65
|54 |        INTEREST
|55 |          RATE          ANNUAL CONTRIBUTION
|56 |+B13                 |    $500 |  $1,000  |  $1,500  |  $2,000 |
|57 |          7.00%       |         |          |          |         |
|58 |          7.50%       |         |          |          |         |
|59 |          8.00%       |         |          |          |         |
|60 |          8.50%       |         |          |          |         |
|61 |          9.00%       |         |          |          |         |
|62 |          9.50%       |         |          |          |         |
|63 |         10.00%       |         |          |          |         |
|64 |         10.50%       |         |          |          |         |
|65 |         11.00%       |         |          |          |         |
|66 |         11.50%       |         |          |          |         |
|67 |         12.00%       |         |          |          |         |
|68 |
|69 |
```

To construct the table, enter the first value (interest rate) into the cells of the first column and the values for the second variable (annual contribution) into the cells of the first row. Also add any column headings or titles required to make the table easier to understand (see Table 8-17).

Now, instead of leaving the first cell in the first row blank as you did in the One-Way Data Table, enter into that cell a *formula* to define the values you want displayed in the body of the data table. In the example, the formula in cell A56 is simply a reference to +B13, the cell in the summary space, which contains the balance at age 65. However, any formula could be entered into cell A56, and whatever that formula may be, the results of the formula are displayed in the cells of the Two-Way Data Table.

Once you have specified the formula and the values, you are ready to enter the Database Data Table command. Do so by typing /**DT**. This time choose **[2]** for a Two-Way Data Table, and proceed to respond to the prompts. The first is:

Enter Table range:

If you have already specified a table range (as you would have done had you just constructed the previous data table), 1-2-3 highlights it as the proposed range. Remember to press the **[BKSP]** key to unlock the cursor for pointing and to shrink the proposed range to the current active cell. Now specify the range for the Two-Way Data Table. If you want, do this by pointing. In the example, the range is A56...E67.

After you press **[ENTER]** to end the specification of the table range, 1-2-3 prompts:

Enter Input cell 1:

Input cell 1 is the worksheet cell into which values from the first *column* of the data table are substituted. Lotus proposes as input cell 1 any input cell previously specified. In the example, this is cell B7, which you specified as the input cell for the One-Way Data Table. In this case, B7 is, in fact, the cell you want to use as Input cell 1.

Accept it by pressing **[ENTER]**. Had another cell been required, you would have used the cursor control keys to point to it.

Next, 1-2-3 prompts you to:

Enter Input cell 2:

Input cell 2 is the worksheet cell into which values from the first *row* of the Two-Way Data Table will be substituted. In the example, the second input cell is the annual contribution. This value is found in the entry space in cell B6. Point to B6 and press **[ENTER]**. As soon as you do, 1-2-3 goes into Wait mode, and after a few moments the values appear in the cells of the data table (see Table 8-18). Again, the value displayed in the cell containing the formula, A56 in this case, displays the value for the formula based on the parameters as actually entered into the worksheet.

Modifying a Data Table

Once you have created a data table, you may want to modify it to display the results of different formulas or to use different values for the input cells. Such changes are easy to make because data tables are defined in terms of a block of cells, *not* in terms of the particular contents of the cells.

The simplest way to change a data table is to replace existing entries with new values or formulas. In the case of the Two-Way Data Table just discussed, you could change the formula in cell A56, and that would change

TABLE 8-18

Completed Two-Way Data Table.

	A	B	C	D	E
49					
50					
51	TWO-WAY DATA TABLE				
52					
53			BALANCE AT AGE 65		
54	INTEREST				
55	RATE		ANNUAL CONTRIBUTION		
56	$200,138	$500	$1,000	$1,500	$2,000
57	7.00%	$54,609	$109,218	$163,827	$218,436
58	7.50%	$60,283	$120,566	$180,849	$241,132
59	8.00%	$66,607	$133,214	$199,820	$266,427
60	8.50%	$73,657	$147,314	$220,971	$294,627
61	9.00%	$81,518	$163,037	$244,555	$326,074
62	9.50%	$90,287	$180,574	$270,861	$361,148
63	10.00%	$100,069	$200,138	$300,207	$400,276
64	10.50%	$110,983	$221,966	$332,949	$443,932
65	11.00%	$123,162	$246,324	$369,485	$492,647
66	11.50%	$136,754	$273,507	$410,261	$547,015
67	12.00%	$151,924	$303,848	$455,772	$607,695
68					
69					

what is displayed in the cells of the table. You could also use the Data Fill command to place a different range of annual contributions in the first row or different interest rates in the first column.

You can also expand the size of a data table by using the Worksheet Insert command to insert additional rows or columns. If you use this command, be sure you insert the rows or columns *between* the first and last rows or first and last columns. If you don't, the newly inserted space will be outside the table range.

Sometimes inserting rows or columns affects material elsewhere on your worksheet. The data tables described in this chapter, for example, are placed below one another, so inserting columns into these tables inserts new columns into the other tables as well. Since you don't want to modify the other tables, use the Move command to move part of the data table over the required number of columns. Remember to leave either the upper left or the lower right corner in place so the range of the data table expands automatically.

The [TABLE] Key

Once you have modified a data table, you are ready to recalculate. To recalculate the last specified data table, simply press the **[TABLE]** function key. This is much faster and easier than entering the Data Table command and accepting all the proposed responses. You can use the **[TABLE]** key at any time to calculate the effects of any change to the worksheet itself or to the data table.

However, if you have defined more than one data table on the worksheet, the **[TABLE]** key recalculates only the most recently used table. To calculate Table 8-15, for example, after defining Table 8-16, you must go back and redefine Table 8-15. To make this task easier, assign a range name to each data table range and to the input cells. You can then use the **[NAME]** Function key to supply the names for the ranges and input cells.

TEN TIPS FOR CONSTRUCTING 1-2-3 WORKSHEETS

The final section of this chapter discusses ten important rules for constructing 1-2-3 worksheets. Some of these rules were introduced in previous chapters; others are introduced here for the first time. In either case, the rules are important. Keep them in mind, and you will increase the speed and efficiency with which you construct accurate, useful 1-2-3 worksheets.

Tip 1: Always Use an Entry Space

The cardinal rule of spreadsheet construction is to *always* use an entry space. An entry space is an area into which the parameters (growth rates, levels of values, etc.) are entered. It is usually located at the top of the worksheet, but it may be anywhere on the worksheet. Furthermore, a worksheet may have as many entry spaces as required to make it easy to use.

Entry spaces build flexibility into your worksheets. When constructing a worksheet, place every parameter into the entry space, and then make an absolute reference to the appropriate cell in the entry space whenever you need that parameter. The formulas that make up the table will contain only references to cells in the entry space; they will *never* contain parameters themselves. Whenever you want to change a parameter, simply change it in the entry space and the parameter changes in *every* formula in which it is used.

Contrast this with a worksheet where the parameters are entered into the formulas. In such a worksheet, you have to change *every* formula containing a parameter *every time* you want to perform a "What If..." analysis. Not only is this a slower, more tedious process, but it creates many opportunities for error. It is unlikely you would try as many values and, thus, you'd be giving up 1-2-3's power to test many alternative assumptions quickly and easily.

Note that the data tables described earlier in this chapter assume you've placed the parameters to be used as entry values into an entry space. If you haven't, you can't use the data table feature.

Tip 2: Use Work Spaces and Summary Spaces

While the entry space is the most important space on your worksheet, you can also improve your worksheets by using *work spaces* for intermediate calculations and *summary spaces* to display important values. You can spread complicated formulas or calculations across several columns of a work space without taking up limited display space on the screen or printing space on a page. The main part of the table can then display the results, rather than the intermediate calculations.

In many worksheets, the main table is actually a summary space in which the important worksheet values are displayed. See Table 8-14, for an example. In other worksheets, you may use a special table to summarize the most important values from the main table. If you locate the summary space near the entry space, "What If..." analysis is easy to perform because both the entry space and the summary space are on the screen at the same time.

Tip 3: Test Your Worksheets

When constructing worksheets, you are likely to make two general types of errors. Test each worksheet to find and eliminate them.

The first type of error occurs when you specify a division by zero or fail to specify a required parameter. Lotus recognizes these errors and either "beeps" and waits for you to correct your mistake or displays the letters **ERR** in the appropriate cell. **ERR** lets you know you've made a mistake, and it ripples through the worksheet to all cells that depend directly or indirectly on the cell that actually contains the error. Thus, you may have to hunt through several cells before you can find the one creating the problem.

The second type of error results from an incorrectly specified cell address in a formula, function, or range. You might, for example, type 1/B2 when you meant to type 1/A2, or you may have specified the range A1..A9 for an @SUM function when you meant to specify A1..A19. These errors are particularly hard to detect because the cell containing the function displays a value, even though it is the *wrong* value.

Perhaps the easiest way to find errors of this type is to enter information into the worksheet that generates predictable results. Often this information is historic. If you have actual values and know how they should be related in the base year, for example, you can enter these values and check the formulas against known results.

Alternatively, you can enter dummy information that calculates predictable values. You can do this for the worksheet as a whole, or you can do it for subsections. To test the @SUM function, you could enter the number 1 into each cell in the range A1..A19. Since the summation is over 19 cells, you'd expect the number 19 to appear in the cell containing the @SUM function. If some other number appears, you know there is an error.

Finally, you can inspect the formulas directly. To inspect a formula, move the worksheet cursor to the appropriate cell, and the contents appears on the status line in the control panel. You can then see if the formula is correct. You can also use the Worksheet or Range Format Text commands to display the formulas in the cells on the worksheet. To make your task easier, print a copy of the worksheet with the formulas displayed. Be sure to expand the column widths, and be sure to use the Borders option of the Print command to supply row numbers and column letters. (See the "Hands On" section in chapter seven.)

Tip 4: Don't Forget What You Know

An electronic spreadsheet with a microcomputer certainly takes the drudgery out of calculations, and it calculates the defined formulas without error—but it is no excuse to ignore your knowledge and your experience. The computer makes no distinction between a loan at a 12% interest rate and one at a 120% interest rate. It takes either interest rate and calculates the results, no matter how silly or unrealistic they may be.

It is very easy to examine many, many alternatives for the parameters that lie behind your worksheets. This is a great strength of a microcomputer, but 1-2-3 does not have a "common sense" command to tell you whether those parameters are realistic. Always judge for yourself whether the assumptions you are making are sensible. So, *think* before you calculate. All you have is your own hard-earned wisdom and good sense to prevent 1-2-3 from burying you in worksheets based on unrealistic assumptions.

Tip 5: Create Your Worksheets by Trial and Error

Constructing a worksheet is not a linear process where an idea is translated directly into a worksheet. In fact, the ease with which worksheets can be modified means that most electronic worksheets are constructed by trial and error. You will often find yourself coming back to improve a worksheet hours or days after it was constructed. And since it is easy to modify a worksheet, you can continue to improve one as long as you want.

Be sure to save partially completed worksheets so you can go back to them should a particular trial end in error. When you have arrived at a suitably constructed worksheet, go back and erase the earlier versions.

Tip 6: Write Notes on Your Worksheets

When constructing a worksheet, write notes about the sources of information, the particular way a worksheet is to be used, and the relationship, if any, between the worksheet and other worksheets. You can also add notes about when the worksheet was last updated or when and to whom copies have been sent. Use the Range Justify command to make entering and organizing these notes easier and more efficient. A little bit of time taken when constructing a worksheet can save hours of frustration, days or months later, when you return to use it.

If someone else is going to use a worksheet, the notes should be a complete set of instructions. If the worksheet is a personal one that only you will use, the notes can be less extensive, but they should still be complete enough to be useful when you read them weeks or months later. If there is any question about what to include in a note, it is better to include too much information than not enough.

Tip 7: Save Often and Always Backup Your Diskettes

It may now sound like a broken record, but saving and saving often is one of the most important things you can do when constructing electronic spreadsheets. Of course, save when you have completed a worksheet, but also save when you are constructing a worksheet. Not only does a copy of a partially completed worksheet prevent the loss of the work that went into creating it, but it allows you to try a new direction, safe in the knowledge that you can always get back to the place from which you began to experiment.

Once you have saved a copy of a worksheet, you *must* go one step further and make a backup copy of the diskette containing the worksheet. This backup copy is the only insurance you have against the failure of the data diskette itself. And diskettes *do fail* because of age, dust, carelessness (like writing on the label with a ball point pen), or stray magnetism. The metal paper clip from a magnetized holder is an ever-present danger. So make backup copies with either your computer's Disk Operating System commands or the Disk Manager section of the Lotus Access System.

Tip 8: Choose Good Filenames and Place Them on All Worksheets

It is important to spend a little time thinking about filenames. As noted in chapter six, good filenames give you as much information as possible about the file. They must be informative and should indicate how a particular file relates to other files. The time you spend choosing a good, informative filename will be repaid each time you avoid loading several files with uninformative filenames in order to find the one you really want.

If you place the exact filename on a worksheet and print it each time you print the worksheet, you will always be able to get back to the electronic copy. Since it is easy to generate multiple variations of a basic worksheet, you will lose track of which file contains which version unless you print the filenames along with the worksheet.

A similar problem arises when you create and distribute many worksheets. You will frequently get requests for modifications of a worksheet or for additional copies. If the filename is on the printout, the request is easy to fulfill. If it's not, you may spend considerable time searching through your library of saved worksheets before you find the right one.

If you have many diskettes (or directories on a hard disk), you can also save time by including the name assigned to the diskette or folder along with the filename. If, for some reason, you don't want this information to appear on a printout, you can use the Range Erase command to remove it just before printing.

Tip 9: Always Issue the Align Instruction before Printing a Worksheet

There are many things to remember when printing a worksheet; to check page parameters and setup strings, and to know that a **[CTRL]-[SCROLL LOCK]** stops printing, while **[CTRL]-[NUM LOCK]** pauses the printer, but the most important thing to remember is to issue the Align instruction just before printing a worksheet.

Recall that 1-2-3 assumes the paper in your printer is properly aligned when 1-2-3 is first loaded. If it isn't, or if you move the paper manually after 1-2-3 has been loaded, the printed worksheet is not correctly positioned on the page. To be sure your worksheets are printed correctly, issue the Align command just before beginning to print with the Go instruction.

Tip 10: Reread This Book (and the Lotus Manual) in Three Months

Whether you are new to 1-2-3 or an old hand, you can profit greatly by rereading this book after you have been working with the program for a few months. The same advice applies to the Lotus 1-2-3 Manual.

If you have had little experience with Lotus, you will have some difficulty separating the detail from what is really important. As your experience grows, you will better appreciate examples, suggestions and advice. You will be able to put things in perspective, and you will be able to relate what this book has to say about using Lotus 1-2-3 to the problems you encounter in your own work.

So pick up this book in three months, and improve your spreadsheet technique.

SELF-TEST

QUESTIONS

1. With what symbol must every 1-2-3 built-in function begin?
2. Can you end a built-in function by typing **[ENTER]** without closing the last parenthesis?
3. Are named ranges treated by 1-2-3 as absolute references or relative references?
4. What symbol identifies a cell reference as an absolute cell reference?
5. How can you designate a named range as an absolute reference?
6. What does the **[ABS]** function key do?
7. Will the Data Fill command replace the contents of any cells in the fill range with the appropriate data fill number?
8. Must you enter the Data Table command before you can lay out the data table?
9. What does the **[TABLE]** function key do?
10. What is the cardinal rule of worksheet construction?

ANSWERS

1. The at symbol **[@]**
2. No. You must always supply the closing parenthesis. If you press **[ENTER]** without closing the last parenthesis, 1-2-3 "beeps" and waits for you to correct your error.
3. All 1-2-3 ranges are treated as relative references. They will adjust when formulas containing the named ranges are copied to other cells.
4. The dollar sign **[$]**. Whenever you see a dollar sign in a cell reference, you know the following reference to a column or row is absolute.

5. To designate a named range as absolute, first enter the formula or function containing the named range into the worksheet. Then edit in a dollar sign before the range name. For example, COST in @SUM(COST) is a relative reference to the range named COST. It adjusts when the function is copied. If you edit in a dollar sign as in @SUM(COST), the reference to the named range does not adjust.

6. When pointing at cell references in Point mode, the **[ABS]** key changes cell references from relative to absolute. The first press provides both absolute column and absolute row references (an absolute reference to a single cell). The next press produces an absolute column, relative row reference; the third press, relative column, absolute row; and the last press returns a relative cell reference.

7. Yes. Be careful not to accidentally replace information with the Data Fill command.

8. No. You must construct the data table *before* entering the Data Table command.

9. The **[TABLE]** function key recalculates the most recently specified data table. You can use this to recalculate a table *after* you have modified it or the worksheet on which it is based.

10. The cardinal rule of worksheet construction is to *always* place parameters into an entry space. This way you can do as much "What If..." analysis as you require by changing assumptions easily, quickly, and without running the risk of introducing errors into the worksheet.

PART C

LOTUS 1-2-3'S DATA COMMAND

The 2 of 1-2-3 is data management; the management of information in a database. Whether it be address lists, orders or suppliers names, it is an important and time consuming task. Theoretically, a 1-2-3 database can have up to 2,047 rows of information in up to 32 columns, but a database of this size would require a very large amount of Random Access Memory (RAM) to store, and it would take several minutes to perform any of the Data command operations. In practice, most personal and managerial databases contain only two to three hundred rows of information, and can be quickly and efficiently managed with 1-2-3's Data command.

The following chapter contains a complete description of the construction and use a 1-2-3 database. Once you have created the database, there are three general operations that you can perform on it:

1. You can **sort** the rows of database into a new order.
2. You can **find** entries in a database.
3. You can **extract** entries to an output space.

In addition to the three major database subcommands, the Data command has Table, Fill, Delete, Unique, and Distribution subcommands. The Table and Fill subcommands were discussed in chapter eight. The Delete subcommand removes all records satisfying your criteria from a database, and the Unique subcommand makes sure that each entry copied to an output range is unique. The Distribution subcommand is used to create a frequency distribution.

Finally, 1-2-3 has a special set of built-in functions called Database Statistical Functions. These are similar to the regular 1-2-3 statistical functions discussed in chapter eight, except that they operate on only those entries which meet the criteria you establish.

By the time you have finished chapter nine, you will have been introduced to all of the features of Lotus' Data command. You will be well on your way to mastering the 2 of 1-2-3.

CHAPTER NINE
THE DATABASE COMMANDS

OBJECTIVES

- To become familiar with the commands and features of Lotus 1-2-3's database function.
- To define and sort a database.
- To set criteria to query a database to find or extract entries.
- To learn to use 1-2-3's special built-in database statistical functions.
- To use the Data Distribution command to prepare a frequency distribution.

INTRODUCTION

Lotus 1-2-3 is a revolutionary product because it successfully integrates into one package the powerful electronic worksheet described in the preceding chapters with a Database command and a Graphics command. This combination gives you immediate access to three powerful analytical tools: the spreadsheet, the database, and the graph.

The Database command, which lets you *sort*, *find*, and *extract* information from the cells of your worksheet, is discussed in this chapter. Also discussed in this chapter are database statistical functions (special built-in functions for use with databases), and the Data Distribution command which is used to create frequency distributions. The Graphics command, discussed in the following chapter, displays and prints information in graphic form.

Two Data commands, Table and Fill, were discussed in the previous chapter because they have many uses on non-database worksheets. The commands do, of course, also have powerful database applications which are discussed in this chapter. If you need more detailed information about constructing data tables or using the Data Fill command, please see the discussion in chapter eight. See Figure 9-1 for the overall Data command tree.

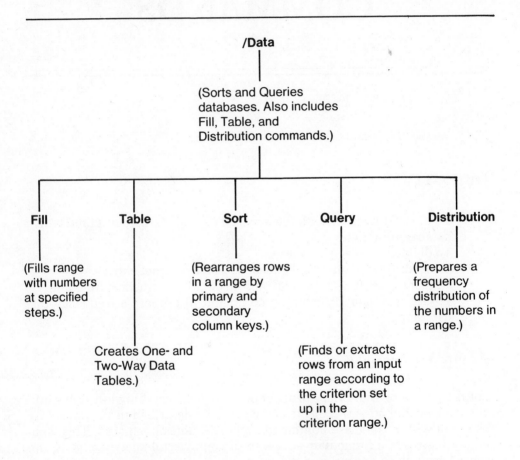

Figure 9-1. The Data command tree.

Symphony

Symphony has all of the features of 1-2-3's Data command, though some of those features are found in other parts of Symphony. The Fill, Table (called What-If), and the Distribution commands have been transferred to the main Sheet command menu. They are no longer considered database commands.

The Symphony database commands are found under Query on the main Sheet command menu. By selecting Query command choices, you can construct and use a Symphony database in exactly the same way that you construct and use a 1-2-3 database. The major difference is that Symphony uses a "setting sheet" which displays the current ranges and sort keys.

Symphony's database commands are also available in a Form environment window. This feature is discussed in detail later in this chapter.

OVERVIEW

What is a Database?

A database is a *collection of information* organized alphabetically, numerically, or by some other system that allows you to find individual entries quickly. Your home and office have many databases. An address book and a dictionary are databases arranged alphabetically. A cook book is a database arranged by type of meal or main ingredient. Calendars are databases arranged by dates, while your checkbook is a database arranged by check number. In business, lists of clients, parts, suppliers, or creditors are databases. So are the Rolodexes and card files on your desk and the file cabinets in your office.

Table 9-1 on the following page contains a small database of all-time batting leaders in professional baseball. It has the two characteristics of any database: it contains information, and it's organized. This database is used throughout this chapter to illustrate the features of 1-2-3's Data command.

TABLE 9-1

Database of All-Time Batting Leaders.

```
      A       B      C      D       E       F       G      H
 1
 2
 3              ALL-TIME BATTING LEADERS
 4                 Ten or more seasons
 5
 6   PLAYER'S NAME    YEARS  GAMES  AT BATS   RUNS   HITS  AVERAGE
 7   ==========================================================
 8       Ty Cobb       24   3,033  11,429   2,244  4,191  0.367
 9   Rogers Hornsby    23   2,256   8,173   1,576  2,930  0.358
10     Joe Jackson     13   1,330   4,981     873  1,772  0.356
11    Pete Browning    13   1,180   4,839     867  1,716  0.355
12     Ed Delahanty    16   1,825   7,493   1,596  2,591  0.345
13    Willie Keeler    19   2,124   8,564   1,720  2,955  0.345
14   William Hamilton  14   1,578   6,262   1,694  2,157  0.344
15     Tris Speaker    22   2,789  10,208   1,881  3,515  0.344
16     Ted Williams    19   2,292   7,706   1,798  2,654  0.344
17    Dan Brouthers    19   1,665   7,493   1,596  2,591  0.343
18    Harry Heilmann   18   2,146   7,787   1,291  2,660  0.342
19      Babe Ruth      22   2,503   8,389   2,174  2,873  0.342
20    Jesse Burkett    16   2,063   8,389   1,708  2,872  0.341
21     Bill Terry      14   1,721   6,428   1,120  2,193  0.341
22     Lou Gehrig      17   2,164   8,001   1,888  2,721  0.340
23    George Sisler    15   2,055   8,267   1,284  2,812  0.340
24
25
```

Figure 9-2 shows the general structure of a 1-2-3 database. The first row of the database *must* contain *field names*. **The field names are like the column headings on an ordinary worksheet; they tell what type of information is entered into each column**. In Table 9-1, the field names tell you that the columns contain information about such things as Games, At Bats, and Hits.

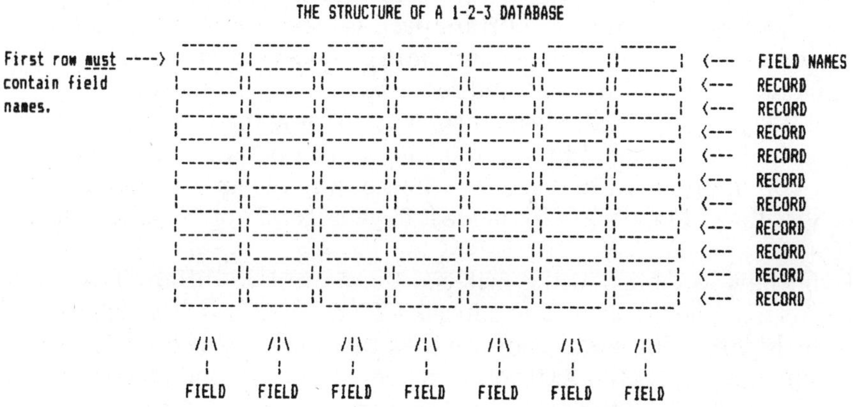

THE STRUCTURE OF A 1-2-3 DATABASE

First row **must** ----> (figure showing grid) <--- FIELD NAMES
contain field <--- RECORD
names.

Figure 9-2. A 1-2-3 database is made up of fields and records. The first row of the database must contain field names. Successive rows contain records.

Successive *rows* of the database contain *records*. **Records contain all the information about a single entry**. If, for example, an entry is a player, as it is in Table 9-1, each record (or row) contains all the information about a particular player.

Finally, *individual* pieces of information (Ty Cobb's Average, for example) are called *fields*. Sometimes the word "field" refers to an *entire column* as in "The At Bats field is next to the Runs field." Other times, "field" refers to a *single cell* in a record, "The number 11,429 is entered into Ty Cobb's At Bats field." Whether "field" refers to a column or a cell within a column will be clear from the context in which it is used.

The most important thing to remember about a database's structure is that the *rows* are the **records** and the columns or *cells* are the **fields**.

What Can You Do with a Database?

You can perform two operations on a database: you can either *sort* it or *query* it. **To sort a database is to rearrange the records**. The batting database, Table 9-1, is sorted by batting average. Ty Cobb is first because he is the player in the database with the highest life-time batting average. If you wished, you could re-sort Table 9-1 by number of hits or years played or alphabetically by player's last name.

The other database operation is called "query." **To query a database is to ask to see those records meeting a particular set of criteria**. Querying has two parts. The first, and most important part, is establishing the *criteria* for the records to be selected. The second part of querying is the method by which you choose to view the selected records.

In Table 9-1, you might establish a criterion to view the records for those hitters who had an average of at least 0.350 or who played in at least 1,500 games. Or you might want to discover whether any players in the database averaged less than .345, played for at least 15 years, and got fewer than 1,900 runs.

Once you have established the criteria, there are two different ways to view records that meet it. First, you can ask 1-2-3 to **Find** those records. Lotus does this by highlighting each record in turn that meets your criteria. Alternatively, you can ask 1-2-3 to **Extract** the selected records and place them in an output range. Once in the output range, you can print extracted records with your printer, or you can copy the records into a separate file with the File Xtract command. Extracted records can also be used to generate graphs displaying the information for only those records meeting your criteria.

SUMMARY

A database is a collection of information arranged into *records* and *fields*. Once you have created a database, you can have 1-2-3 perform several different operations. First, 1-2-3 can rearrange or *sort* the records with the Data Sort command. Next, you can query the database. To do this, you establish *criteria* to select particular records, then instruct 1-2-3 to either *find* or *extract* the records that meet these criteria.

THE DATA SORT COMMAND

The Data Sort command, Figure 9-3, shows the simplest operation you can perform on a database. You use it to arrange data. Alphabetically is a common arrangement, but other orders are possible. "Reverse" telephone directories, for example, are ordered by area code or street address.

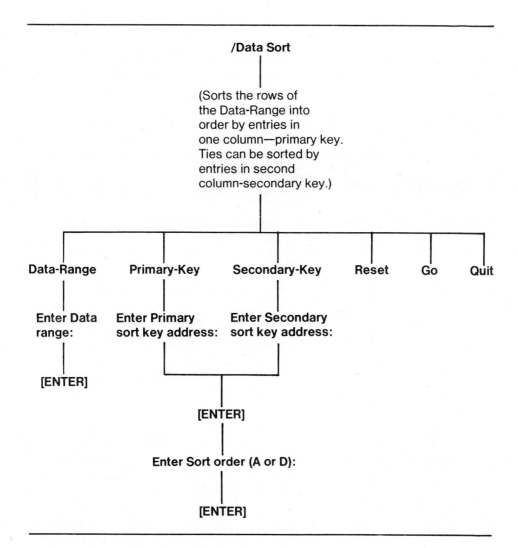

Figure 9-3. The Data Sort command tree.

You will also want to sort data for analytical purposes. In the All-Time Batting Leaders database, sorting by different columns provides insight into who really was the best baseball player of all time. The rankings differ substantially when the players are arranged by Runs (Babe Ruth is second; Lou Gehrig is third) as compared to Average (Ruth is 12th; Gehrig is 15th), or by At Bats (where Peter Browning is last instead of fourth when the ranking is by Average). Re-sorting is one of the easiest ways to analyze information in a database.

Using the Data Sort Command

To sort a database you must supply three pieces of information: the *data range*, the *primary key*, and the *order*, ascending or descending. (Descending is the proposed order.)

Data Range The first parameter, the *data range*, is the range of cells containing the records to be sorted. It *must not* include the field names. If it does, the field names are sorted into the database along with the records.

Symphony

> Unlike the 1-2-3 data range, the range for a Symphony sort *includes* the row of field names at the top of the database. Symphony simply ignores the first row of a database when performing a sort operation.

Figure 9-4 contains a 1-2-3 screen displaying the All-Time Batting Leaders database. Look at the control panel. Note that the Data Sort command has been entered and that the prompt on the prompt line is asking for the data range. The correct data range is A8..H23. Note that both the field names in row 6 and the double dashes in row 7 are omitted from the data range.

As with any 1-2-3 range, you can either type in the addresses, point to the range, or supply a range name. Lotus remembers the last specified data range and proposes it the next time you enter the Data Sort command. Lotus also saves data ranges as part of each worksheet file. After you have specified the data range, Lotus does not return to the Ready mode, but continues to display the Sort command submenu so you can specify the other parameters.

Primary Key Next, you must designate one column of the data range as the *primary key*. This is the column on which the rows (records) of the data range will be sorted. If, for example, you wanted to sort an address database alphabetically by last name, you would designate the column containing the last names as the primary key. In Figure 9-4, if you wanted to sort the players by the number of career hits, you'd move the worksheet cursor to any cell in column G and press **[ENTER]**. That would designate the Hits field as the primary key.

Ascending or Descending Finally, you must decide whether you want the database sorted in ascending or descending order. Ascending order is 1, 2, 3 ... or A, B, C... Descending order is the opposite. Descending is the proposed

```
A8: "Ty                                                              MENU
Enter Data range:A8..H23
---------------------------------------------------------------------
!         A       B       C       D       E       F       G       H   !
!1 !
!2 !
!3 !                   ALL-TIME BATTING LEADERS
!4 !                     Ten or more seasons
!5 !
!6 ! PLAYER'S NAME      YEARS   GAMES  AT BATS   RUNS    HITS  AVERAGE
!7 ! ================================================================
!8 !       Ty Cobb        24    3,033  11,429   2,244   4,191   0.367
!9 !   Rogers Hornsby     23    2,256   8,173   1,576   2,930   0.358
!10!     Joe Jackson      13    1,330   4,981     873   1,772   0.356
!11!    Pete Browning     13    1,180   4,839     867   1,716   0.355
!12!     Ed Delahanty     16    1,825   7,493   1,596   2,591   0.345
!13!   Willie Keeler      19    2,124   8,564   1,720   2,955   0.345
!14! William Hamilton     14    1,578   6,262   1,694   2,157   0.344
!15!    Tris Speaker      22    2,789  10,208   1,881   3,515   0.344
!16!    Ted Williams      19    2,292   7,706   1,798   2,654   0.344
!17!    Dan Brouthers     19    1,665   7,493   1,596   2,591   0.343
!18!   Harry Heilmann     18    2,146   7,787   1,291   2,660   0.342
!19!     Babe Ruth        22    2,503   8,389   2,174   2,873   0.342
!20!   Jesse Burkett      16    2,063   8,389   1,708   2,872   0.341
```

Figure 9-4. Database ready to sort. Prompt line shows the data range is being specified.

order (1-2-3 places "D" on the prompt line), and you can select it by pressing **[ENTER]**. In the example in Figure 9-4, you'd like the player with the greatest number of hits to appear as the first record, so choose Descending by typing a **[D]** or accept the proposed order by pressing the **[ENTER]** key. The other players are then ranked in descending order.

Secondary Key While the preceding three pieces of information (data range, primary key and ascending or descending) are the only inputs *required* to perform a data sort, you do have an additional option. If you wish, you can select another field as the *secondary key* to sort any ties that result from the primary key sort.

In a mailing list, for example, you might want all people in the same Zip code alphabetized by last name. To achieve this, designate the column containing the last name fields as the secondary key. Again, you can choose whether the secondary key is to sort in ascending or descending fashion. There aren't likely to be any ties in the number of Hits over a career in Figure 9-4, so it isn't necessary to specify a secondary key.

Symphony

In addition to Primary and Secondary Keys (what Symphony calls 1st and 2nd Keys), you can specify a 3rd Key when sorting a Symphony database.

Sorting the Data Range After you have designated the input range, the primary key, the optional secondary key, and specified whether the sort is to be ascending or descending, you are ready to sort the data range. To do this, select Go from the command line of the Data Sort submenu. (See Figure 9-3.) Lotus enters the Wait mode, the indicator light flashes, and in a few moments (depending on the size of the data range) the rearranged records are displayed.

Problems with Blanks, Brackets, and Formulas

While the Data Sort command is simple to use, you do need to know the order in which 1-2-3 places items so you won't be surprised by the results. Table 9-2 contains the actual sorting sequence used by 1-2-3 when executing the Data Sort command.

The blank character can introduce the most perplexing problems since, to 1-2-3, a blank is as much a character as an "A" or a "1." Blanks appear before letters in an ascending sort and after them in a descending sort. Since blank characters are sometimes placed before an entry (called a "leading blank") to position a label in a cell, the resulting sort can produce unexpected results. For example "[Blank]Zebra" would appear before "Apple" in an ascending sort!

To make matters worse, it is often difficult to tell whether a label's position is due to blanks or to the label-alignment character. Lotus ignores the label-alignment character, but uses the blank as a character when sorting. To check for leading blanks, move the worksheet cursor to the cell and view the contents on the status line.

TABLE 9-2

Lotus sorts by letters, numbers, characters, and blanks. Be particularly aware of leading and trailing blanks.

Ascending Sort	Descending Sort
{Blank}	Numbers: 9 to 0
! " # $ % & ' ( ) * + , − . /	∼ } {
	Lower case letters: z to a
Numbers as forced text entry. (e.g. 1A, 34B)	_] \ [
: ; < = > ? @	Capital letters: Z to A
Capital letters: A to Z	@ ? > = < ; :
[\ ] ^ _	Numbers as forced text entry. (e.g. 34B, 1A)
Lower case letters: a to z	/ . − , + *) (' & % $ # " ' !
{¦} ∼	{Blank}
Numbers: 0 to 9	

Upper and lower case letters can also cause a list to sort in unexpected ways since 1-2-3 treats the two types of letters as completely different characters. Upper case letters appear before lower case letters in an ascending sort, so the word "Zebra" would appear before the word "aardvark." Likewise, in a descending sort, upper case letters appear after lower case ones and "zoo" would appear before "Amphitheater."

Another problem arises with numbers entered as forced text entries. They appear before letters in an ascending sort (values appear after) so that "1" as a forced text entry appears before "Alphabet" or "Apple," both of which appear before "1" as a value entry. This may not be what you expect.

Entries containing formulas are sorted by their displayed value, though that value may **change** after the formula is sorted into its new location. If you can avoid it, it is best *not* to use formulas that refer to cells in rows other than the row containing the formula. Formulas that refer only to cells in the row containing the formula (or absolute references to cells outside the data range) present no problems since the cells are in the same row both before and after sorting.

Apart from numbers, letters, and blanks, the various symbols and characters are sorted in unusual ways. Parentheses come before capital letters in an ascending sort, but square brackets come after. It is, of course, the reverse in a descending sort. If you have any questions about the order in which 1-2-3 places items when sorting, consult Table 9-2.

Getting Back to Where You Started From

Once you have sorted a database, it isn't possible to simply undo the sort and return to the previous order. However, if the original order was itself the result of a sort, you can sort the database to the previous order. The Batting Leaders database, for example, was originally arranged by Average (descending order), so you can return to that order by sorting on the Average column.

There may be times, however, when the original database was not sorted. An example would be a database in which you record requests as they come into your office. If you don't include the date on which the request was entered into the database, there may be no way to sort the database into the order in which the requests were received.

To be able to sort by order entered, use the Data Fill command to create a long column of consecutive numbers immediately to the right or left of the records. Include this column of numbers in the data range, and they will provide an "index" corresponding to the order in which the records were entered into the database. As new entries are made, expand the data range to include both new index numbers and new records. You can re-sort on the index column whenever you want the requests sorted by the sequence in which they were placed into the database.

THE DATA QUERY COMMAND

The Data Query command is at the heart of 1-2-3's database functions. With it you specify criteria and then *find* or *extract* records that satisfy your requirements. See Figure 9-5 for the Data Query command tree. Other options of the Query command can be used to eliminate entries from a database (Delete), erase range specifications (Reset), and exit the command (Quit).

The Input Range

You *must* construct the database first. Only after the records and fields have been entered into 1-2-3 worksheet cells can you use the Data Query command. Recall the database structure illustrated in Figure 9-2. Place the field

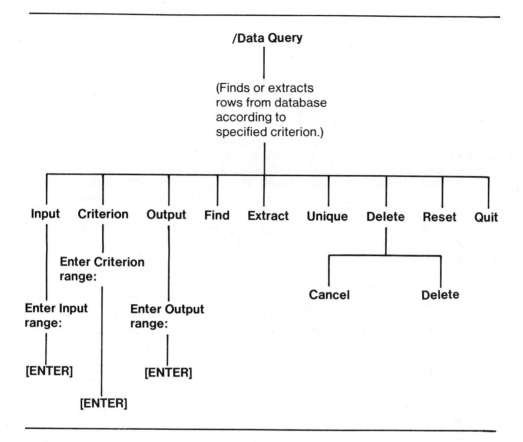

Figure 9-5. The Data Query command tree.

names at the top of the columns. If you use multiple row field names, *only* that text in the single row directly above the database is used as field names by the database function. Be particularly careful not to include two identical field names. Once the field names have been specified, enter each record into successive rows.

When creating the database, remember that you have all 1-2-3's worksheet construction tools at your disposal. In particular, remember that you can use the Worksheet Insert and Delete commands to insert or delete rows and columns. You can use the Copy and Move commands, and you can also use the Format commands to determine the appearance of the entries in the database.

Figure 9-6 on the following page contains a 1-2-3 screen displaying the by now familiar Batting Leaders database. Notice that the field names

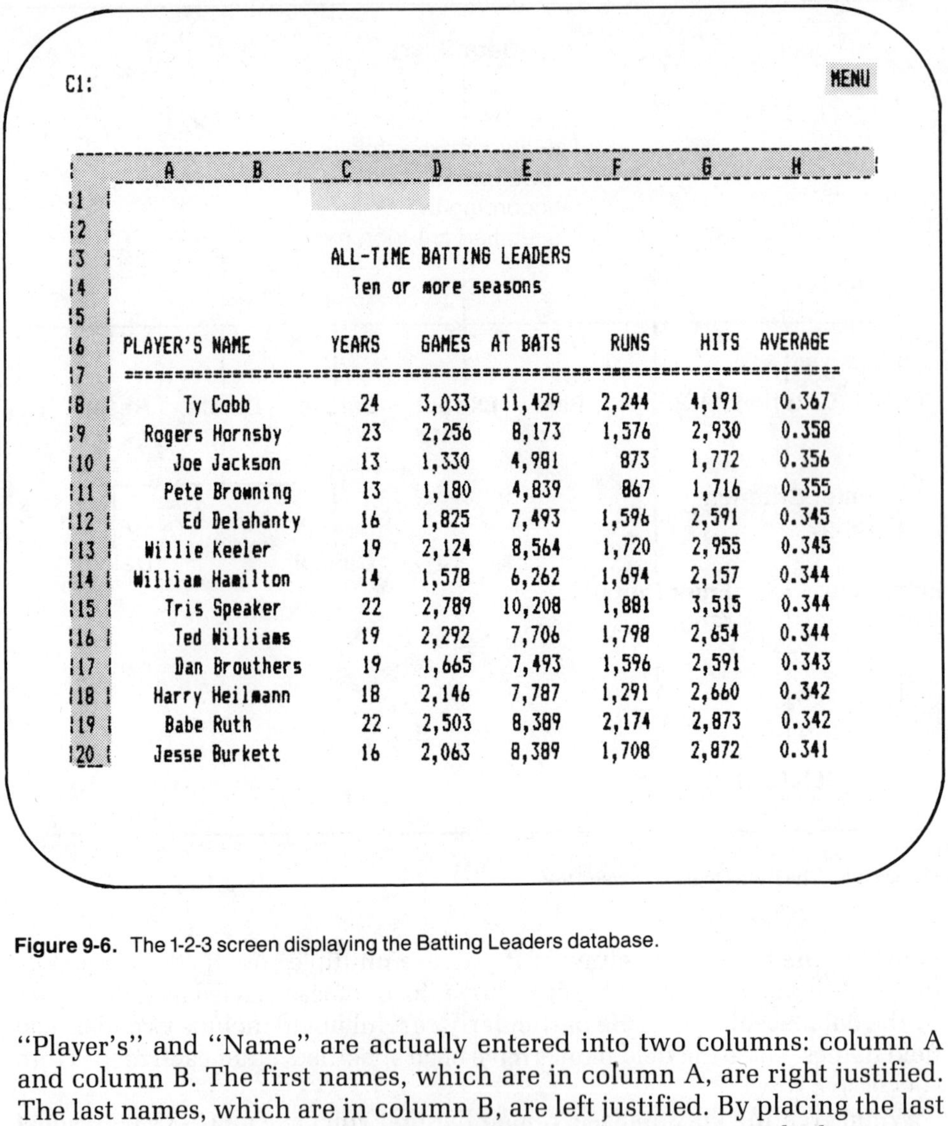

```
C1:                                                                    MENU

     _____
     :      A        B        C        D        E        F        G        H    :
   :1 :
   :2 :
   :3 :                    ALL-TIME BATTING LEADERS
   :4 :                    Ten or more seasons
   :5 :
   :6 : PLAYER'S NAME     YEARS   GAMES  AT BATS   RUNS    HITS  AVERAGE
   :7 : ==================================================================
   :8 :      Ty Cobb        24   3,033  11,429    2,244   4,191   0.367
   :9 :  Rogers Hornsby     23   2,256   8,173    1,576   2,930   0.358
   :10:   Joe Jackson       13   1,330   4,981      873   1,772   0.356
   :11:  Pete Browning      13   1,180   4,839      867   1,716   0.355
   :12:   Ed Delahanty      16   1,825   7,493    1,596   2,591   0.345
   :13: Willie Keeler       19   2,124   8,564    1,720   2,955   0.345
   :14: William Hamilton    14   1,578   6,262    1,694   2,157   0.344
   :15:  Tris Speaker       22   2,789  10,208    1,881   3,515   0.344
   :16:  Ted Williams       19   2,292   7,706    1,798   2,654   0.344
   :17:  Dan Brouthers      19   1,665   7,493    1,596   2,591   0.343
   :18: Harry Heilmann      18   2,146   7,787    1,291   2,660   0.342
   :19:   Babe Ruth         22   2,503   8,389    2,174   2,873   0.342
   :20: Jesse Burkett       16   2,063   8,389    1,708   2,872   0.341
```

Figure 9-6. The 1-2-3 screen displaying the Batting Leaders database.

"Player's" and "Name" are actually entered into two columns: column A and column B. The first names, which are in column A, are right justified. The last names, which are in column B, are left justified. By placing the last names in a separate column, it is possible to sort or query on the last name, something that couldn't be done had you entered the entire name into a single column, unless you had entered them last name first.

Also, notice that row 7, the first **record** (and the second **row**) of the input range, is a row of double dashes. This separates the field names from the records. Keep in mind that when querying a database, 1-2-3 will evaluate the double dashes in the second row as a zero in any formula used to specify a criterion. (Text is always evaluated as zero in formulas and functions.) This is usually not a problem, but sometimes you'll establish a criterion that selects the double dashes along with other, desired records.

The Criterion Range

The most important part of querying a database is setting up the criteria. Criteria are *tests* that are applied to successive fields in a database. Lotus can specify many different types of criteria. As with the database itself, the contents of the criterion range must be entered into the worksheet before you enter the Data command.

You can specify *exact criteria* for finding those players in the Batting Leaders database who have played for exactly 16 years. Or you can specify *relative criteria*. With relative criteria you can find all the players who have played for at least 20 seasons.

Exact Criteria

The place to begin setting criteria is with exact criteria which are the most straightforward. With exact criteria, you want to view only those records that meet your requirements exactly. You want only Babe Ruth's record or only the records for those players who have played for a certain number of years.

Table 9-3 shows a criterion range set up to find players who have played exactly 16 years. All criterion ranges have two parts. The first is a row of field names which must *always* be entered into the first row of the criterion range. The second part of the criterion range is a row or set of rows immediately below the row containing the field names. These rows contain the actual criteria. Table 9-3 has only one row below the field names, but, as you will soon see, there may be more than one row of criteria.

TABLE 9-3

Criterion range. Row 31 contains the field names and row 32 the criteria.

	A	B	C	D	E	F	G	H
30								
31	PLAYER'S NAME		YEARS	GAMES	AT BATS	RUNS	HITS	AVERAGE
32			16					
33								
34								

The field names in the criterion range must be **exactly** the same as the field names in the input range, otherwise the query will not work. To assure that the field names *are* the same in both ranges, use the Copy command to copy the field names from the input range to the criterion range. By using the Copy command, you can be sure that leading **and** trailing blanks are the same in both places. Lotus also makes a distinction between upper and lower case letters in field names. To 1-2-3, "YEARS" and "Years" are different. Avoid problems by copying the field names rather than attempting to re-enter them correctly into the criterion range.

Now look at cell C32 in Table 9-3. It contains the value 16. This is the criterion for finding those records that have 16 entered into the YEARS field. Lotus uses the criterion by applying it to successive cells in column C (the YEARS column). Whenever it finds a match, it selects the record. Whenever it doesn't find a match, it skips over the record.

To specify an exact criterion, simply enter it into the cell below the appropriate field name. If the field contains text, the criterion will be text. If the field contains values, the criterion will be a value. Remember, 1-2-3 recognizes blanks, capital letters, and lower case letters as *distinct* characters. Thus, "Ruth," "ruth," and "{blank}Ruth" are *three* different criteria. Only "Ruth" would match an entry in the database in Table 9-3.

Table 9-4 shows several examples of exact criteria. Study each criteria to see what records it would select. In each case, only records that satisfy the criteria *exactly* will be selected. All other records in the database will be passed over by the query operations.

Relative Criteria

In many situations, an exact criteria is too restrictive. You may not want to see those batting leaders who have played exactly 16 seasons. Rather you may want to see those who have played for **at least** 16 seasons. Or you might be interested in all players whose last names **begin** with B, but which may have any letters in the rest of their name. The criteria that would find these records are called *relative criteria* because the criteria is specified relative to a particular value, such as 16 or B.

Lotus has different tools for specifying relative criteria depending on whether the field contains values or labels. For values, the tools are the logical operators: greater than [>], greater than or equal to [> =], less than [<], less than or equal to [< =], and not equal to [< >]. For labels, the characters [?], [*], and [~] are used to define relative criteria.

TABLE 9-4

Four different criterion ranges, each with a different exact criterion.

	A	B	C	D	E	F	G	H
30								
31	PLAYER'S NAME		YEARS	GAMES	AT BATS	RUNS	HITS	AVERAGE
32		Ruth						
33								
34								

	A	B	C	D	E	F	G	H
30								
31	PLAYER'S NAME		YEARS	GAMES	AT BATS	RUNS	HITS	AVERAGE
32			22					
33								
34								

	A	B	C	D	E	F	G	H
30								
31	PLAYER'S NAME		YEARS	GAMES	AT BATS	RUNS	HITS	AVERAGE
32						873		
33								
34								

	A	B	C	D	E	F	G	H
30								
31	PLAYER'S NAME		YEARS	GAMES	AT BATS	RUNS	HITS	AVERAGE
32								0.344
33								
34								

Table 9-5 shows the Batting Leaders database with a relative criterion entered into cell C32. The criterion is formula +C7 > =16, and it is displayed with the Range Format Text command.

TABLE 9-5

Criterion range with relative criterion entered into cell C32.

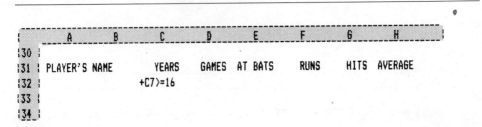

Note that the cell reference in the criterion is to the first record (the second row) in the input field. Lotus searches down the Years column, applying the criterion to each entry. When a value is greater than or equal to 16, the record is selected. When the value is less than 16, the record is rejected. Table 9-6 contains a number of examples of relative criteria applied to value entries.

When it comes to specifying relative criteria for text fields, 1-2-3 has three special characters or *wild cards*. They are the question mark **[?]**, the asterisk **[*]**, and the tilde **[∿]**. Each character can be used to define criteria that will accept a range of label entries. Here is how they work:

The Question Mark. When the question mark, **[?]**, is used in a criterion, it means **any character may occupy that spot**. For example, the criterion **?at** would select bat, cat, rat, and hat. It would not accept brat, frat, or scat.

The Asterisk. The asterisk, **[*]**, is a very powerful wild card. When it is used in a criterion, it means **any character may occupy the place of the asterisk and any character or characters may appear after the asterisk**. For example, the criterion **B***, selects any word beginning with a capital "B." Better, Both, Baltimore, and Bolivia would all be selected by the **B*** criterion.

The Tilde. The tilde **[∿]** is the opposite of the asterisk. Used in a criterion, it means to **select any entry, except entries that match what follows the tilde**. For example, the criterion **∿Ruth** would select all players whose last name was *not* Ruth.

TABLE 9-6

Criterion ranges containing different relative criteria.

	A	B	C	D	E	F	G	H
30								
31	PLAYER'S NAME		YEARS	GAMES	AT BATS	RUNS	HITS	AVERAGE
32			+C7<16					
33								
34								

	A	B	C	D	E	F	G	H
30								
31	PLAYER'S NAME		YEARS	GAMES	AT BATS	RUNS	HITS	AVERAGE
32				+D7<1500				
33								
34								

	A	B	C	D	E	F	G	H
30								
31	PLAYER'S NAME		YEARS	GAMES	AT BATS	RUNS	HITS	AVERAGE
32					+E7>=5000			
33								
34								

	A	B	C	D	E	F	G	H
30								
31	PLAYER'S NAME		YEARS	GAMES	AT BATS	RUNS	HITS	AVERAGE
32								+H7<>0.344
33								
34								

You can combine wild cards in the same criterion. For example ∿**B*** would accept any entry that didn't begin with a B, while **?a*** would accept any entry whose second letter is an "a."

The three wild cards allow you to set up complicated criteria for searching label fields. However, when using the wild cards, be careful to avoid criteria that select records you didn't want selected. Lotus will follow your instructions to the letter (and the character), so make sure the criteria you establish are really the criteria you wish to establish. It is always good practice to check the selected records for entries you didn't intend to select. If there is a problem, redefine your criteria and repeat the query operation.

Multiple Criteria

In many situations, you will want to establish criteria that apply to several fields at one time. There are two general types of multiple criteria. You may want the selected records to satisfy **every** criteria you establish, or you may want selected records that satisfy **any** one of the criteria. These two ways to specify criteria are called "AND" and "OR" criteria, respectively.

In the Batting Leaders database, the AND criteria might be used to select all players who have played in at least 2,000 games, and who have at least 2,500 hits, and whose last names begin with B. Only those players who satisfied *all* the criteria would be selected. Failure to satisfy any one of the criteria would cause the record to be rejected.

The OR criteria selects any player who has played in at least 2,000 games, or who has at least 2,500 hits, or whose last name begins with B. Meeting *any* one of the three criteria would qualify a record for selection. Only those records that failed to meet all the criteria would be rejected.

You instruct 1-2-3 to treat your criteria as AND criteria or OR criteria by the way you construct the criterion range. Each criterion in a **single row** of the criterion range is treated as **AND**. Criteria in **different rows** are treated as **OR**.

Table 9-7 shows the entries you would make to find records meeting the two criteria discussed in the preceding paragraphs. The first criterion range has the criteria entered into a single row; therefore, all the criteria must be satisfied by any record selected. The second criterion range contains three rows of criteria; therefore, a record can be selected by meeting the criteria in row 1, or row 2, or row 3.

TABLE 9-7

When the criteria are in the same row, all the criteria must be met by a selected record. When the criteria are in different rows, a record can be selected by meeting all the criteria in any one row.

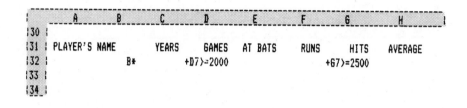

"AND" Criteria

	A	B	C	D	E	F	G	H
30								
31	PLAYER'S NAME		YEARS	GAMES	AT BATS	RUNS	HITS	AVERAGE
32		B*		+D7>=2000			+G7>=2500	
33								
34								

"OR" Criteria

	A	B	C	D	E	F	G	H
30								
31	PLAYER'S NAME		YEARS	GAMES	AT BATS	RUNS	HITS	AVERAGE
32				+D7>=2000				
33							+G7>=2500	
34		B*						
35								

When you specify the criterion range, you must include all the rows that contain criteria. In the first example, the criterion range consists of two rows, row 31 and row 32. In the second example, the criterion range contains four rows: rows 31, 32, 33, and 34.

You can combine AND criteria and OR criteria in the same criterion range. For example, you might want players whose Last Names begin with C **or** R, whose Average is at least .345, **and** whose Years are less than 23. In Table 9-8 on the following page, the C and R criteria are in different rows while the 23 and .345 criteria are in the same row.

TABLE 9-8

AND and OR criteria combined in the same criterion range.

	A	B	C	D	E	F	G	H
30								
31	PLAYER'S NAME		YEARS	GAMES	AT BATS	RUNS	HITS	AVERAGE
32		C#	+C7<23					+H7>=0.345
33		R#	+C7<23					+H7>=0.345
34								

One caution when setting criteria: **never** include in the criterion range a row containing *only* blank cells. Each blank cell accepts *all* entries in that field, and a complete set of blank criteria would accept all fields in all records. Thus, the entire database would be selected, regardless of any other criteria you may have established, since all records are passed by the all blank row.

Extensions Whenever you use a formula in a criterion, be sure that cell references to fields within the database are **relative**, while references to cells outside the database are **absolute**. This requirement will be clear when you understand how 1-2-3 applies a criterion. It begins with the first cell in the particular field and evaluates the criterion for that field. It selects the record if the result is true (true formulas evaluate to 1). The cell is rejected if the formula evaluates to false (zero).

After testing the first cell, 1-2-3 moves down one record and tests the next cell in the field by *adjusting* the cell references so that they apply to that field. You usually want references to cells within the database to adjust, but you would want to use the same value for each record from a cell somewhere else on the worksheet.

The next point has to do with the location of the criterion range. It may be anywhere on the worksheet. Since formulas are typically wider than value entries, you'll often need extra column width to view them. Therefore, it is best to locate the criterion range in a place where you can expand the columns in that range without disturbing either the database or any other entries. This way, you can widen the columns so that formulas entered as criteria can be viewed under the Range Format Text command.

In the preceding examples, the entire row of field names was copied as the first row of the criterion range. This isn't necessary. You need the field names for only the fields in which you wish to specify criteria. You can omit the other field names. However, the entire list of field names serves to remind you of the possible fields in which criterion may be specified and, for that reason, you may want to include all field names in your criterion ranges.

Finally, a criterion can be changed by simply editing the old criterion or by typing a new criterion and entering it into the appropriate cell in the criterion range. As with all changes, these changes must be made *outside* the Data Query command. You cannot change criterion (or any other entry, for that matter) from inside the command.

SUMMARY

You now know about the four types of criteria you can use with 1-2-3 databases: exact, relative, AND, and OR. Establishing the criteria is the hardest part of using the Data Query command. Until you become comfortable specifying criteria, test each criterion by identifying a record you expect to be selected, and then verify that it is, indeed, selected. (The Find command, is the easiest way to perform this task.)

If you have trouble specifying a criterion, write out what you want to use as a criterion and then translate the words into formulas that 1-2-3 understands. Specifying individual elements of multiple criteria and then testing each element is also a good idea when you are first becoming familiar with specifying criteria. (The **[QUERY]** function key can be a great aid in doing this. See the discussion that follows).

Finally, it is quite easy to specify criteria that none of the records in your database satisfy. If this happens, you get a "beep" to indicate that none of the entries in the input range have been selected. Begin relaxing your requirements until 1-2-3 selects the records you are looking for.

Using the Data Find Command

The hard work is over. You have created the database and entered the criteria. You are now ready to use the Data Query command. Begin by typing /DQ. The command line displays a submenu with the Query options:

Input   Criterion   Output   Find   Extract   Unique   Delete   Reset   Quit

The first three choices; Input, Criterion, and Output, are the three ranges you need to specify. Each time you finish specifying a range, 1-2-3 returns to the Query command submenu so you can specify another range.

The first step is to specify the input range. This range *must* include the single row of field names at the top of the database. The control panel in Figure 9-7 shows that the input range is ready to be specified. The correct range is A6..H23 and, as you know, you can specify it by typing cell addresses, pointing with the cursor, or by supplying a range name. If you have already specified an input range, 1-2-3 proposes it. (The last input range is also stored with the worksheet.) If you want to accept the proposed range, press **[ENTER]**; otherwise supply your own.

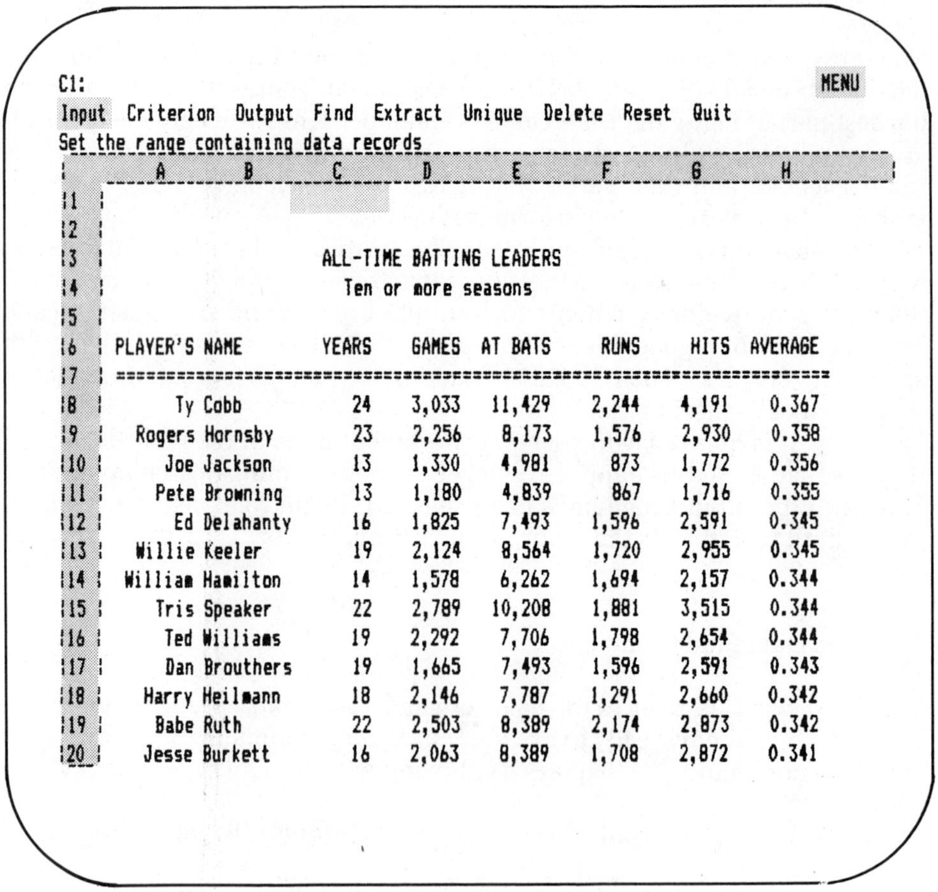

```
C1:                                                              MENU
Input Criterion Output Find Extract Unique Delete Reset Quit
Set the range containing data records
         A        B        C        D        E        F        G        H

 1
 2
 3                         ALL-TIME BATTING LEADERS
 4                         Ten or more seasons
 5
 6   PLAYER'S NAME      YEARS    GAMES  AT BATS    RUNS    HITS  AVERAGE
 7   ==================================================================
 8         Ty Cobb        24    3,033   11,429   2,244   4,191   0.367
 9    Rogers Hornsby      23    2,256    8,173   1,576   2,930   0.358
10       Joe Jackson      13    1,330    4,981     873   1,772   0.356
11      Pete Browning     13    1,180    4,839     867   1,716   0.355
12       Ed Delahanty     16    1,825    7,493   1,596   2,591   0.345
13     Willie Keeler      19    2,124    8,564   1,720   2,955   0.345
14    William Hamilton    14    1,578    6,262   1,694   2,157   0.344
15      Tris Speaker      22    2,789   10,208   1,881   3,515   0.344
16      Ted Williams      19    2,292    7,706   1,798   2,654   0.344
17      Dan Brouthers     19    1,665    7,493   1,596   2,591   0.343
18    Harry Heilmann      18    2,146    7,787   1,291   2,660   0.342
19       Babe Ruth        22    2,503    8,389   2,174   2,873   0.342
20     Jesse Burkett      16    2,063    8,389   1,708   2,872   0.341
```

Figure 9-7. The 1-2-3 screen with the Input range ready to be specified.

If you are adding entries to an existing database, you can stretch the proposed range to include the new entries. Remember, the period key **[.]** moves the blinking bar from one corner of the proposed range to an adjacent corner. Use the period to position the cursor in the correct corner, and then stretch the proposed range over the database.

After you specify the input range, proceed to specify the criterion range. It must include at least two lines, one of field names and at least one row below the field names for criteria.

When you have specified at least the input and criterion ranges, you are ready to use the Query Find command (Find command, for short). This command locates and highlights records in the database that meet your criteria. You view the records on the screen, but they aren't copied to an output space for future processing, printing, or analysis. (Copying to the output range is performed by the Extract option.) To use the Find command, select Find from the Query submenu by typing an **[F]** or by moving the command line cursor to Find and pressing **[ENTER]**.

A typical use of the Find command is with a telephone database where you want to find someone's telephone number. You don't need a copy of the record; you just want to view it while placing your call. Just specify the name, enter the Data Query Find command, and bingo, it is on the screen.

In addition to highlighting, which makes it impossible to mistake the selected record for some other record, notice that the left-most cell in the highlight record contains a flashing underline character. This character indicates the "active field." You can use the **[RIGHT ARROW]** and **[LEFT ARROW]** keys to move the underline character to the left or the right. This way you can scroll the screen to expose all the fields of a record that is too wide to view on the screen at one time.

When you have finished viewing a particular record, press the **[DOWN ARROW]** key, and the next record meeting your criteria is highlighted. If you want to view previously viewed records, press the **[UP ARROW]** key. Finally, **[HOME]** and **[END]** move the cell pointer to the first and last record in the database, regardless of whether those entries satisfy your criteria or not.

Table 9-9 on the next page shows the Batting Leaders database with criteria entered into rows 29 and 30. The first record selected is Ty Cobb's, and it is highlighted. Can you predict what will be the next record selected? And the next?

To end the Find command, press the **[ESC]** key and you'll return to the Query submenu. From there you can perform other Data Query operations. To exit the Data command altogether, select Quit from the Query submenu. As you know, you can also always terminate a command by typing **[CTRL]-[SCROLL LOCK]** or by pressing the **[ESC]** key a sufficient number of times.

TABLE 9-9

The Find command locates and highlights those records in the input range that satisfy the criteria in the criterion range.

	A	B	C	D	E	F	G	H
1								
2								
3			ALL-TIME BATTING LEADERS					
4			Ten or more seasons					
5								
6	PLAYER'S NAME		YEARS	GAMES	AT BATS	RUNS	HITS	AVERAGE
7	===							
8	Ty Cobb		24	3,033	11,429	2,244	4,191	0.367
9	Rogers Hornsby		23	2,256	8,173	1,576	2,930	0.358
10	Joe Jackson		13	1,330	4,981	873	1,772	0.356
11	Pete Browning		13	1,180	4,839	867	1,716	0.355
12	Ed Delahanty		16	1,825	7,493	1,596	2,591	0.345
13	Willie Keeler		19	2,124	8,564	1,720	2,955	0.345
14	William Hamilton		14	1,578	6,262	1,694	2,157	0.344
15	Tris Speaker		22	2,789	10,208	1,881	3,515	0.344
16	Ted Williams		19	2,292	7,706	1,798	2,654	0.344
17	Dan Brouthers		19	1,665	7,493	1,596	2,591	0.343
18	Harry Heilmann		18	2,146	7,787	1,291	2,660	0.342
19	Babe Ruth		22	2,503	8,389	2,174	2,873	0.342
20	Jesse Burkett		16	2,063	8,389	1,708	2,872	0.341
21	Bill Terry		14	1,721	6,428	1,120	2,193	0.341
22	Lou Gehrig		17	2,164	8,001	1,888	2,721	0.340
23	George Sisler		15	2,055	8,267	1,284	2,812	0.340
24								
25								
26								
27								
28			*************CRITERION RANGE******************					
29	PLAYER'S NAME		YEARS	GAMES	AT BATS	RUNS	HITS	AVERAGE
30					+E7>7000			
31								
32								
33								

Using the Data Extract Command

You will often want to have a list of all the records in the database meeting your criteria. You might want to print this list, or you might want to save it into its own worksheet file with the File Xtract command. You might want to subject the information in the selected records to further analysis, or you might want to use them as input to a graph to display the information visually. You can perform all these tasks with the Data Extract command.

Using the Extract command is much like using the Find command except that the selected records are copied to an output range rather than highlighted in the database. To use the Extract command, you must first use the Output option on the Query command submenu to define the location of an output range.

Like the input and criterion ranges, the output range begins with a row of field names which must be entered before you begin the Data command. Below the field names are a number of rows into which to copy the extracted records. Once again, the field names in the output range **must** be identical to the field names above the input range.

If a field name isn't the same in both places, 1-2-3 does **not** copy the information from fields in the column with the mismatched field names. So use the Copy command to make sure the field names in the output and the input range are identical. Don't rely on your ability to retype the field names; if you do, you are inviting trouble.

You can specify the output range itself in two different ways. The easiest is to specify as the output range **only** the row of cells containing the output field names. Lotus then uses as many rows below the field names as it requires to copy the extracted records. However, 1-2-3 automatically erases **everything** in the columns below the output field names down to the bottom edge of the worksheet at row 2,048. If you choose the first option, be certain there is nothing below the row of output field names that you would mind having erased.

The alternative is to specify the output range as a **block of cells**. If you do this, Lotus erases the entries in the specified cells and does not affect the entries below the last specified row. If the output range is not large enough to accommodate all the selected records, you receive a *Too many records for output range* error message. When you respond to the message by pressing the **[ENTER]** key, 1-2-3 fills the output range with as many selected records as will fit. To extract all the selected records, you must return to the Data Query command, expand the size of the output range, and then repeat the operation.

To execute the Extract command, choose the Extract option from the Query submenu. Do this by typing **[E]** when the submenu is displayed, or move the command line cursor to Extract and press **[ENTER]**. As you begin the Extract command, 1-2-3 enters the Wait mode. The mode indicator flashes, and in a few moments, the records matching your criteria appear in the output range.

Note that the records in the output range do not contain any formulas or functions that may have been part of the database's structure. Only displayed

values are copied to the output range. Table 9-10 shows the Extract command applied to the Batting Leaders database.

TABLE 9-10

The Extract command selects all records that meet the criteria and copies them to the output range.

	A	B	C	D	E	F	G	H	
27									
28			**********CRITERION RANGE****************						
29	PLAYER'S NAME		YEARS	GAMES	AT BATS	RUNS	HITS	AVERAGE	
30					+E7>8500				
31									
32									
33			**********OUTPUT RANGE****************						
34	PLAYER'S NAME		YEARS	GAMES	AT BATS	RUNS	HITS	AVERAGE	
35	Ty Cobb		24	3,033	11,429	2,244	4,191	0.367	
36	Willie Keeler		19	2,124	8,564	1,720	2,955	0.345	
37	Tris Speaker		22	2,789	10,208	1,881	3,515	0.344	
38									
39									

Omitted and Rearranged Field Names. In the previous example, the field names in the output range were the same in number and order as the field names in the input range. However, you can omit field names from the output range. If you do, the omitted fields do not appear. See Table 9-11 for an example. You can use this technique to eliminate unnecessary or unwanted information from the selected records.

You can also rearrange the order in which the fields appear in the output range by simply rearranging the order of the output range field names. See Table 9-12 for an example.

This technique can be used with a regular 1-2-3 worksheet as well as with a database worksheet. Just rearrange the field names, specify a blank row in the criterion range (this causes all records to be selected), and presto, the columns of your worksheet are in a new order.

Remember, however, that only **values**, not formulas or functions, are copied to the output range, thus extracting a worksheet to reorder its columns destroys the structure behind the worksheet. This is not a problem *if* you do the operation just before you print the worksheet **and** *if* you keep a copy of the worksheet with its formulas and functions intact in a file or elsewhere on the same worksheet.)

TABLE 9-11

The field names in the output range determine which fields are copied. If you omit a field name, that field is omitted from the output range.

	A	B	C	D	E	F	G	H
27								
28			***********CRITERION RANGE****************					
29	PLAYER'S NAME		YEARS	GAMES	AT BATS	RUNS	HITS	AVERAGE
30					+E7>8500			
31								
32								
33			***********OUTPUT RANGE****************					
34	NAME	AT BATS	RUNS	HITS	AVERAGE			
35	Cobb	11,429	2,244	4,191	0.367			
36	Keeler	8,564	1,720	2,955	0.345			
37	Speaker	10,208	1,881	3,515	0.344			
38								
39								
40								

TABLE 9-12

You can rearrange the order of the columns in the output range by rearranging the order of the field names.

	A	B	C	D	E	F	G	H
27								
28			***********CRITERION RANGE****************					
29	PLAYER'S NAME		YEARS	GAMES	AT BATS	RUNS	HITS	AVERAGE
30					+E7>8500			
31								
32								
33			***********OUTPUT RANGE****************					
34	NAME	PLAYER'S	AVERAGE	RUNS	HITS	GAMES	AT BATS	YEARS
35	Cobb	Ty	0.367	2,244	4,191	3,033	11,429	24
36	Keeler	Willie	0.345	1,720	2,955	2,124	8,564	19
37	Speaker	Tris	0.344	1,881	3,515	2,789	10,208	22
38								
39								
40								

Other Data Query Operations

In addition to the Find and Extract operations discussed above, 1-2-3 has four other options on its Data Query submenu. Two options, Quit and Reset, are straightforward. Quit terminates the Data command and returns the worksheet to the Ready mode. The Reset option clears all remembered input, criterion, and output ranges. It gives you a clean slate of ranges to work with.

The other two options, Unique and Delete, perform data management tasks. The Unique option is exactly like the Extract option. except that it makes sure each record is copied into the output range only once. The Delete option erases records from your database that meet your criteria. Records below removed records move up to fill the space so no blank rows remain in the database.

When using the Delete option, be particularly careful when specifying relative criteria or when using wild cards. Delete takes out **every** record that meets your criteria—whether you intended it to or not. To avoid deleting the wrong records, use the specified criteria to first perform an extract operation on the database. You can then check the extracted records to be sure none are records you want to keep. When you are satisfied that the criteria has selected only those records you wish to erase, choose the Delete option from the Query command submenu to remove the unwanted records from your database.

The [QUERY] Function Key

Lotus has an important feature for performing the same query operation (Find, Extract, Delete, or Unique) over and over. This is the **[QUERY]** function key which repeats the last defined Data Query command. When you use the **[QUERY]** key, 1-2-3 remains in Ready mode. You can enter new criteria into the appropriate cell in the criterion range and press **[QUERY]** to have the criteria applied to the most recently defined Data Query command.

In a telephone number database, for example, you can enter one name, find it, then enter another and find it. You don't have to type the several keystrokes required to enter and exit the Data Query command itself.

To use the **[QUERY]** key, you must define all the ranges required for the particular Query operation, and you must also perform the operation at least one time from the Data Query command submenu.

Symphony

You can use the Query command in a Sheet environment to construct and use a Symphony database in exactly the same way you construct and use a 1-2-3 database. However, Symphony also provides an easy to use and powerful alternative method of database construction. This method is the Generate command in a Form environment.

Simply put, the Form environment is a data entry form made up of the field names used in your database. The form takes up the entire window (see Figure 9-8 on the next page) while the spreadsheet to which it is linked, disappears.

To use the form to make an entry into the database, type an entry in the appropriate field. When you press the **[ENTER]** key, the cursor moves from field to field. If necessary, you can come back and change an entry. When all the entries are correct, you press the **[INS]** key, and the entry is inserted into the database. A blank data entry form then appears, ready for your next entry. Symphony makes creating a database as simple as filling in the blanks.

The Form environment can be used, among other things, to establish criteria (the criteria are typed into the appropriate fields) and display selected records. (This works like 1-2-3's Find command.) You can also display successive records in the entry form by pressing the **[PgUp]** and **[PgDn]** keys or by using the **[GOTO]** key to go to a particular record number. (Records are numbered consecutively beginning with the second row of the database.)

By far the easiest way to generate a database and its accompanying data entry form is with the Generate command on the main menu of a Form environment window. This command generates all of the ranges and settings required to set up a form and the accompanying database.

Here are the steps you must go through to generate a database in a Form environment.

1. Begin in a Sheet window. Start by typing the field names you want to use in your database. Arrange them in either a row or a column. Be sure there are no entries from the initial location of the worksheet cursor down to the bottom of the worksheet for a number of columns equal to the number of field names you will be using. If there are entries in this area, Symphony will refuse to generate the database.

```
            A         B         C         D         E         F         G         H
 1 : Name
 2 : Address
 3 : City
 4 : State
 5 : Zip
 6 : Phone
 7 :
 8 : Name _____
 9 : Address _____
10 : City _____
11 : State _____
12 : Zip _____
13 : Phone _____
14 :
15 : Name      Value     Type      Default   Formula   Validity  Input     Prompt
16 : Name                L:9                                               Enter Name
17 : Address             L:9                                               Enter Address
18 : City                L:9                                               Enter City
19 : State               L:9                                               Enter State
20 : Zip                 L:9                                               Enter Zip
21 : Phone               L:9                                               Enter Phone
22 :
23 : Name      Address   City      State     Zip       Phone
24 :      0         0         0         0         0         0
25 :
26 : Name      Address   City      State     Zip       Phone
27 :
28 :
29 :
30 :
31 : Name      Address   City      State     Zip       Phone
32 :
33 :
```

Figure 9-8. Symphony Form environment.

2. Use **[ALT]-[TYPE]** to switch to the Form environment. You will be greeted by the message **(No Definitions range defined)**, but don't worry. You'll take care of that next.
3. Press **[MENU]** to display the Form environment menu and then select Generate.
4. A series of prompts are now displayed. They are:

Select default field type:

Default field length:

Name of Data-base settings sheet

Accept the proposed responses to each of these prompts by pressing the **[ENTER]** key or, if appropriate, type in another response.
5. Finally, you will be prompted:

Range of Field names:

At this point, the spreadsheet behind the Form environment is displayed so you can use the cursor control keys to point to the field names you typed into the spreadsheet.
6. After you have pointed to the field names, press **[ENTER]**, and you are finished. The screen returns to the Form environment, and your field names are displayed as a data entry form. The underline characters (See Figure 9-8) following each field name, nine if you accepted the default field length, show the maximum length of each entry. You can now make the first entry into you database, and Symphony will take care of the rest.

To understand what happened when you generated the form, look at Figure 9-9 on the next page. This is what you would see when you switch from the Form environment to the Sheet environment. The original field names are in rows 1 to 6. Below the field names, Symphony has created, an Entry range (rows 8 to 13), a Definition range (rows 15 to 21), an Above Report range (rows 23 and 24), a Criterion range (rows 26 to 30), and a Database range (row 31 to the bottom of the worksheet).

The Database and Criterion ranges are familiar concepts; the other ranges are new to Symphony. The Entry range is the text and underline characters used in the Form environment. The Above Report range is the labels to be printed above a report generated from this database. And, finally, the Definition range passes data back and forth automatically between the entry form and the database.

The Definition range is the heart of Symphony's Form environment. It contains columns labeled Value, Type, Default, Formula, Validity, Input, and Prompt. Only Type and Prompt are filled in. Type is the type and length of entry that will be accepted in a field. Prompt is the text displayed at the top of the screen when the cursor is on a

```
Inserting Record 1                    New Record                          FORM
Enter Name
┌─────────────────────────────────────────────────────────────────────────┐
│Name_____                                                               │
│Address_____                                                            │
│City_____                                                               │
│State_____                                                              │
│Zip_____                                                                │
│Phone_____                                                              │
│                                                                           │
│                                                                           │
│                                                                           │
│                                                                           │
│                                                                           │
│                                                                           │
│                                                                           │
│                                                                           │
│                                                                           │
│                                                                           │
│=MAIN=================================================================MAIN=│
05-Jan-85  9:53 AM                          CALC
```

Figure 9-9. Entries behind Form environment.

particular field. You can change a field type by typing in a different letter (L for label, N for number, etc.), and you can change the field length by changing the number after the colon. (Alternatively, you can change the field length by changing the number of underline characters in the Entry range.) You can change the prompt by simply editing new text into the appropriate cell in the Prompt column.

The other columns in the Definition range have more esoteric uses. The Default column places your specified default value in the specified field. The Formula column lets you specify a formula to calculate the actual entry into the database. It can, for example, convert values entered in Dollars into Yen by multiplying by the appropriate exchange rate. The Value and Input columns are used by Symphony and should contain no user entries.

Symphony normally arranges the entries in the form window in a column as shown in Figure 9-9. You can, however, rearrange the labels and the underlines in the Entry range in any manner you wish. When you do combine two or more field names on a single line, you must edit the entries into *one* long label. For example, to have the field names "City" and "State" in Figure 9-9 appear on a single line, you'd have to enter the long label "City_____State___" into the appropriate cell. You would also have to delete the row containing "State" from the Entry range to avoid the duplication of field names.

The commands and options discussed in the previous paragraphs just scratch the surface of Symphony's Form environment. However, the steps described will allow you to quickly generate a database and its associated form. These steps are keys that unlock the power of Symphony's Form environment.

THE DATABASE STATISTICAL FUNCTIONS

Lotus has seven special built-in statistical functions for use with databases (see Table 9-13 on the following page).The functions are designated as database functions by a "D" before the function name (e.g., @DSUM). The functions perform the same type of statistical operation (summation, for example) as the regular built-in functions. The difference is that **the database statistical functions only operate on designated fields in those records selected by your criteria**.

In the Leading Batters database you can, for example, have @DSUM calculate the total number of hits by players who have played 15 or more seasons. Or you can have @DMAX find the player with the highest batting average among those players who have played less than 18 years and who have played in more than 1,600 games. You can use the database statistical functions to create tables of statistics on the selected records.

The database statistical functions can also be combined with the data table function to produce data tables where several successive criteria are used to select the records. An application of this type is presented in the Hands On section at the end of this chapter.

Using the Database Statistical Functions

The database statistical functions are used much like their non-database counterparts, except that you must supply **three** separate pieces of information. (Note that each of the three arguments is separated from the other by a comma.)

TABLE 9-13

Database statistical functions. Each function must have three arguments: the location of the input range, the offset, and the location of the criterion range.

FUNCTION	DESCRIPTION
@DCOUNT	Counts number of non-blank cells in the offset field of selected records.
@DSUM	Sums values in the offset field of selected records.
@DAVG	Averages values in the offset field of selected records.
@DVAR	Calculates variance of values in the offset field of selected records.
@DSTD	Calculates standard deviation of values in the offset field of selected records.
@DMAX	Finds maximum value in the offset field of selected records.
@DMIN	Finds minimum value in the offset field of selected records.

@FUNCTION NAME (Input Range, Offset, Criterion range)

You are already familiar with the input range and the criterion range. They have exactly the same meaning here as they do when used with the Data Query operations. The input range is the database (including the field names) and the criterion range is the range of cells containing field names and the criteria established for querying a particular input range.

The new piece of information required by the database statistical functions is the "offset." "Offset" is a complicated way of asking for the column containing the fields for which you want the statistics calculated. To make things a little more confusing, Lotus designates the left-most column in the input range as "Offset 0" so that the second column is "Offset 1," the third "Offset 2," and so on.

Table 9-14 shows the offsets for the Leading Batter's database. **When specifying an offset, remember to begin counting at zero with the left-most column of the input range**.

Other than the need to specify the input range, the offset, and the criterion range, the database statistical functions can be used like any other built-in function. They can be copied with the Copy command, but if you do intend to copy one of the functions, be sure to designate the input and criterion ranges as absolute, otherwise they adjust when the copies are made. Lotus recalculates the database statistical functions whenever you press the **[QUERY]** key to repeat a data query operation. Thus, you can change your criteria and have the new statistics calculated at the press of a single key.

TABLE 9-14

In a database statistical function, the "offset" refers to the column containing the fields on which the function operates. Note that the first column in the input range is offset zero.

```
:       A       B       C       D       E       F       G       H
:1 :
:2 :                    ALL-TIME BATTING LEADERS
:3 :                      Ten or more seasons
:4 :
:5 :              OFFSET is given by number above field name
:6 :
:7 :       0        1       2       3       4       5       6       7
:8 :  PLAYER'S NAME      YEARS   GAMES  AT BATS  RUNS    HITS  AVERAGE
:9 :  ================================================================
:10 :     Ty Cobb        24     3,033  11,429   2,244   4,191  0.367
:11 :  Rogers Hornsby    23     2,256   8,173   1,576   2,930  0.358
:12 :    Joe Jackson     13     1,330   4,981    873    1,772  0.356
:13 :   Pete Browning    13     1,180   4,839    867    1,716  0.355
```

Table 9-15 on the next page contains examples of several database statistical functions. The text of each function is displayed immediately to the right of the cell containing the function. Note the use of absolute range names in the functions.

THE DATA DISTRIBUTION COMMAND

The last feature of the Data command (see the command tree in Figure 9-10 on page 275) is the Data Distribution command. This command is used to create a count of values falling within specified ranges in a distribution. This count is called a *frequency distribution*, and it is often graphed as a bar graph.

TABLE 9-15

The database statistical functions at the bottom of this table calculate the specified statistics for those records selected by the criteria in the criterion range.

```
      A       B      C       D       E       F       G       H
 1
 2                 ALL-TIME BATTING LEADERS
 3                   Ten or more seasons
 4
 5            OFFSET is given by number above field name
 6
 7      0       1      2       3       4       5       6       7
 8  PLAYER'S NAME     YEARS   GAMES  AT BATS  RUNS    HITS  AVERAGE
 9  ================================================================
10      Ty Cobb        24    3,033   11,429   2,244   4,191   0.367
11   Rogers Hornsby    23    2,256    8,173   1,576   2,930   0.358
12     Joe Jackson     13    1,330    4,981     873   1,772   0.356
```

```
23     Bill Terry      14    1,721    6,428   1,120   2,193   0.341
24     Lou Gehrig      17    2,164    8,001   1,888   2,721   0.340
25   George Sisler     15    2,055    8,267   1,284   2,812   0.340
26
27
28            ***********CRITERION RANGE****************
29  PLAYER'S NAME     YEARS   GAMES  AT BATS   RUNS    HITS  AVERAGE
30                                    +E9>=8500
31
32   For players who have been at bat
33        at least 8,500 times
34
35  Number of players:                     3 <-- @DCOUNT($INPUT,7,$CRITERION)
36  Total number of games played:      7,946 <-- @DSUM($INPUT,3,$CRITERION)
37  Average number of games played:    2,649 <-- @DAVG($INPUT,3,$CRITERION)
38  Average number of times at bat:   10,067 <-- @DAVG($INPUT,4,$CRITERION)
39  Average batting average:           0.352 <-- @DAVG($INPUT,7,$CRITERION)
40  Maximum batting average:           0.367 <-- @DMAX($INPUT,7,$CRITERION)
41
```

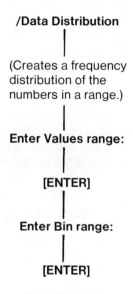

/Data Distribution

(Creates a frequency
distribution of the
numbers in a range.)

Enter Values range:

[ENTER]

Enter Bin range:

[ENTER]

Figure 9-10. Data Distribution command tree.

Symphony

The Distribution command is *not* part of Symphony's database commands. Instead, the command is a subcommand of the Range command in a Sheet environment window.

Using the Data Distribution Command

Assume you'd like to create the frequency distribution for At Bats from the
information in the Batting Leaders database. Before entering the command,
you must place values into a column of cells to determine the intervals into
which the numbers from the At Bats field will be counted. This column is
called the *Bin Range* since it serves as "bins" into which to count the values.

The values that define the bins must be in strictly increasing order. If the intervals in the bin range are regular (as they often are), you can use the Data Fill command to specify them.

You must leave a blank column of cells immediately to the right of the bin range. Furthermore, these blank cells must extend one row *below* the last value in the bin range. This column of cells is where Lotus places the "count," and the last cell (the one below the last cell in the bin range) is where 1-2-3 places the count for all values that are larger than the largest value in the bin range. All values smaller than the smallest value in the bin range (the value in the first cell) are counted into the first cell. See Table 9-16 for an example of the bin and count ranges for the Data Distribution command.

TABLE 9-16

Data Distribution command used to generate a frequency distribution of the At Bats field in the Batting Leaders database.

	I	J	K	L	M	N	
1							
2							
3							
4							
5				AT BATS			
6			Frequency Distribution				
7			==================================				
8				Bin	Count		
9				Range	Range		
10				5,000	2		
11				6,000	0		
12				7,000	2		
13				8,000	4		
14				9,000	6		
15				10,000	0		
16					2		
17							
18							
19							
20							

Once you have specified the values in the bin range, you are ready to use the Data Distribution command. Begin by typing /**DQ**. Then select Distribution from the Data Query submenu. The prompt line reads:

Values range:

Lotus is asking for the range of values to be tabulated. Supply it by pointing, typing cell addresses, or, if you've given it a name, selecting the name from the name list with the **[NAME]** function key. The values range can be a block as well as a row or column. In the Batting Leader's database, the information is in cells E3..E24.

Once you have specified the values range, press **[ENTER]** and the following prompt appears:

Bin range:

After you have specified the bin range (K10..K15 in the example), press **[ENTER]** again. Lotus enters the Wait mode, tabulates the values in the values range, and displays the count one column to the right of the bin range.

Lotus remembers the values and bin ranges, so you can easily repeat the Data Distribution operation. You can, for example, change the intervals in the bin range and then recount the values into different intervals. Should you need to, the bin range can be expanded or contracted with the Worksheet Insert and Delete commands and with the Move command.

An obvious use of the Data Distribution command is to create a frequency distribution which is then graphed to create a histogram. In the next chapter, you'll learn to construct 1-2-3 graphs, but it should come as no surprise that the range of cells into which the count is placed can be used as the input range for a bar graph. You can even use the bin range as the labels for the bars.

HANDS ON: USING THE DATA COMMAND

Table 9-17 on the following page contains a small database of expense records. Each row contains an entry for the month, the person, and the expense. In its current form, it is difficult to tell what expenses have been incurred by each person each month. The information would be easier to understand and use if the total expenses for each person for each month were summarized into a table.

You could use the Sort command to reorder the database or the Extract command to extract the records for each person for each month, but these operations would have to be repeated several times to get the raw informa-

TABLE 9-17

Sample database of expenses by person and month for June, July, and August.

```
 ┌─────────────────────────────────────────────────────────────────────┐
 │      A        B        C      D      E        F              G        │
│1 │                                                                     │
│2 │    ***INPUT RANGE***                     **CRITERION RANGE**        │
│3 │    Month    Person Expenses              Month      Person          │
│4 │    ============================                                     │
│5 │ June       Jones    $36.15                                          │
│6 │ July       Smith    $29.54                                          │
│7 │ August     Jones    $15.47                                          │
│8 │ July       Smith   $161.00                                          │
│9 │ June       Smith   $115.31                                          │
│10│ August     Smith    $87.69                                          │
│11│ August     Jones    $13.45                                          │
│12│ June       Smith   $251.78                                          │
│13│ July       Jones     $0.36                                          │
│14│ July       Jones   $147.98                                          │
│15│ August     Smith    $36.25                                          │
│16│ June       Smith    $12.54                                          │
│17│ June       Jones    $98.73                                          │
│18│ August     Smith    $64.12                                          │
│19│ July       Jones    $91.54                                          │
│20│ July       Jones   $125.79                                          │
│21│                                                                     │
│22│                                                                     │
│23│                                                                     │
```

tion. The raw information would still have to be processed before you had a complete record of expenses by person. If the database contained several hundred records, the task could take quite some time.

Luckily, 1-2-3 has a better way to produce summary tables from databases. This better way is to use a *data table*. In the last chapter, the application of data tables to regular 1-2-3 worksheets was explained. From that discussion, you know that a data table works by substituting successive entries from a specified range into specified cells (called "input cells"). Lotus then recalculates the worksheet and displays the results in the data table. (See the discussion in chapter eight for the details of constructing and using data tables.)

Data tables can be constructed for use with databases, but instead of substituting successive values, the data table can substitute successive *criteria*. The criteria can be values or, as in the following example, the criteria can be labels. Database statistical functions can then be used to calculate summary statistics for those records selected by each criteria.

Table 9-18 shows a Two-Way Data Table that has been constructed to the right of the database from Table 9-17. From the discussion of data tables in the last chapter, you know that the formula to be evaluated in each cell of a two-way table is entered into the upper-left cell of the data table range. In Table 9-18, the cell is E10, and the formula is @DSUM(A3..C20,2,F3..G4). Also, you know that the first argument of the @DSUM function is the input range for the database. The next argument is the offset which is the column in the input range to be summed. The last argument is the criterion range.

TABLE 9-18

A Two-Way Data Table used to summarize expenses for each month for each person in the input range.

```
         A      B       C      D      E       F        G         H
 1
 2      ***INPUT RANGE***              **CRITERION RANGE**
 3      Month   Person Expenses        Month      Person
 4      ============================
 5    June    Jones   $36.15
 6    July    Smith   $29.54
 7    August  Jones   $15.47           ***TWO-WAY DATA TABLE***
 8    July    Smith   $161.00              MONTHLY EXPENSES
 9    June    Smith   $115.31
10    August  Smith   $87.69    1287.7     Smith     Jones     Totals
11    August  Jones   $13.45     June    $379.63   $134.88    $514.51
12    June    Smith   $251.78    July    $190.54   $365.67    $556.21
13    July    Jones   $0.36      August  $188.06    $28.92    $216.98
14    July    Jones   $147.98
15    August  Smith   $36.25     Total   $758.23   $529.47  $1,287.70
16    June    Smith   $12.54
17    June    Jones   $98.73
18    August  Smith   $64.12     Formula in cell E10: @DSUM(A3..C20,2,F3..G4)
19    July    Jones   $91.54
20    July    Jones   $125.79
21
22
23
```

The entries in the first column of the data table; June, July, and August, are the three months for which expense records have been recorded. These labels need to be substituted into cell F4 in the criterion range. Do this by specifying F4 as Input Cell 1 when designating the parameters for the Data Table command.

Input Cell 2, the other parameter that varies in a two-way data table, is given by the entries in the first row of the data table. These are the names of the two persons in the database for whom expense information has been gathered, Smith and Jones. Specify G4 as Input Cell 2.

Each cell in the data table is at the intersection of a name and a month; therefore, the value in that cell shows the total expenses claimed by each person for each month, just the information you were looking for.

Note that the value displayed in cell E10 is the value of the formula @DSUM(A3..C20,2,F3..G4) when both cells in the criterion range are blank. The value displayed in the upper-left cell is the value for the formula evaluated under whatever entries have been made into the input cells on the worksheet—not the values that are substituted into those cells by executing the Data Table command. Also, notice that the Totals in column H and in row 15 are familiar @SUM functions that provide total expenses by month and by person.

To use the data table in Table 9-18, specify the table range as E10..G13, and specify Input cell 1 as F4 (the cell under Month in the criterion range), and Input cell 2 as G4 (the cell under Person in the criterion range). When you specify the last input cell, the command executes and the summary totals are displayed.

The Two-Way Data Table just described can be used as a model for other combinations of data tables and database statistical functions. If you substituted the @DAVG or @DMAX function in cell E10 for the @DSUM function, you will have the average monthly expenditure or the maximum monthly expenditure for each person for each month. If you wanted these figures for each person over all three months, you could have them by constructing a One-Way Data Table. The persons' names would be entered into the cells in the first column, and the required database statistical functions would be entered into the appropriate cells of the first row.

Data tables for use with databases are as easy to construct as the data tables used with regular electronic spreadsheets. In conjunction with database statistical functions, data tables become powerful tools for expanding the analysis and presentation of information stored in 1-2-3 databases.

Just remember to use the Copy command to enter the criteria into the appropriate cells of the data table. Like all criteria, 1-2-3 considers upper and lower case letters and leading and trailing blanks when searching for matches. The only way to be sure that the criteria you specify in the data table are the same as the entries in the database is to use the Copy command to copy them from the database to the cells of the data table.

SELF-TEST

QUESTIONS

1. What is a record?
2. What is a field?
3. Should you include the field names in the data range of the Sort command?
4. Should you include the field names in the input range when performing a query operation?
5. Is it good practice to retype the field names when entering them into the criterion or output ranges?
6. When can you use the **[QUERY]** key?

ANSWERS

1. A record corresponds to a row in a 1-2-3 database. It is all the information about a particular entry.
2. A field corresponds to a cell in a record in a 1-2-3 database. A field contains a single piece of information about a particular entry. All the cells in a column of a database are sometimes called a field.
3. No. If you include the field names, they are sorted along with the records.
4. Yes. The field names must be included in the input range of the Query command.
5. No. Always use the Copy command to copy the field names from the input range to the criterion and output ranges. The field names must be *exactly* the same in all three places. The Copy command is the best way to avoid making mistakes.
6. Whenever 1-2-3 is in Ready mode, pressing the **[QUERY]** key executes the last defined Data Query command.

PART D
LOTUS 1-2-3'S GRAPH COMMAND

The 3 of 1-2-3 is graphics. With the Graph command, you can create graphs based on the numbers in your spreadsheet, and you can instruct 1-2-3 to remember the specifications of a graph for viewing or for printing later.

Graphs have two purposes. First, graphs can be used as part of a presentation. They can be distributed at meetings, and they can be incorporated into memos and reports. Presentation-quality graphs clearly and forcefully convey the meaning behind the numbers in your spreadsheets. If you have a color plotter or color printer, 1-2-3 can create color graphs to make your point even more dramatically.

The second purpose of a 1-2-3 graph is often overlooked. Graphs are, in their own right, an important form of analysis. When you create a graph, you get a quick, overall perspective on your worksheet. This perspective can give you insights that are often difficult to obtain from the numbers alone. Analytical graphs, in contrast to presentation-quality graphs, are usually "quick-and-dirty" affairs. Since you do them to gain insight, you aren't concerned with elaborate labels, legends, or special type faces—features that go into making a presentation-quality graph.

Keep in mind the two uses for a 1-2-3 graph as you read the following chapter. Use presentation and analytical graphs to increase the impact of your oral and written presentations and to improve your analysis.

CHAPTER TEN
THE GRAPH COMMANDS

OBJECTIVES

- To master the steps required to specify a 1-2-3 graph.
- To learn the options available for enhancing the display of 1-2-3 graphs.
- To understand the difference between a graph saved for viewing and a graph saved for printing.
- To become familiar with the options available for printing a 1-2-3 graph.
- To master printing 1-2-3 graphs.

INTRODUCTION

The 1-2-3 Graph command can create five different types of graphs; bar, line, stacked-bar, Pie, and XY graphs.

The bar, line, and stacked-bar graphs are used to compare relative magnitudes. The magnitudes are graphed along the vertical axis. The categories in which the information is presented are listed along the horizontal axis. These categories may be time periods (month, quarter, year, etc.), divisions, or regions.

Pie graphs (sometimes called pie charts) display the relationship between a whole and its parts.

The final graph type, the XY graph, displays the relationship between two numerical magnitudes, one on each axis.

Symphony

In addition to the five 1-2-3 graph types, Symphony can draw a high-low, open-close graph (often used to graph stock prices), and it can explode one or more sections of a pie chart for emphasis. With Symphony, you can also assign a cross hatching pattern to each segment of a pie chart.

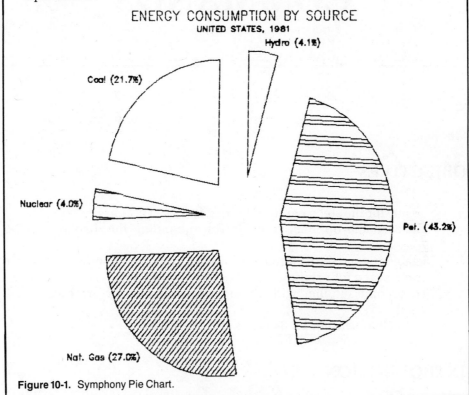

ENERGY CONSUMPTION BY SOURCE
UNITED STATES, 1981

Hydro (4.1%)

Coal (21.7%)

Nuclear (4.0%)

Pet. (43.2%)

Nat. Gas (27.0%)

Figure 10-1. Symphony Pie Chart.

When you first encounter the 1-2-3 Graph command (see Figure 10-2 for the command tree), you may be overwhelmed by its large number of choices, but don't worry. Creating a 1-2-3 graph actually requires only *two* pieces of information, and, if you wish, 1-2-3 will supply one of them. To create a graph, you first select one of the five graph types or accept the line graph which is 1-2-3's proposed graph type, and secondly, you specify at least one data range (A to F). Then to see how your graph looks, select View from the Graph command main menu. That is all; just a graph type and at least one data range. All the other choices on the Graph command main menu are options, options you exercise *only* when you need a special feature.

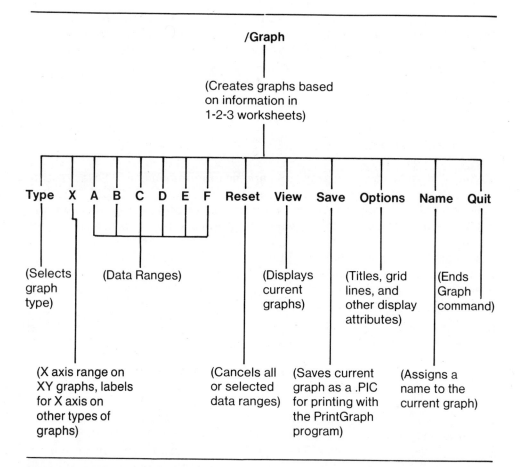

Figure 10-2. The Graph command tree.

Symphony

Just as you have access to Symphony's database command through two routes (Sheet and Form environments), you have access to Symphony graphs through two different routes. When in the Sheet environment, you can select Graph from the Sheet menu and proceed to specify a graph. Alternatively, you can designate a window as a Graph window, and then press the **[MENU]** function key. This gives you access to the same Settings choices available from the Graph option of the Sheet menu. Both routes accomplish the same thing, but the 1-2-3 user who is learning to use Symphony will find the Graph option in a Sheet window more familiar.

A Word About Hardware

If your system has a single graphics-capable monitor such as a Texas Instruments Professional Computer, a Compaq computer, or an IBM Personal Computer with a color/graphics monitor adapter and a graphics monitor, 1-2-3 switches back and forth between the graph and the worksheet. To view the most recently specified graph, select View from the Graph command main menu or press the **[GRAPH]** function key when 1-2-3 is in Ready mode. Lotus replaces the worksheet on your monitor with the graph. When you are ready to return to the worksheet, press any key, and 1-2-3 returns to the worksheet.

Symphony

Symphony doesn't have a **[GRAPH]** function key. It does have a key named **[DRAW]**, but this key *does not* perform the same function. Instead, it redraws all windows and will not redraw a graph that isn't in its own Graph environment window. To draw a Symphony graph, you must select Preview from the Graph submenu of the Sheet command or, if you are in a Graph window, the graph will be drawn automatically each time you return to the main menu from a submenu.

Also, if you have the hardware to display text and graphics on the *same* monitor, Symphony can draw a graph in one window while displaying other environments (Sheet, Doc, Form, etc.) through other windows on the same screen. Thus, for example, you can have a graph, a spreadsheet, and a memo displayed on your screen at the same time.

If you have a two-monitor system, perhaps an IBM PC with a Monochrome Display and a graphics monitor (which may or may not be a color monitor), Lotus displays the worksheet on the Monochrome display and the graph on the graphics monitor. There is no need to switch back and forth between the two; the graph is displayed on the graphics monitor until it is redrawn by selecting View or by pressing the **[GRAPH]** key when in Ready mode.

To get a printed version of a 1-2-3 graph, you need a graphics-capable printer such as one of the Epson brand dot-matrix printers or a plotter such Hewlett-Packard's HP7470A Plotter. If you don't have a graphics-capable monitor, but do have a printer capable of printing 1-2-3 graphs, you can still specify and print graphs. You won't be able to view the graphs before printing, but you will have available the full range of printing options.

CREATING A 1-2-3 GRAPH

Create the Worksheet First

A 1-2-3 graph cannot exist independently of the worksheet that contains the information to be graphed. Thus, the *first* step in creating a 1-2-3 graph is to create the worksheet. Pay particular attention to the row labels and column headings because you have the option of using the text from these cells as labels for your graph. To be effective labels, however, they must be short since the space around a graph is at a premium.

You can also use the worksheet title and subtitle to title your graphs, but if you used leading blanks to center the titles on the worksheet, these blanks will cause the automatic centering feature of the Graph command to incorrectly align the titles. If you are going to use entries from the worksheet as titles, don't use leading blanks. Also, don't plan on inserting or deleting rows or columns that move the cells containing the labels. If you do, 1-2-3 *does not* adjust the cell references in the graph specification.

Select a Graph Type

Once you have a worksheet to the point where you would like to draw a graph, enter the Graph command by typing **/G**. Figure 10-3 shows a 1-2-3 screen with the command line displaying the Graph command main menu. The first choice, Type, is highlighted, and the prompt line reads, "Set graph type."

Select Type and choose one of the five available graph types. Bar is a good all-purpose choice, but one of the other choices may be more appropriate for the task at hand.

Once you have selected a graph type, 1-2-3 returns control to the Graph command menu rather than to the Ready mode. This allows you to continue to make the choices necessary to specify your graphs.

```
B6: 1970                                                          MENU
Type X A B C D E F  Reset  View  Save  Options  Name  Quit
Set graph type
         A        B        C        D        E        F        G        H
 1 :
 2 :
 3 :         Doctorate Degrees Conferred
 4 :             1970 to 1980
 5 :
 6 :             1970     1975     1980
 7 :
 8 : Total     29,475   32,913   30,982
 9 :
10 : Male      25,349   25,705   21,594
11 : Female     3,979    7,208    9,388
12 :
13 :
14 :
15 :
16 :
17 :
18 :
19 :
20 :
```

Figure 10-3. When you select the Graph command from the slash command main menu, the choices for the Graph command are displayed in the control panel.

Specify a Data Range

Graphs visually display data, so before you can ask 1-2-3 to draw a graph, you must tell it where to find the data to be graphed. Data is specified in ranges A, B, C, D, E, and F. (See the overall command tree in Figure 10-2.) To specify one of the six data ranges, select a letter, and 1-2-3 prompts you to "enter first (or second, etc.) data range." Don't leave a blank data range between two other data ranges because 1-2-3 leaves room for that range and a blank space will appear on your graphs. For example, don't specify range A and C and leave range B blank.

Pie graphs use data in only the A data range so if you are drawing a pie graph, 1-2-3 ignores any other data ranges you may have specified. Graphs of the XY type require you to specify the data to be plotted along the X-axis as the X data range. Other graph types do not use the X option as a data range. (See the discussion that follows on X Range Labels.) The other six data ranges (A to F) can also be used with XY graphs.

In the example in Figure 10-3, assume you'd like to see a bar graph of total doctorates awarded in each of the three years. To specify this graph, select "Bar" as the graph type, and then specify B8..D8 as the A data range.

View Your Graph

The final step is to view your graph. Do this by selecting View from the Graph command main menu. See Figure 10-4 on page 292 for the bar graph you've just specified. If you have a two-monitor system, the graph appears on the graphics monitor. If you have a one-monitor system, the worksheet disappears and the graph takes its place on the screen. When you are ready to continue specifying options for the graph, press any key, and the worksheet and the Graph command main menu reappear.

Symphony

From the Graph command in a Sheet window, the minimum requirements for a Symphony graph—type, data range, and Preview (Symphony's term for "View")—are the same as for a 1-2-3 graph. In a Graph window, you only need the type and at least one data range. The graph will be drawn as soon as you return to the main menu in the Graph window.

Note that you cannot use the **[GRAPH]** function key to view a graph while you are still in Menu mode. The function key *only* works from the Ready mode where it is an easy, efficient way to view a graph after making a change in the assumptions behind the worksheet. Changing assumptions and view-

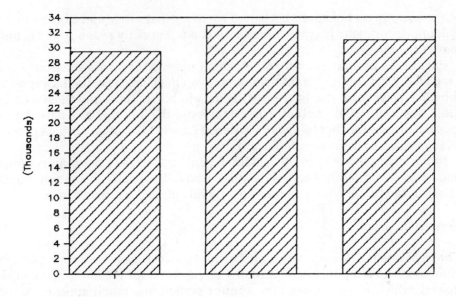

Figure 10-4. Bar graph of the total doctorates conferred 1970 to 1980.

ing the results with the **[GRAPH]** key is called "What if...?" graphing. It shows in visual terms what happens to a worksheet's values when the underlying assumptions change.

X Range Labels

While you are still in the Graph command main menu, you can proceed to add labels, titles, legends, and other information to your graph. All these additions are optional. And don't use an option if it clutters up a graph or if it otherwise makes the graph difficult to read or understand.

There is, however, one feature you will want to chose for every bar, line, or stacked-bar graph. This is the X option on the main Graph command menu. Use it to specify labels for the tick marks on the X-axis. Lotus automatically scales the vertical or Y-axis and displays numbers near the tick marks. It also supplies the words "Thousands" or "Millions" when appropriate. Labels for the X or horizontal axis are a different matter. Lotus doesn't supply them automatically. Instead, you must tell 1-2-3 where to find the labels for the X-axis tick marks. To do this, choose X from the Graph command main menu and proceed to specify the cells containing the values or labels to be used along the X-axis. In the example, the column headings, 1970 to 1980, are the logical labels for the X-axis, so specify the range of cells B6..D6 as the X range. The result is the graph in Figure 10-5.

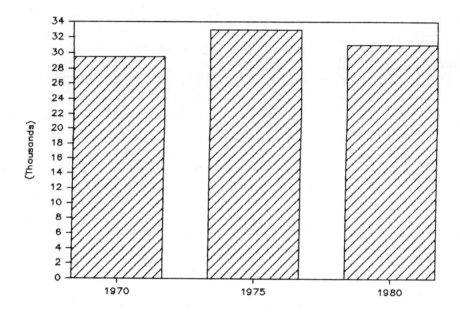

Figure 10-5. X axis labels added to graph in Figure 10-3.

The X range can cause some confusion because the type of information specified as the X range differs from graph type to graph type. On bar graphs (including multiple bar graphs) and on line and stacked-bar graphs, the content of the X range, as in the preceding example, is used to label the tick marks along the horizontal axis.

In contrast, on an XY graph, the X range is a true data range. Graphs of the XY type plot numerical values on *both* axes, and the X-axis data on an XY graph is specified under the X data range. You *must* specify data for the X range of an XY graph, and you may have up to six data ranges, A through F, plotted against the X-axis data range.

Finally, pie charts don't have X and Y axes, so labels or data specified under the X data range is ignored when 1-2-3 draws a pie chart.

If you find use of the X data range confusing, just remember that the X range provides *labels* for the tick marks on the horizontal axis for *all* graph types *except* the XY graph and the pie chart. For the XY graph, the X range is a data range. The pie chart has no X-axis, so any entry in the X range is irrelevant and is ignored by 1-2-3.

OPTIONS

Once you have chosen a graph type and specified at least one data range, you are ready to add additional options to your graph. Options should enhance the appearance and clarity of your graph. If an option doesn't do that, abandon it and try another.

To begin entering options, select the Options choice on the main Graph command menu. See Figure 10-6 for a command tree of the Graph options.

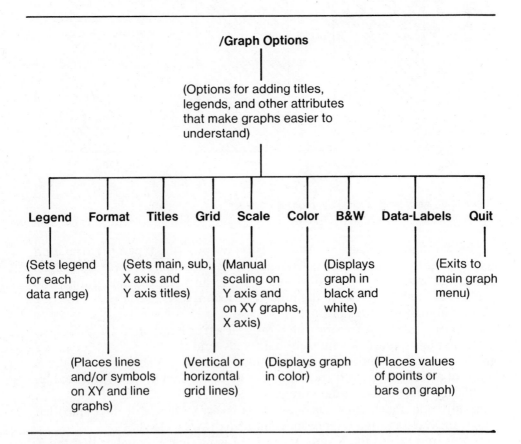

Figure 10-6. The Graph options command tree.

Major Options

Two choices on the Options submenu, Legend and Titles, are choices you will probably want to make with most graphs you create. The other options are more specialized.

Legends Each bar, line, stacked-bar, or XY graph assigns a different cross-hatching pattern or color (if you are displaying the graph in color) to each data range. The Legend option labels each pattern or color. The legends are displayed along the bottom of the graph and are essential for comprehending a multiple bar, stacked-bar, or line graph.

Figure 10-7 shows a multiple bar graph. In Part A, the graph is displayed without legends. Notice how difficult it is to understand the graph. Which bar goes with which data range? In Part B, the same graph is displayed with legends that make it much easier to understand.

To specify a legend, begin by selecting a data range. You are then prompted to type the legend. Legends may be no longer than 15 characters. If there are several data ranges, they *must* be much shorter. If you have specified all six data ranges, for example, you must keep each legend to a *single character*. If the legends are too long, they are truncated. If a legend is truncated, simply re-enter the Options Legend command and edit the legend until it fits in the allotted space.

While you can specify a legend by typing letters or numbers in response to the Legend prompt, you can also specify a legend by referring to a cell on the worksheet. To specify a cell address as the location of a legend, precede the cell address with the backslash character. For example, if you wanted to use the contents of cell A5 as a legend, type \ **A5** in response to the Legend prompt.

Using references to cells on the worksheet has two advantages. First, it establishes a direct link between the legends and the labels on your worksheet. This link helps coordinate the information on the graph with the information on the worksheet. Secondly, while in the Ready mode, you can modify the legend by editing the information in the cell. You can then display the graph with the **[GRAPH]** function key. This method of adjusting the appearance of several legends is easier than re-entering the text of each legend through the Graph command.

Titles The second option you will almost always use is the Titles option. This option lets you specify a main title, a subtitle, an X-axis title, and a Y-axis title. The main title is centered above the worksheet, and the subtitle, if any, is centered under it. On the screen, the main and subtitles appear in the same size type. When printed, however, main titles are in larger type, and subtitles in smaller type.

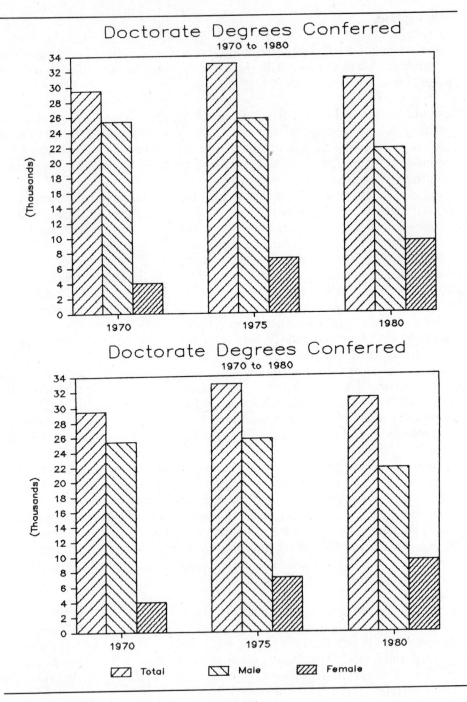

Figure 10-7. Multiple bar graph without and with legends.

Like legends, titles can be typed in response to the prompt, or they can be supplied by referring to a spreadsheet cell. Again, if you refer to a cell, precede the reference with a backslash (e.g. \ **A3**). See Figure 10-8 for an example of a graph with several titles.

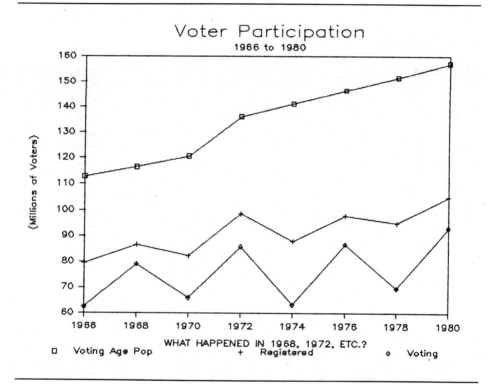

Figure 10-8. Graph with titles.

If the data on your worksheet is in thousands or millions, you need not supply the words "Thousands" or "Millions" as Y-axis titles. Lotus automatically labels the Y-axis with the appropriate word whenever it rounds the numbers. On the other hand, if the numbers on the worksheet are already rounded, you will need to supply the appropriate Y-axis label.

Minor Options

The other options on the Options command submenu are more specialized (see Figure 10-6). Unlike the Legend and Title options just discussed, they are used only in special cases.

B&W and Color The B&W and Color options switch the display between black and white and color. Black and white graphs use different cross-hatching patterns to separate different bars. Color graphs use different colors for this purpose. If you intend to plot or print a graph in color, you must choose the color option before you save the graph. If you cannot print or plot in color, you *must* select B&W before you save the graph for printing. Otherwise, the cross-hatch pattern is omitted and the different parts of your graph will be indistinguishable from one another.

Data Labels These are values placed on a graph to give the exact value for a bar, a segment of a stacked-bar graph, or a data point on a line or XY graph. It is often hard to read exact values off a graph, so data labels are used to provide the information directly (see Figure 10-9). However, use data labels sparingly because their number and position can clutter a graph to the point where it is very difficult to read. If this happens, eliminate or reposition the data labels.

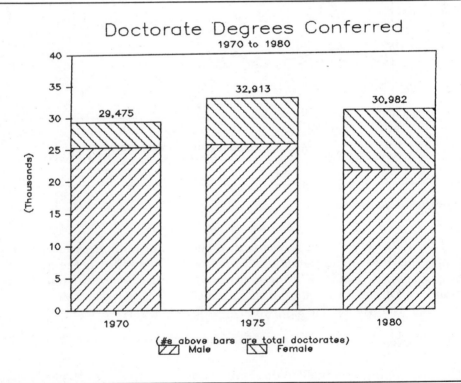

Figure 10-9. Stacked-bar graph with data labels.

Grid The Grid option serves some of the same functions as data labels and has some of the same drawbacks. With the Grid option, you specify either horizontal or vertical lines (or both) to form a grid. This makes it easier to estimate the value of a data point or the height of a bar. Again, the rule is to use grids when they help and not to use them when they make your graph harder to understand.

Scale Lotus normally scales the axis automatically. The Scale option lets you set scales manually. Scaling the horizontal axis manually applies only to XY graphs as other types of graphs don't use the horizontal scale to display values. A typical use of the Scale option is to gain a little "head room" at the top of the graph to display data labels. Without manual scaling, it is sometimes difficult to display these data labels without having them write over the top border.

Once you have chosen to scale an axis, you are prompted to provide the upper and lower limits, and you are given an option to format the values displayed along the axis. The format options (Currency, Percent, Fixed, etc.) are the same options available under the Range or Worksheet Format commands. You can choose to have the values on an axis formatted, even if you choose to accept the automatic scaling of the axis.

The last Scale option is called "Skip." It allows you to specify a "skip factor" for the tick marks on the horizontal axis. That is, you can choose to have every other (2), every fifth (5), or every tenth (10) tick mark labeled. The skip factor ranges from 1 (every tick mark) to 2,048. When you choose a skip factor greater than 1, intervening tick marks appear, but they are not labeled. If you have many data points in a data range, you may end up with so many labels on an axis that they write over one another. With a little experimenting, you will arrive at the appropriate skip factor to prevent this.

Quit Quit returns you to the Graph command main menu. Once there, you can select View to see the effect of choices made while in the Options submonu. You can also return to the Graph command main menu by pressing the **[ESC]** key once.

Format The Format choice is a bit confusing. This "Format" is not the same as the "Format" discussed under the Scale option. This format doesn't affect the display of values. Rather, it sets certain attributes of the lines and data points on line and XY graphs. It lets you choose whether to have the data points connected by lines or to omit the lines. The latter option produces a "scatter plot" of the data points. You can also use Format to draw different symbols (diamond, triangle, cross, etc.) at the data points in each data range in a line or XY graph.

As noted at the beginning of this section, except for the Legend and Titles options, the choices on the Options submenu are specialized. Some apply to only a few of the graph types (Format, for example), while others are only useful in certain situations (Scale, for example). If you need additional information on little-used options, use the **[HELP]** function key.

Symphony

Symphony uses the same set of options for specifying a graph as does 1-2-3, but the way Symphony presents the graph options is much easier to use (see Figures 10-10 and 10-11). These settings sheets are for the Symphony graph shown in Figure 10-1.

```
Switch to 2nd-Settings                                                 MENU
Switch  Type  Range  Hue  Format  Data-Labels  Legend  Cancel  name  Quit
,-----------------------------------------------------------------------,
|     Type:      Pie                                                    |
|                                                                       |
|  Range              Hue  Format  Data-Labels         Legend           |
|                                                                       |
|  X  A4..A8           1                                                |
|  A  C4..C8           2                                                |
|  B  D4..D8           3                                                |
|  C                   4                                                |
|  D                   5                                                |
|  E                   6                                                |
|  F                   7                                                |
'=============================================Graph 1st-Settings: MAIN=='
```

Figure 10-10. First Settings Sheet.

```
Switch to 1st-Settings                                              MENU
Switch  Titles  Y-Scale  X-Scale  Other  Name  Quit
|----------------------------------------------------------------------|
| Titles                                        Type:  Pie             |
|   First    ENERGY CONSUMPTION BY SOURCE  X-Axis                      |
|   Second   UNITED STATE, 1981            Y-Axis                      |
| Y-Scale                    X-Scale                   Other           |
|   Type     Automatic         Type     Automatic       Grid    None   |
|   Lower                      Lower                     Hide    No     |
|   Upper                      Upper                     Color   Yes    |
|   Format   6                 Format   6                Skip    1      |
|   Exponent Automatic         Exponent Automatic        Origin  0      |
|   Width    9                                           Aspect  1      |
|==================================================Graph 2nd-Settings: MAIN==|
```

Figure 10-11. Second Settings Sheet.

When you select either 1st-Settings or 2nd-Settings, one of the screens in Figure 10-10 or 10-11 appears. Each screen has a set of submenu choices. Each time you complete a choice, assign a Range, for example, the result appears in the table. You can switch between the two settings screens by selecting Switch from either menu.

SAVING GRAPHS FOR VIEWING AND PRINTING

Unless you do something to preserve a set of graph specifications, those specifications are *lost* when you specify another graph, and they are not saved when you save the worksheet. Furthermore, two distinct and quite different operations save a graph for viewing and a graph for printing. A graph saved for printing cannot be viewed with the Graph command unless it is also saved for viewing. Likewise, a graph saved for viewing cannot be printed with the PrintGraph utility unless it is also saved for that purpose.

A graph saved for viewing changes whenever the data in its data ranges changes. A graph saved for printing is like a snapshot. It contains the information at the time the graph was saved, but it is unaffected by subsequent changes in data ranges or other graph specifications.

Naming Graphs for Viewing

To save the specifications of a graph for *viewing* later, you must *name* the graph. Once a name has been assigned to a graph, the graph specifications are stored with the name. You view the graph later by selecting the name. Furthermore, when a worksheet is saved with the File Save or File Xtract command, the graph names and accompanying specifications are also saved.

Symphony

Symphony also requires you to assign names to the graphs (actually, the settings sheets) that you wish to view again. However, in an improvement over 1-2-3, the program does assign a default name to the *first* graph you specify. It is therefore automatically saved for viewing. If you define settings sheets for additional graphs based on the same window, you must assign these additional graphs their own names. Otherwise, the new settings replace the original settings and the original settings are lost.

The distinction between graphs saved for viewing (named graphs) and graphs saved for printing is continued in Symphony. To save a Symphony graph for printing, you select Image-Save from either the Sheet Graph command menu or from the menu in a Graph window. The graph's specifications are then saved in a .PIC file for printing later with Symphony's PrintGraph utility.

Before a graph can be named, it must be displayed on your screen. Once the graph is displayed, choose the Name option from the Graph command main menu. When you do, the following choices appear:

Use Create Delete Reset

To name a graph, select Create, and then specify the name for the graph. Like other 1-2-3 names, you can use up to 15 characters, and you can use most of the symbols, letters, and characters available on the keyboard. Letters are treated as upper case regardless of how they are entered.

You can view any named graph by selecting the Use option from the above list. This option displays the names of all the named graphs based on the current worksheet. See Figure 10-12 on the following page for a 1-2-3 work-

sheet with graph names displayed on the prompt line. You can then choose
from that list the name of the graph you want to make current. Once chosen,
the graph appears on the screen; you don't have to select View from the main
menu to have the graph drawn.

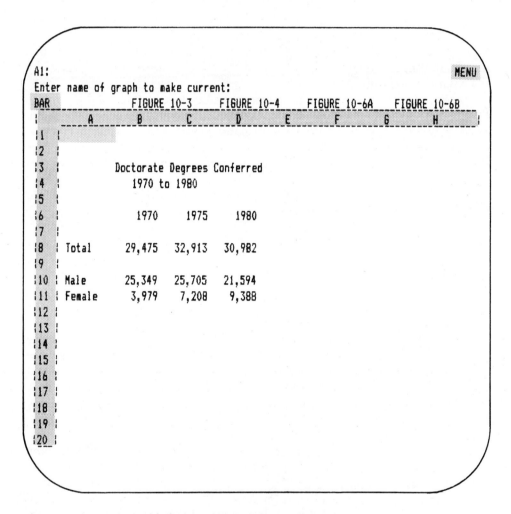

```
A1:                                                                    MENU
Enter name of graph to make current:
BAR                  FIGURE 10-3      FIGURE 10-4     FIGURE 10-6A   FIGURE 10-6B
  !       A         B        C         D        E        F        G        H      !
 !1  !
 !2  !
 !3  !             Doctorate Degrees Conferred
 !4  !                1970 to 1980
 !5  !
 !6  !                1970     1975     1980
 !7  !
 !8  ! Total        29,475   32,913   30,982
 !9  !
 !10 ! Male         25,349   25,705   21,594
 !11 ! Female        3,979    7,208    9,388
 !12 !
 !13 !
 !14 !
 !15 !
 !16 !
 !17 !
 !18 !
 !19 !
 !20 !
```

Figure 10-12. Worksheet with a list of the named graphs displayed in the control panel.

As noted, named graphs are stored along with the worksheet, so they are available whenever you reload the worksheet. If you change the specifications while viewing a named graph, these changes can be made to appear on the graph with the View option (or with the **[GRAPH]** key when you are in Ready mode). *But the changes are not incorporated into the specifications of the named graph unless you use the Name Create option to assign the old name to the new graph.* If you don't rename the graph, the next time you use that particular graph name, 1-2-3 creates a graph from the settings (ranges, titles, legends, etc.) *originally* stored with the graph. A common error is to call up a named graph, make some changes, and then forget to save the changes by reassigning the graph name.

Finally, as previously noted, saving a graph by naming it is *not* the same as saving a graph for printing. To save a graph for printing, you must use the Save option on the main Graph command menu. Before describing that procedure, a few words about the other choices under the Name option: Reset and Delete. Reset clears all assigned graph names. It is a devastating action. Don't use it unless you are certain you want to eliminate *all* graph names. Delete cancels graph names one-by-one. It is the preferred way to eliminate graph specifications that are no longer needed.

Saving Graphs for Printing

To save a graph for printing, begin by displaying it on your monitor. Once displayed, select the Save option from the main Graph command menu. You are then asked to supply a filename. Like all 1-2-3 filenames, this filename must begin with a letter, and it can contain only letters, numbers, and the underline character. The filename cannot exceed eight characters, and it cannot contain blanks. Lotus automatically adds the filename extension .PIC to graph files. The extension indicates a "picture" file containing a graph for printing.

Once a graph has been saved as a .PIC file, further changes to the worksheet such as new data and changes in titles or legends, have **no effect** on the graph as saved for printing. To incorporate changes, you *must* save the modified graph.

If you try to save a graph under an existing filename, you are asked whether you want to replace the existing file. If you are updating a graph, replace the existing file. If you don't want to replace the file, press **[ESC]** to back up one level. Enter a new filename and proceed to save the graph.

PRINTING GRAPHS WITH THE PRINTGRAPH UTILITY

Once you have created and saved a graph as a .PIC file, you are ready to print it or plot it. Once printed, you can cut and paste the graph into a report or you can make additional copies for distribution. In either case, 1-2-3 has a broad range of options available to help make your graphs an effective addition to a memo, a spreadsheet, or an oral presentation.

Since you must end a 1-2-3 work session to print a graph, a common practice is to accumulate all the graphs from a work session and then print all of them once you are finished working with 1-2-3. If you do this, keep a list of the filenames of the graphs you want to print. Your data diskette can contain many .PIC graphs and, without a list, it will be difficult to identify those particular graphs you want to print.

When you are ready to print a graph, Quit the 1-2-3 worksheet and transfer program control to the Lotus Access System. From this menu, select the PrintGraph option, and 1-2-3 prompts you to place the PrintGraph diskette in the A drive. The PrintGraph diskette contains the programs necessary to supply special type fonts, printer configurations, and other parameters necessary to create a printed or plotted copy of a 1-2-3 graph. If you have a hard disk, 1-2-3 will automatically access the PrintGraph programs.

The Main PrintGraph Screen

Once you have loaded the PrintGraph files, 1-2-3 displays the main PrintGraph screen (see Figure 10-13). Like other 1-2-3 screens, the control panel at the top contains a series of choices:

Select   Options   Go   Configure   Align   Page   Quit

The main body of the screen displays the current parameters for use when printing a graph. The parameters displayed in Figure 10-13 on the next page give an excellent overview of the options available for printing 1-2-3 graphs.

Look at the left column. Under the heading Selected Graphs is a *print queue* or list of filenames for those graphs that were selected for printing with the Select option.

The next column contains a list of colors assigned to the overall grid and to each data range. The current configuration is for an Epson FX80 dot-matrix printer, so all color assignments are black. Had a plotter or a color printer been in use, different colors could have been assigned to each element.

```
Copyright 1982, 1983 Lotus Development Corp.  All Rights Reserved.     MENU
-----------------------------------------------------------------------------
Select  Options  Go  Configure  Align  Page  Quit
Select Pictures
=============================================================================
SELECTED GRAPHS    COLORS            SIZE:    HALF            DIRECTORIES

   FIG10_3         Grid:     Black   Left margin:    .750     Pictures
   FIG10_4         A Range:  Black   Top margin:     .395     B:\
   FIG10_6A        B Range:  Black   Width:         6.500     Fonts
   FIG10_6B        C Range:  Black   Height:        4.691     A:\
   FIG10_7         D Range:  Black   Rotation:       .000
                   E Range:  Black                            GRAPHIC DEVICE
                   F Range:  Black   MODES
                                                              Epson FX80/1
                   FONTS             Eject:   No              Parallel
                                     Pause:   No
                   1: Block1                                  PAGE SIZE
                   2: Block1
                                                              Length  11.000
                                                              Width    8.000
```

Figure 10-13. Main PrintGraph screen with the main PrintGraph menu in the control panel. The current selections are displayed in the lower portion of the screen.

Below the colors specifications in the second column is a listing of the fonts to use when printing titles and legends. Lotus lets you choose from four different type fonts: Block, Italic, Roman, and Script. Font 1 is used for the main title, and Font 2 is used for legends and the other titles (sub, X axis, and Y axis).

The next column contains specifications for the size of the printed graph. You can have graphs printed full size or half size, or you can choose the size manually. In Figure 10-13 you can see that Half is the selected graph size, and the parameters for printing a half-size graph on 8-by-11 inch paper are listed.

The next set of specifications, Modes, are listed below the size parameters. The modes are Eject and Pause. If you select Yes for the Eject mode, 1-2-3 ejects each sheet after printing the graph. Selecting No means the printer does not advance to the top of the next page automatically, thus graphs are printed one after another without regard to page breaks.

The Pause mode tells 1-2-3 whether to pause after printing a graph and before printing the next graph in the print queue. If you select No for Pause, 1-2-3 prints graphs one after another without stopping. When the graph size is Half and you have also selected No for Eject, two graphs are printed on each page until all the graphs in the queue have been printed.

The right column in Figure 10-13 contains information about the location of the .PIC files and the files containing the fonts. These and other choices in the right-hand column are changed by selecting Configure from the menu. See Figure 10-14 on the following page for the Configure command tree. You seldom need to change these settings, but if you do and you are using diskettes, the location is a disk drive. If you are using a hard disk, the location will be a directory on the hard disk.

Lotus lets you configure your PrintGraph program to work with a wide range of printers and plotters. The configuration operation is extremely easy to perform. Just select Configure from the main PrintGraph menu and then select the name of your printer from the list displayed on the screen. That's all there is to the configuration process. When you return to the main PrintGraph screen, the name you selected appears in the right column under Graphic Device. If you want to use the changes the next time you load the PrintGraph program, you must save them by selecting Save from the Configuration submenu.

Symphony

You must select your printer and plotter type during the installation procedure you perform when first preparing the Symphony diskettes for use. Unlike 1-2-3, you cannot change printer or plotter types from the PrintGraph utility.

The final piece of information on the main PrintGraph screen is the size of the paper you are using. In Figure 10-13 you can see that 1-2-3 is set up to use standard 8-by-11 inch paper. You can set the size to accommodate the paper size you are using in your printer or your plotter.

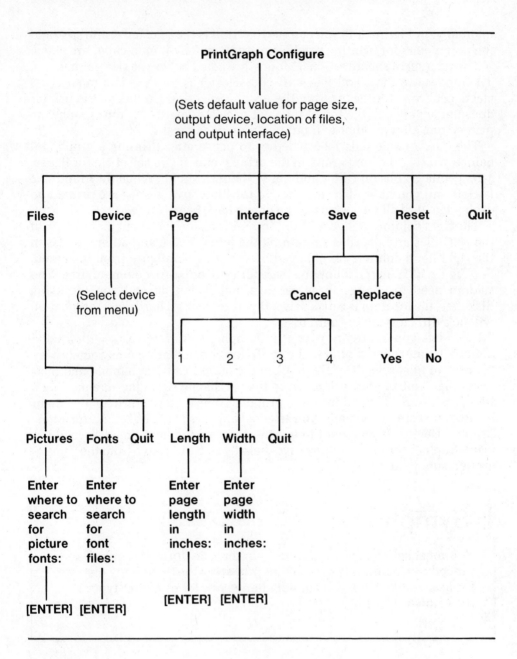

Figure 10-14. The Configure command tree of the PrintGraph utility.

Symphony

The operation of Symphony's PrintGraph utility closely parallels that of 1-2-3's PrintGraph utility. The major changes have to do with the names assigned to the various options. For example, Select is renamed Image-Select, and Colors is renamed Hue. The layout of the main PrintGraph screen has been changed a bit, but anyone familiar with the 1-2-3 screen will have little trouble adjusting. In fact, once you have learned how to print 1-2-3 graphs, you will have little trouble transferring that knowledge to Symphony.

Printing A Graph

After you have set all of the parameters on the main PrintGraph screen to the correct values, printing a 1-2-3 graph is simple. First you must choose the graphs you want to print. Do this by choosing Select from the PrintGraph menu. When you do, the screen changes to display the filenames for all the .PIC files in the Pictures directory (see Figure 10-15 on the following page). As the directions on the right of the screen indicate, the [UP ARROW] and [DOWN ARROW] keys move the highlight from one filename to the next.

When you have highlighted a filename you'd like printed, press the [SPACE BAR] and the filename is marked with a cross-hatch [#]. To preview the graph before printing it, press the [GRAPH] key when the filename is highlighted and the graph will appear on the screen. When you have selected all the files you want to print under the current set of parameters, press [ENTER] to return to the main PrintGraph menu. You can now proceed to actually print the graphs.

Symphony

To preview a Symphony graph, highlight it and press the [DRAW] function key.

Printing a graph is much like printing a worksheet with the Print command. Align tells 1-2-3 that the print head is at the top of a page. It is good practice to issue the Align instruction just before beginning to print a graph.

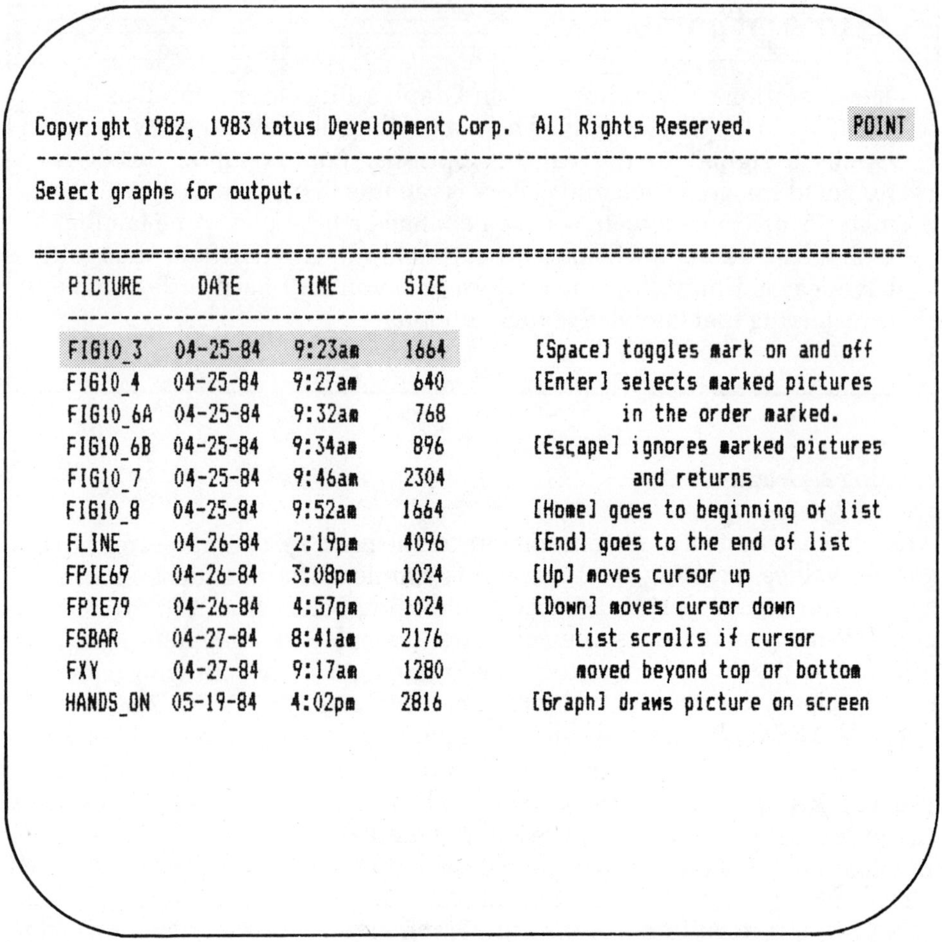

```
Copyright 1982, 1983 Lotus Development Corp.  All Rights Reserved.      POINT
-----------------------------------------------------------------------------
Select graphs for output.


=============================================================================
    PICTURE    DATE     TIME     SIZE
    -------------------------------------
    FIG10_3   04-25-84  9:23am   1664      [Space] toggles mark on and off
    FIG10_4   04-25-84  9:27am    640      [Enter] selects marked pictures
    FIG10_6A  04-25-84  9:32am    768          in the order marked.
    FIG10_6B  04-25-84  9:34am    896      [Escape] ignores marked pictures
    FIG10_7   04-25-84  9:46am   2304          and returns
    FIG10_8   04-25-84  9:52am   1664      [Home] goes to beginning of list
    FLINE     04-26-84  2:19pm   4096      [End] goes to the end of list
    FPIE69    04-26-84  3:08pm   1024      [Up] moves cursor up
    FPIE79    04-26-84  4:57pm   1024      [Down] moves cursor down
    FSBAR     04-27-84  8:41am   2176          List scrolls if cursor
    FXY       04-27-84  9:17am   1280          moved beyond top or bottom
    HANDS_ON  05-19-84  4:02pm   2816      [Graph] draws picture on screen
```

Figure 10-15. When you choose Select from the main PrintGraph menu, the screen is replaced with a listing of all the .PIC files on the current data diskette or picture directory.

The Page option advances the paper to the top of the next page, and the Go option gets the process underway.

After you select Go, 1-2-3 reads in the graph specifications for the first graph in the Selected Graphs list. Fonts are supplied, and after a few moments, your printer or plotter begins creating the first graph in the queue.

To pause in the middle of printing a graph, press the **[CTRL]-[NUM LOCK]** keys. When you are ready to resume printing, press any key, and 1-2-3 finishes printing the graph.

To stop printing a graph altogether, press the **[CTRL]** and **[BREAK]** keys at the same time. Lotus enters Error mode, and the printing process is terminated. To return to Menu mode, press the **[ENTER]** key. You can then correct the problem that caused you to cancel printing. When ready, resume printing by once again selecting Go from the PrintGraph main menu.

HANDS ON: USING THE GRAPH COMMAND

In the last ten chapters, you have learned about the commands and features of Lotus 1-2-3. You know how to use 1-2-3's many tools to construct and use electronic spreadsheets. You know how to create a database and get the most out of the Query, Find and Data Table commands. In this chapter, you have learned to use the 1-2-3 Graph command to create and print graphs. You now have a formidable kit of tools with which to solve almost any problem involving information or numbers and to print or display your conclusions in professional reports, memos, and presentations.

Lotus' individual elements are certainly powerful tools, but when combined, their usefulness is much more than the sum of their parts. The following Hands On exercise uses a graph to present the information generated by the database and the data table constructed in the "Hands On" section in the last chapter (Tables 9-17 and 9-18). The data table in the "Hands On" section of that chapter uses regular worksheet functions to summarize information. These summaries are included in the graph. The Hands On exercise in this chapter combines all the elements of 1-2-3 into a unified solution to a common business problem.

Table 10-1 contains the database and data table constructed in chapter nine. Recall that to construct this table, you simply enter the information into the database, copy the field names to the criterion range, and enter the labels for the first column and the first row of the Two-Way Data Table.

You then enter the Data command and define the input range, the criterion range, and the parameters for the data table. Recall that the two inputs for the data table are the names in columns F and G and the months in rows 11, 12, and 13. They are substituted into the criterion range under Date and Person. The database statistical function in cell E10, @DSUM, calculates the values for the cells in the data table. Standard worksheet @SUM functions in column H and row 15 calculate the totals. For more details about this table's construction, see the "Hands On" section in chapter nine.

TABLE 10-1

Database and data table constructed in Hands On section of Chapter Nine.

```
       A        B        C        D       E        F         G         H
 1
 2         ***INPUT RANGE***                    **CRITERION RANGE**
 3         Month   Person Expenses              Month     Person
 4         ============================
 5    June     Jones    $36.15
 6    July     Smith    $29.54
 7    August   Jones    $15.47                 ***TWO-WAY DATA TABLE***
 8    July     Smith   $161.00                    MONTHLY EXPENSES
 9    June     Smith   $115.31
10    August   Smith    $87.69      1287.7     Smith     Jones    Totals
11    August   Jones    $13.45       June     $379.63   $134.88   $514.51
12    June     Smith   $251.78       July     $190.54   $365.67   $556.21
13    July     Jones     $0.36       August   $188.06    $28.92   $216.98
14    July     Jones   $147.98
15    August   Smith    $36.25       Total    $758.23   $529.47  $1,287.70
16    June     Smith    $12.54
17    June     Jones    $98.73
18    August   Smith    $64.12     Formula in cell E10: @DSUM(A3..C20,2,F3..G4)
19    July     Jones    $91.54
20    July     Jones   $125.79
21
22
23
```

A graph of the information in the data table in Table 10-1 would make that information easier to grasp. The first step in creating a 1-2-3 graph is to select a graph type. Do this by entering the Graph command and choosing the Type option. The available graph options are line, bar, stacked-bar, XY, and pie. A bar graph is used in this Hands On exercise, but you may want to choose one of the other graph types. Switching between graph types is as easy as selecting a different type of graph. Once the data ranges are specified, you will certainly want to try the other graph types.

The second step in creating a 1-2-3 graph is to specify the data ranges. You want your bar graph to show the expenses for Smith and Jones for each month, so the first data range (the A data range) will be F11..F13, the expenses for Smith for June, July, and August. The second data range (the B data range) is G11..G13, the expense information for Jones. Look at the data table (Table

10-1), and you will see that the total expenses for each month have been calculated in column H. To include this information in your graph, designate the range H11..H13 as the C data range.

You have now supplied a graph type and three data ranges. You have the minimum information necessary to draw a 1-2-3 graph, so your next step is to view the graph. Do this by selecting View from the Graph command main menu. View your graph frequently to make sure the options you select are producing a useful graph. If an option doesn't work out, change it until you have something that does. The result of your labors to this point is the graph in Figure 10-16.

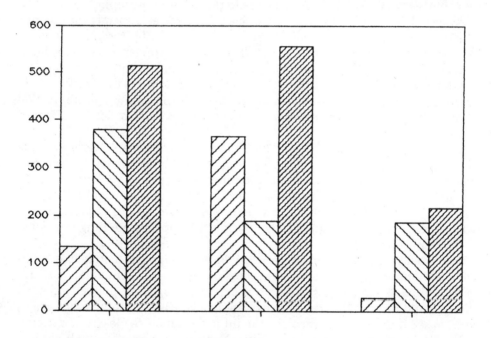

Figure 10-16. Graph based on data table in Table 10-1.

This graph looks fine, but it is a bit difficult to understand without a title, X-axis labels, and legends. Add these descriptive labels to your graph. The particular labels you choose for your graph are those that suit your needs and the purpose to which the graph will be put. If the graph is for personal, analytical use, you may not need to supply a full set of labels, On the other hand, if the graph is to be used as part of a presentation or a report to be circulated throughout your office, you will certainly want to take advantage of 1-2-3's ability to dress up the graph's appearance. Assume your graph will be circulated, so you'll want a professional appearance.

To add titles to your graph, select Options from the main Graph command menu. Then select Titles from the Options submenu. You can type in the titles, or you can specify them by placing a backslash character before a reference to a label cell on your worksheet. A good main title would be the text from cell G8, MONTHLY EXPENSES. To use this as the main title, type \ G8 in response to the prompt for the main title. A good subtitle would be the names of the months; June, July, and August. This text doesn't appear on the table, so type the words in response to the Subtitle prompt.

While still in the Options submenu, select Legends and specify the legends to go with each data range. The legends are Smith for the A range, Jones for the B range, and Total for the C range. These words appear in various places in Table 10-1. Can you find the cells that contain each of these legends?

After you have provided the legends, select Quit from the Options submenu (or press **[ESC]**) and return to the main Graph command menu. You haven't seen the result of your handiwork, so select View to see the effect of your choices (see Figure 10-17).

Are you satisfied, or is something missing from your graph? Something *is* missing because the tick marks on the X-axis don't have any labels. You can guess that the first three graphs apply to June, but a professional graph would provide this information directly. To specify X-axis labels, select X from the main Graph command menu and specify the range of cells containing the words June, July, and August. Can you find the appropriate range in Table 10-1? (It's in column E.)

Your final graph is displayed in Figure 10-18 on page 316. You may want to add additional information. The numbers on the Y-axis, for example, could be formatted to dollars, or the actual expenses for each person for each month could be added to the bars as data labels. Also try some other graph types to see if one of them displays the information more clearly or dramatically. Try as many options as you like. View the graph after each choice. Retain an option when it improves your graph; drop it when it makes the graph cluttered or otherwise difficult to read or understand.

Once you have arrived at a satisfactory specification, remember to save the graph in **two** different ways. Use the Name option from the Graph command menu to assign a name to your graph and preserve the graph specifications for later viewing. To distribute your graph, you need to print it, so it must be saved as a .PIC file with the Save option on the Graph command menu.

If you don't have a color printer or plotter and if you have been viewing the graph in color, you **must** select the B&W option from the Options submenu

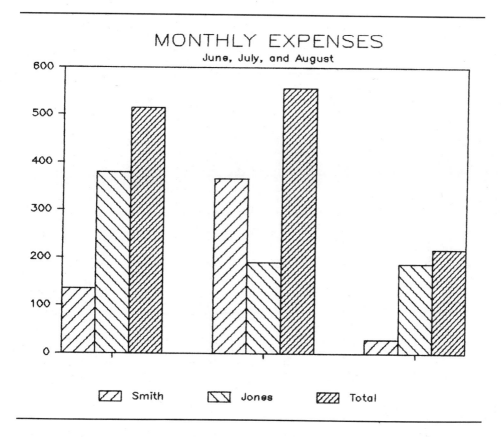

Figure 10-17. Graph from Figure 10-13 after adding titles and legends.

before saving the graph. If you don't save it as a black and white graph, the cross-hatch patterns are not saved, and the printed graph will be difficult to read. If you have a color plotter, you can save a graph as either a B&W graph (with cross-hatching) or as a Color graph. Color graphs are printed with solid colors in each bar.

Whenever you want to use this worksheet, simply retrieve it with the File command. Once the worksheet has been loaded, you don't need to enter the Graph command to display the last specified graph. All you need do is press the **[GRAPH]** key, and the last specified graph appears.

To add additional information to your database, use the Move command or the Worksheet Insert Row command to move the last entry (row 20 in Table 10-1) down the necessary number of rows. Using either command automatically adjusts the range specifications in the @DSUM function (cell E10) to the enlarged input range. After you have entered the new expenses, press

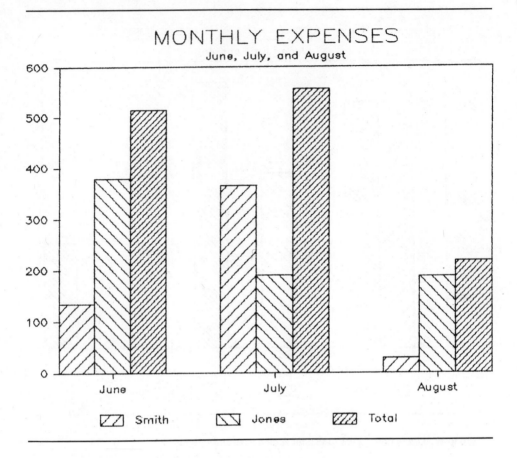

Figure 10-18. Final form of graph based on data table in Table 10-1.

[TABLE], and the data table is recalculated. Next press [GRAPH], and your bar graph is redrawn to reflect the additional information.

To add additional months or sales persons, use the Move command to expand the data table. (You can also use the Insert command, provided using it doesn't affect entries elsewhere on the worksheet.) The specifications for the table as well as the ranges of the other functions adjust automatically. When you redraw the graph, the X-axis labels (the months) reflect new months because those labels were entered as a range and that range specification adjusts automatically. However, the legends, which refer to salespersons, aren't entered as a range. They are entered individually, so you may have to respecify the legends. The last step is to edit the subtitle to include new months.

Remember that once these changes have been made, you *must* rename the graph so the new specifications replace the old ones, and you must save the new graph as a .PIC file for printing. If you don't rename the graph, the next time you press the **[GRAPH]** key or select the name of the original graph, you will get the original specifications. Updated information is, of course, used to draw the graph, but new elements, such as the legends and subtitles, are not included. To print the new graph, you must save the new graph as a .PIC file.

In this "Hands On" section, you have seen the easy, natural integration of the graphics, database, and spreadsheet functions of 1-2-3. As you become familiar with these three functions, you will find many opportunities for creating worksheets that integrate different features. In fact, you will soon find the separation between spreadsheet, database, and graphics receding into the background as Lotus becomes an integrated decision-support tool, an easy-to-use tool that is a natural extension of your analytical mind. Use this tool to organize information, analyze problems, and prepare the results for display and distribution. At that point, doing your job with Lotus 1-2-3 will become as easy as...well...1, 2, 3.

SELF-TEST

QUESTIONS

1. What are the two general purposes to which a 1-2-3 graph may be put?
2. What two pieces of information are required to draw a 1-2-3 graph?
3. What information goes in the X data range?
4. The pie chart plots information from only one data range. Which data range is it?
5. What is the difference between saving a graph with the Save option and naming it with the Name option?
6. Can you view graphs saved with the Save option?
7. If you change the specifications for a named graph, are the changes saved automatically?
8. What does the **[GRAPH]** key do?
9. What filename extension is applied to graphs saved for printing?
10. Assuming you have a color monitor, how do you get 1-2-3 to display your graph in color?

ANSWERS

1. Graphs can be used for *analysis* or for *presentation*. Analytical graphs give quick insights into the information on a spreadsheet. Presentation-quality graphs are used in memos, reports and presentations to make your points clearly and dramatically.
2. A graph type and at least one data range.
3. On bar, stacked-bar, and line graphs, X-axis labels are specified by means of the X data range. On XY graphs, the X data range is used to specify a range of data. On pie graphs, the X data range is not used at all.
4. The A data range. If data has been specified in other ranges, it is ignored when the pie chart is drawn.
5. Graphs saved with the Save option can be printed or plotted with the PrintGraph program. Graphs named with the Name option can be viewed again by selecting the graph name with the Graph Name Use option.
6. Graphs saved with the Save option cannot be viewed from within the 1-2-3 program. However, a saved graph can be viewed before printing from within the Select option of the PrintGraph program.
7. No. It is most important to realize that modifications to a named graph are not saved unless the changed graph itself is assigned a name.
8. When 1-2-3 is in Ready mode, pressing the **[GRAPH]** function key displays the last defined graph. Within the Select option of the PrintGraph utility, pressing **[GRAPH]** displays the highlighted graph.
9. Graphs saved for printing are assigned the .PIC extension.
10. To display a graph in color, select Color from the Options submenu.

EPILOGUE

DO YOU REALLY NEED A SYMPHONY WHEN YOU CAN MAKE SUCH BEAUTIFUL MUSIC WITH A TRIO?

As you know by now, Lotus also has a "big brother" called *Symphony* which adds two more features to 1-2-3's three modes—spreadsheet, database, and graphics. Those two features are: word processing, and telecommunications. Like 1-2-3, Symphony is built on the framework established by its spreadsheet mode. However, Symphony's spreadsheet is potentially much large than 1-2-3's, more than two million cells in 256 columns and 8,192 rows.

Symphony also has the ability to create and manage windows. You can have one mode—word processing, for example—operating in one window, and another mode—spreadsheet—operating in another. You can expand or contract windows, and you can move from window to window (hence, from mode to mode) at the press of a single key. Symphony can use cell references to manipulate label cells in the same way 1-2-3 manipulates value cells. With Symphony you can have text returned from a lookup table, and you can specify functional relationships that combine text from two or more cells into one long label. Finally, Symphony has time functions (hour, minute, and second) as well as data functions, and it has the ability to deal with many foreign languages and international currencies.

Is Symphony Less Than the Sum of Its Parts?

It is impossible to list all the ways Symphony goes 1-2-3 one better, but on a point by point comparison Symphony is almost always superior to 1-2-3. Each feature is more powerful, has more options, or is more elegantly designed than the corresponding feature in 1-2-3. Furthermore, Symphony gives you powers—word processing, telecommunications, database forms generation, and windows—that are simply not available in 1-2-3.

Despite this dominance of features (or rather because of it) you may discover Symphony to be less than the sum of its parts. Symphony's power comes at a price. Simply put, there is a trade-off between extra features and ease of use. For example, 1-2-3 has about 200 options or choices that you can make while using the program; Symphony has over 500.

Windows are another example. They are wonderful if you need them, and if you are willing to spend the time required to master the commands used to create and manage them. Likewise with telecommunications and word processing. Both are excellent features.

In theory, you can ignore those parts of Symphony that you do not need. And if you can successfully resist the temptation to stray from your areas of competence, then you can avoid the pitfalls associated with the need to master a large number of commands. But this temptation will be difficult to resist once you know that somewhere in Symphony there is a function or a feature that will help solve a particular problem. Of course, if you do resist the temptation, you will not be taking full advantage of Symphony.

In addition to the problems generated by a large number of command choices, Symphony costs several hundred dollars more than 1-2-3. The price difference, however, understates the actual difference in cost. Symphony requires a minimum of 320K of Random Access Memory (RAM) compared to 1-2-3's requirement of a minimum of 192K, so you must buy an expansion board and more memory to use Symphony. But the difference doesn't stop there. A machine with the same amount of RAM (320K, for example) can build and store a larger worksheet with 1-2-3 than it can with Symphony because 1-2-3's program code is smaller and, hence, it leaves more RAM for worksheet construction.

How Big a Band Do You Really Need?

In the final analysis, the decision of whether to move up to Symphony or to stay with 1-2-3 comes down to an evaluation only you can make. Do you need Symphony's additional features? And if you do, are you willing to spend the time and energy required to master the program? If your answer is "Yes" to *both* questions, then Symphony is the program for you.

On the other hand, if you are like many users, and your needs are met by the features of 1-2-3, then your answer should be "No." In this case, choosing Symphony over 1-2-3 would be like buying a Cadillac when all you need to get around town is a Honda. By using 1-2-3 you will have a powerful, elegant spreadsheet program at your disposal. And you will avoid the many, possibly confusing, choices Symphony presents to the user who doesn't need to make a loud noise with all those instruments.

APPENDIX A
KEY ASSIGNMENTS

Throughout *Lotus™ 1-2-3™ From A to Z* references have been made to specific keys to press because specific instructions are easier to understand and easier to follow. However, a dilemma arose when choosing key names for these instructions because 1-2-3 is available on many different computers with many different keyboards.

Should key names from a specific machine be adopted? Or should all of the keys for the more popular machines be listed for each instruction? The first alternative was considered too narrow, the second too cumbersome. Instead, it was decided to use generalized, easy to understand key names. The instructions would then be clear, and any translation required for a specific machine would be easy and natural.

Examples of these generalized key names are **[ENTER]** for the key that tells 1-2-3 to move text or a value into a spreadsheet cell, and **[SHIFT]** for the key that shifts keys to their upper case mode. Likewise, "function keys" have been referred to by their functional name rather than by a function key designation on a particular machine. Thus **[HELP]** and **[EDIT]** were used, instead of F1 and F2 which are the particular key names on the IBM PC and many other computers.

Even though the exact set of key names used in the text doesn't appear on any specific machine, they do closely parallel the key names used on the IBM Personal Computer keyboard. This was a conscious choice since microcomputers with an IBM PC-style keyboard account for a substantial majority of machines using Lotus 1-2-3. If you are using one of these machines, you will find the instructions in the text particularly easy to follow.

Lotus 1-2-3 is becoming available on more and more microcomputers and many of these machines have keyboards that are quite different from the IBM-style keyboard. To help you translate the generalized instructions used in this book to specific keystrokes for specific machines, Steve Miller, the

Publishing Coordinator at Lotus Development Corporation, has prepared a guide to keyboard assignments on the most popular machines. Those assignments are reproduced on the following pages.

The first column on each page contains a listing of the key names used in this book. Succeeding columns contain the keystroke or strokes required to produce the same action on a particular machine. In general, machines with relatively few keys require more keystrokes. For example, instead of a single key to produce the **[{]**, the Grid Compass requires you to press three keys: **[CODE]-[SHIFT]-[,]**.

In the following listing, names apply to specific key names on specific machines. Where machines use symbols rather than key names, those symbols have been reproduced.

Lotus 1-2-3, version 1A, is currently available on the following machines:

IBM PC	TI PROFESSIONAL COMPUTER	GRID COMPASS
IBM XT	WANG PROFESSIONAL COMPUTER	HP 110 & 150
IBM 3270	BYTEC HYPERION	TANDY MODEL 2000
COMPAQ	DEC RAINBOW 100 & 100+	IBM PCjr
COLUMBIA MPC	CONVERGENT TECHNOLOGIES'	AT&T PC 6300
	NGEN WORKSTATION	
	ZENITH Z-100 & Z-150	

Lotus also runs on machines that are 100% IBM PC compatible.

Since 1-2-3 is being made available on more and more microcomputers, you must check with your Lotus 1-2-3 dealer for the latest list of machines. One thing you can be sure of, whatever machine Lotus runs on, the program itself presents the same screen appearance, the same range of functions and commands, and the same elegant structure and remarkable ease of use.

GENERIC 1-2-3	SYMBOL USED IN TEXT	IBM PC, IBM XT, COMPAQ and other IBM compatible computers
Enter	[ENTER]	[←]
Cursor Control		
Up Arrow	[UPARROW]	[↑]
Down Arrow	[DOWNARROW]	[↓]
Left Arrow	[LEFTARROW]	[←]
Right Arrow	[RIGHTARROW]	[→]
Big Up	[PgUp]	PgUp
Big Down	[PgDn]	PgDn
Big Right	[TAB]	[⇆]
Big Left	[SHIFT]-[TAB]	[⇧]-[⇆]
End	[END]	End
Home	[HOME]	Home
Function Keys		
Help	[HELP]	F1
Edit	[EDIT]	F2
Name	[NAME]	F3
Absolute	[ABS]	F4
GoTo	[GOTO]	F5
Window	[WINDOW]	F6
Query	[QUERY]	F7
Table	[TABLE]	F8
Calc	[CALC]	F9
Graph	[GRAPH]	F10
Other Keys		
Escape	[ESC]	Esc
Break	[CTRL]-[BREAK]	Ctrl-Break
Delete	[DEL]	Del
Backspace	[BKSP]	[←]
Caps Lock	[CAPS LOCK]	Caps Lock
Num Lock	[NUM LOCK]	Num Lock
Scroll Lock	[SCROLL LOCK]	Scroll Lock
Shift	[SHIFT]	[⇧]
Alt	[ALT]	Alt
Macro Step	[ALT]-[F1]	Alt-F1
Space	[SPACE BAR]	[space bar]
\	[\ ]	\
{	[{]	{
}	[}]	}
~	[~]	~
¦	[¦]	¦

SYMBOL USED IN TEXT	TEXAS INSTRUMENTS PROFESSIONAL COMPUTER	WANG PROFESSIONAL
[ENTER]	RETURN	RETURN or EXEC
Cursor Control		
[UP ARROW]	[▲]	[↑]
[DOWN ARROW]	[▼]	[↓]
[LEFT ARROW]	[◄]	[←]
[RIGHT ARROW]	[►]	[→]
[PgUp]	ALT-[▲]	SHIFT-[↑]
[PgDn]	ALT-[▼]	SHIFT-[↓]
[TAB]	TAB or ALT-[►]	TAB or SHIFT-[→]
[SHIFT]-[TAB]	SHIFT-TAB or ALT-[◄]	BACKTAB or SHIFT-[←]
[END]	F12	NEXT/END
[HOME]	HOME	HOME
Function Keys		
[HELP]	F1	HELP
[EDIT]	F2	2/
[NAME]	F3	3
[ABS]	F4	4
[GOTO]	F5	GO TO or 5/GoTo
[WINDOW]	F6	6
[QUERY]	F7	7
[TABLE]	F8	8
[CALC]	F9	9
[GRAPH]	F10	10
Other Keys		
[ESC]	ESC	CANCEL or 12/ESCAPE
[CTRL]-[BREAK]	CTRL-BREAK	SHIFT CANCEL
[DEL]	DEL	DELETE
[BKSP]	BACKSPACE	BACKSPACE or ERASE
[CAPS LOCK]	CAPS LOCK	LOCK
[NUM LOCK]	not available	not available
[SCROLL LOCK]	F11/Scroll	11/SCROLL LOCK
[SHIFT]	SHIFT	SHIFT
[ALT]	ALT	GL/ALT
[ALT]-[F1]	ALT-F1	SHIFT HELP
[SPACE BAR]	**[space bar]** or SPAC	**[space bar]**
[\ ]	\	2ND /
[{]	{	2ND [
[}]	}	2ND]
[~]	~	2ND -
[:]	¦	2ND !

SYMBOL USED IN TEXT	IBM 3270	VICTOR 9000
[ENTER]	[↵]	RETURN
Cursor Control		
[UP ARROW]	[↑]	[↑]
[DOWN ARROW]	[↓]	[↓]
[LEFT ARROW]	[←]	[←]
[RIGHT ARROW]	[→]	[→]
[PgUp]	PgUp	SHIFT-[↑]
[PgDn]	PgDn	SHIFT-[↓]
[TAB]	[→] or Ctrl [→]	TAB or SHIFT-[→]
[SHIFT]-[TAB]	[↑][→] or Ctrl-[←]	SHIFT TAB or SHIFT-[←]
[END]	End	WORD-[→]
[HOME]	Home	WORD-[←]
Function Keys		
[HELP]	PF1	1
[EDIT]	PF2	2
[NAME]	PF3	3
[ABS]	PF4	4
[GOTO]	PF5	5
[WINDOW]	PF6	6
[QUERY]	PF7	7
[TABLE]	PF8	8
[CALC]	PF9	9
[GRAPH]	PF10	10
Other Keys		
[ESC]	Esc	[♀]
[CTRL]-[BREAK]	Break	CLR/HOME
[DEL]	Del	DEL
[BKSP]	[←]	BACKSPACE
[CAPS LOCK]	Caplk	LOCK
[NUM LOCK]	Numlk	not available
[SCROLL LOCK]	Scrlk	ALT SCRL
[SHIFT]	[↑]	SHIFT
[ALT]	Alt	ALT
[ALT]-[F1]	Alt PF1	ALT 1/Help
[SPACE BAR]	[space bar]	[space bar]
[\ ]	\	\
[{]	{	{
[}]	}	}
[~]	~	~
[¦]	¦	¦

SYMBOL USED IN TEXT	ZENITH Z-100	GRID COMPASS
[ENTER]	RETURN or ENTER	RETURN
Cursor Control		
[UP ARROW]	[↑]	[↑]
[DOWN ARROW]	[↓]	[↓]
[LEFT ARROW]	[←]	[←]
[RIGHT ARROW]	[→]	[→]
[PgUp]	SHIFT-[↑]	CODE-[↑]
[PgDn]	SHIFT-[↓]	CODE-[↓]
[TAB]	TAB	TAB or CTRL-[←]
[SHIFT]-[TAB]	SHIFT TAB	SHIFT TAB or CTRL-[　]
[END]	F11 or DEL LINE	CODE-TAB or CODE-SHIFT-[↓]
[HOME]	HOME	CODE-SHIFT-[↑]
Function Keys		
[HELP]	F1	CODE-1
[EDIT]	F2	CODE-2
[NAME]	F3	CODE-3
[ABS]	F4	CODE-4
[GOTO]	F5	CODE-5
[WINDOW]	F6	CODE-6
[QUERY]	F7	CODE-7
[TABLE]	F8	CODE-8
[CALC]	F9	CODE-9
[GRAPH]	F10	CODE-10
Other Keys		
[ESC]	ESC	ESC
[CTRL]-[BREAK]	SHIFT BREAK	CODE-CTRL-[↓]
[DEL]	DELETE	CODE[-]
[BKSP]	BACKSPACE	BACK SPACE
[CAPS LOCK]	CAPS LOCK	SHIFT ESC
[NUM LOCK]	not available	not available
[SCROLL LOCK]	f12	not available
[SHIFT]	SHIFT	SHIFT
[ALT]	CTRL SHIFT	CODE
[SHIFT]-[F1]	SHIFT F1	CODE-SHIFT-1
[SPACE BAR]	[space bar]	[space bar]
[\ ]	\	CODE-SHIFT
[}]	}	CODE-SHIFT-[,]
[{]	{	CODE-SHIFT-[.]
[~]	~	CODE-[;]
[¦]	¦	CODE-SHIFT-[;]

SYMBOL USED IN TEXT	HP 150	HYPERION
&ENTER]	RETURN	RTN
Cursor Control		
[UP ARROW]	[▲]	[↑]
[DOWN ARROW]	[▼]	[↓]
[LEFT ARROW]	[◄]	[←]
[RIGHT ARROW]	[►]	[→]
[PgUp]	Prev or CTRL-[▲]	PGUP
[PgDn]	Next or CTRL-[▼]	PGDN
[TAB]	Tab or Ctrl-[►]	TAB or CTRL-[→]
[SHIFT]-[TAB]	Shift-Tab or Ctrl-[◄]	SHIFT-TAB or CTRL-[←]
[END]	Select	END
[HOME]	[↖]	HOME
Function Keys		
[HELP]	f1	F1
[EDIT]	f2	F2
[NAME]	f3	F3
[ABS]	f4	F4
[GOTO]	f5	F5
[WINDOW]	f6	F6
[QUERY]	f7	F7
[TABLE]	f8	F8
[CALC]	/Calc	F9
[GRAPH]	/Graph	F10
Other Keys		
[ESC]	ESC	ESC
[CTRL]-[BREAK]	Break or Shift-Stop	CTRL BREAK
[DEL]	Delete Char	DEL
[BKSP]	Backspace	RUBOUT
[CAPS LOCK]	Caps	CAPS LOCK
[NUM LOCK]	not available	NUM LOCK
[SCROLL LOCK]	/Scroll Lock	BRK
[SHIFT]	Shift	SHIFT
[ALT]	CTRL-Shift	ALT
[SHIFT]-[F1]	Shift-f1	ALT-F1
[SPACE BAR]	[space bar]	[space bar]
[\ ]	\	\
[}]	{	{
[{]	}	}
[~]	~	~
[¦]	¦	¦

SYMBOL USED	DEC RAINBOW
IN TEXT	
[ENTER]	Return or Enter
Cursor Control	
[UP ARROW]	[⬆]
[DOWN ARROW]	[⬇]
[LEFT ARROW]	[⬅]
[RIGHT ARROW]	[➡]
[PgUp]	Prev Screen or Shift-[⬆]
[PgDn]	Next Screen or Shift-[⬇]
[TAB]	Tab
[SHIFT]-[TAB]	Shift Tab
[END]	Select/End
[HOME]	Find/Home
Function Keys	
[HELP]	Help
[EDIT]	Do
[NAME]	Name
[ABS]	Abs
[GOTO]	Go To
[WINDOW]	Window
[QUERY]	PF1
[TABLE]	PF2
[CALC]	PF3
[GRAPH]	PF4
Other Keys	
[ESC]	F11
[CTRL]-[BREAK]	Break
[DEL]	Remove
[BKSP]	[⌫] or F12
[CAPS LOCK]	Lock
[NUM LOCK]	not available
[SCROLL LOCK]	Addtnl Options
[SHIFT]	Shift
[ALT]	Ctrl-Shift
[SHIFT]-[F1]	Shift-Help
[SPACE BAR]	[space bar]
[\ ]	\
[{]	{
[}]	}
[~]	~
[:]	
:	

APPENDIX B
THE TYPING ALTERNATIVE

OVERVIEW

Lotus 1-2-3 has an important advanced feature that can make repetitive typing tasks easier and automate any worksheet operation. This feature goes by a number of names: *typing alternative, keyboard macro,* or *macro,* for short. It is simply a series of text characters that 1-2-3 understands as instructions in exactly the same way the program understands typing a key as an instruction (hence typing "alternative"). For example, if the characters "/C" are found in a typing alternative, they will instruct 1-2-3 to enter the slash command Copy. The letters "WRITE", which do not define a command or a function, would appear on the entry line as if you had typed.

The instructions in a typing alternative can be *any* series of key strokes. Hence, it can reproduce any action you can produce by pressing keys on the keyboard; copying cells, specifying ranges, entering letters, setting up the printer, printing worksheets, or saving files. The list is as great as the list of commands and functions available with 1-2-3. And therein lies the great power of the typing alternative—it's an electronic you. Anything you can do, it can do faster, more efficiently, and without error.

The typing alternative is actually a kind of computer programming language, and like any computer language, it is very, very *literal*. You must give the typing alternative exact instructions, so you must know *exactly* what keys are pressed to achieve each action. As noted, the instructions are entered as text (you must force the text entry if necessary), and you must be aware of non-displaying keys like the space bar, the function keys, and the **[ENTER]** key. To help out, 1-2-3 has assigned particular names to many keys.

Because the **[ENTER]** key is the most often used special key, Lotus has assigned that key a character of its own: the tilde **[~]**. Whenever 1-2-3 encounters a tilde in a keyboard macro, it acts as if the **[ENTER]** key has been pressed. All other named keys are placed in brackets, {}. (See Table B-1 for a list.)

TABLE B-1

The special designations for named keys for use with the Typing Alternative.

TYPING ALTERNATIVE DESIGNATION	DESCRIPTION
(~)	**[ENTER]**
{Esc}	**[ESC]**
{Up}	**[UP ARROW]**
{Down}	**[DOWN ARROW]**
{Right}	**[RIGHT ARROW]**
{Left}	**[LEFT ARROW]**
{Home}	**[HOME]**
{End}	**[END]**
{PgUp}	**[PgDn]**
{Bs}	**[BKSP]**
{Del}	**[DEL]**
{Edit}	**[EDIT]**
{Abs}	**[ABS]**
{Name}	**[NAME]**
{GoTo}	**[GOTO]**
{Window}	**[WINDOW]**
{Table}	**[TABLE]**
{Graph}	**[GRAPH]**
{Query}	**[QUERY]**
{Calc}	**[CALC]**
{?}	Pause for manual input until user presses **[ENTER]**.

Symphony

Symphony's Typing Alternative has one particular feature whose power will be immediately apparent to anyone who has tried to construct a 1-2-3 macro. Symphony can *learn* your key strokes as you make them. To use this feature, you specify a Learn range and then you press **[ALT]-[LEARN]**. After that, Symphony copies keystrokes as they are typed into the appropriate cells in the Learn range. This ability to "learn" keystrokes as you type them makes the specification of a set of macro commands considerably easier with Symphony than with 1-2-3.

Since Symphony has many more special function keys than does 1-2-3, it also has a correspondingly longer list of special named key indicators. Symphony has other features. For example, you can specify several repetitions of the same key stroke, {**Left**} for example, as {**Left 5**} without having to repeat the entire command the required number of times. You can also assign macros to function keys (1-2-3 limits you to the keys A to Z). In addition to these examples, Symphony has a large library of specialized macro commands. Some manage display and string (label) functions; others are used to manage tele-communications links. All in all, Symphony gives you a set of macro commands and functions to match the power and elegance of the rest of the program.

There are several commands that are unique to the typing alternative. One is a question mark in brackets {?}. Whenever this character is encountered, 1-2-3 pauses and lets you enter information from the keyboard. You can type whatever you want, and execution of the keyboard macro continues at the next press of the **[ENTER]** key. A typical use of {?} is to pause in the middle of an entry so you can supply a needed piece of information.

Lotus also provides a number of commands for use only within a keyboard macro. These include an If function for branching, a GoTo function for changing the order of execution of a macro (not to be confused with the **[GOTO]** function key which moves the worksheet cursor), a Quit function for ending execution of a macro, and a Menu function for creating custom menus. Each of the **/X** commands is explained in detail in Table B-2 on the following page.

TABLE B-2

Lotus provides a set of /X commands for use within a keyboard macro. Note that the tilde at the end of some commands is part of the command and must be entered in the keyboard macro.

/X COMMAND	DESCRIPTION
/XIformula~	Formula contains a logical comparison. If the comparison is TRUE, continue processing on the same line; if FALSE, move down one line and continue processing.
/XGlocation~	Transfers processing within the keyboard macro to the specified location. Doesn't move the worksheet cursor.
/XQ	Terminates execution of the keyboard macro.
/XCrange~	Transfers processing to a subroutine in the specified range.
/XR	Returns processing to the main keyboard macro after transfer to a subroutine.
/XNmessage~range~	Displays a message in the control panel and accepts a number input which is placed in the range.
/XLmessage~range~	Displays a message in the control panel and accepts a label input which is placed in the range.
/XMrange~	Displays a user-defined menu from the specified location in the control panel.
[ALT] - [HELP]	In this mode, a macro is executed one step at a time. This is helpful in discovering mistakes.

Source: *Lotus 1-2-3 Manual*, Lotus Development Corporation, Cambridge, Massachusetts, 1983.

Once you have created the macro, the next step is to use the Range Name Create command to assign a special range name to the cell containing the first instruction. This special name *must* consist of a back slash $< \backslash >$ and one of the letters of the alphabet. The effect is to assign the macro to one of the letter keys.

If, for example, you name a macro $\backslash$ A, the macro will be assigned to the "A" key on the keyboard. In addition to the letters, the number zero [0], can also be used to name a macro (as in $\backslash$ 0). Macros with the $\backslash$ 0 name are special macros. They will automatically execute as soon as the worksheet containing them is loaded into your computer's memory.

To use a macro with a name other than \ 0, you just press **[ALT]** and the appropriate letter key. For example, to execute the macro assigned to the "A" key you would press **[ALT]-[A]**. Lotus then begins to read the keyboard macro and to execute the instructions. It begins with the first cell containing the macro, and it executes keystrokes in that cell from left to right until it runs out of characters. (Up to 240 characters can be stored in a single cell.)

When 1-2-3 completes the keystrokes in the first cell, it moves to the cell below. If there are more keystrokes to execute, it keeps going. It repeats this process, executing keystrokes in a cell and then moving down one cell, until it reaches a *non-label cell* or executes the /XQ (Quit) command. At that point, 1-2-3 stops processing instructions, exits the typing alternative, and returns control to the keyboard. The non-label cell ending the macro may contain a value, or it may simply be a blank cell.

In summary, to create a keyboard macro:

1. Enter the text which describes the instructions. Enter this text into successive cells in a column. All cells must be text cells so force text entries when necessary.
2. Name the first cell in the column with the Range Name Create command. The name must be a backslash **[\ ]**, followed by one of the twenty-six letters of the alphabet or, for automatic macros, the number zero.
3. To execute the macro, position the worksheet cursor in the appropriate cell; then press the **[ALT]** key and the letter assigned to the macro.

Finding Mistakes in Your Macros: [ALT]-[HELP]

A problem exists with Lotus' macro facility because you must write the macro from *memory*. You must remember that /CA1...A3∿D4∿ is the correct sequence of key strokes (with **[∿]** substituted for **[ENTER]**) required to copy the range A1..A3 into the column beginning with D4. One misplaced letter, one omitted tilde, and the macro will not execute.

Everyone makes errors when entering all but the simplest keyboard macros. To find the errors in your macro, Lotus has a feature you will find invaluable. It is the single step function. When you press **[ALT]-[HELP]** the word **STEP** appears at the bottom of the screen and the letters **SST** appear in the mode indicator at the top. *Lotus is ready to execute any of the macros on the current worksheet one character at a time.*

To select the macro you want to step through, press **[ALT]** and the appropriate letter key. Then press any of the keys on the keyboard and the first step or letter of the macro will execute. Each time you press a key, another step in the macro executes, and you can see exactly what is happening by observing the control panel and the screen. If you have made an error in your macro, 1-2-3 will ''beep'' when it reaches it. An error message is displayed, and the program refuses to go any further. Press any key, and you will be out of the step-by-step execution mode. You can then move the worksheet cursor to the appropriate cell in the macro. Then use the **[EDIT]** key to edit in the correction.

You can continue to test other macros on the current worksheet until you are satisfied that they are all error free. When you are ready to exit the step mode, press the **[ALT]-[HELP]** keys a second time. The word STEP disappears from the bottom of the screen and the letters SST disappear from the mode indicator.

HANDS ON: TYPING ALTERNATIVE

When constructing worksheets, you will often find that you are typing a particular phrase or function over and over again. For example, a database often has a field for the date, and each time you enter the data function, you have to type **@DATE(**. If you make many entries during the same month, October 1984 for example, you will have to type **@DATE(85,10** over and over. A short keyboard macro can automate this typing task and reduce the number of keystrokes you have to type.

Table B-3 shows the macro (in cell A1) and a simple database of orders. To create the macro, the first thing you'd do is enter *as text* **@DATE(85,10,{?}~**. Notice that the last character is the tilde. It will be interpreted by 1-2-3 as **[ENTER]**. Also, notice that {?} has been inserted in the place where the number of the day will go. When 1-2-3 executes this macro, it pauses after entering **@DATE(84,10**, and allows you to supply the day number from the key board. After you press **[ENTER]**, 1-2-3 completes the date formula by adding the closing parenthesis and executing **[ENTER]**.

Now that you have entered the macro as text, you must name it with a name that is a backslash followed by one of the letters A to Z. One of the most convenient names to use for a macro is \ **Z** because the **[Z]** key is close to the **[ALT]** key, and the two keys are easy to press together.

To use this macro, move the worksheet cursor to a cell into which you wish to place a date (cell A10, for example). Then invoke the macro by typing **[ALT] -[Z]**. As you do, the characters **@DATE(84,10** appear on the command line, and 1-2-3 pauses for you to enter the day number. Do so, press **[ENTER]**, and the date formula appears in the current cell. A formula that would have taken more than a dozen keystrokes to create and enter has been completed with only four or five.

TABLE B-3

Worksheet with macro in cell A1.

```
|       A         B          C         D        E         F        |
|1 | @DATE(85,10,{?})` 
|2 |
|3 |
|4 |
|5 |
|6 |              INVOICE
|7 |   DATE       NUMBER      ITEM      PRICE   NUMBER    AMOUNT
|8 | ================================================================
|9 |  10-Oct-85      142     Ribbons    $7.36      24     $176.64
|10|                 253       Paper   $35.25       3     $105.75
|11|                 267   Diskettes    $2.70      40     $108.00
|12|                 189       Cases    $1.50      10      $15.00
|13|
|14|
|15|
|16|
|17|
|18|
|19|
|20|
```

The preceding example shows how you can use the typing alternative to simplify repetitive typing tasks. The next example shows how to automate a more complicated process. The example also illustrates the use of several of the special macro functions.

In this example, you will create a keyboard macro that takes names and addresses from an address list database, reformats the information into the layout appropriate for a mailing label, and automatically prints the label. The macro then moves on through the list of names and addresses, printing each label in turn, until it reaches the last entry in the list. Then the macro stops, and control is returned to the keyboard.

The general plan is to create a master mailing label (address and return address) and then to write a typing alternative which first copies each address into the mailing label and then prints the label.

To begin, you need some data. Table B-4 gives what you need: a dozen hypothetical addresses. You might have entered these addresses directly into the cells, perhaps before incorporating them into a database. Or you might use the Data Query Extract command to select them from a database according to a particular criteria.

TABLE B-4
The names and address to be used in the mailing labels created by the Typing Alternative.

	A	B	C	D
1				
2	NAME	STREET ADDRESS	CITY/STATE	ZIP CODE
3	David Moss	946 Piedmont Ave.	Oakland, CA	94832
4	Erin Williams	915 Contra Costa Ave.	Berkeley, CA	94707
5	Mary Stewart	5842 3rd Avenue	Irvine, CA	92714
6	Samuel Burkhart	320 Cedar St. Apt 7	Chestnut Hill, Mass.	2167
7	Jordan Black	1030 Apple Way	Renton, WA	98055
8	Ann Witherspoon	54 Burbank Avenue	North Hollywood, CA	91603
9	Stephen Summers	P.O. Box 3542	Alexandria, VA	22301
10	Peter Andrews	12092 North N Street	Fargo, ND	58102
11	Sally Smith	3050 Winter Street	West Bloomfield, Mich.	48033
12	Robert Parker	31464 Riverside Drive	Plano, TX	75074
13	Fisher Montrose	605 Buena Vista Way	Ellenwood, GA	30049
14	Charlie Chaplan	P.O. Box 1328	Boca Raton, FL	33432
15				
16				
17				
18				
19				
20				

Table B-5 shows the master mailing label. It is located in columns E to H and in rows 22 to 28 of the worksheet. The return address is typed in since that doesn't change from label to label. Table B-6 contains a listing of the keyboard macro. It is entered into the worksheet beginning with cell H5.

TABLE B-5

The keyboard macro copies the elements of the address into the appropriate cells in Columns G.

```
|     E               F              G              H         |
|19 |                                                        |
|20 |            MASTER MAILING LABEL                        |
|21 |                                                        |
|22 |  MicroOZ                                               |
|23 |  Frank L. Baum, President                              |
|24 |  Emerald City, Kansas                                  |
|25 |                      -------------------                |
|26 |                      :Charlie Chaplin :                |
|27 |                      :P.O. Box 1328   :                |
|28 |                      :Boca Raton, FL  :                |
|29 |                      :        33432   :                |
|30 |                      -------------------                |
```

TABLE B-6

Keyboard macro for printing address labels.

LINE-BY-LINE DESCRIPTION OF MACRO	KEYBOARD MACRO
Sets up printer	/PPCAOS \ 015∿OUQRf22.g28∿Q
Copy address to label area	/C∿g25∿{right}/C∿g26∿{right}/C∿g27∿{right}/C∿g28
Prints, and advances three lines	/PPLLLGQ
Move to next address	{down}
Copies Zip Code to cell F16	/C∿f16∿
Tests for more addresses	/Xif16 < > 0∿{end}{left}/XGh6
DONE!	DONE!!!!∿
Non-label cell. Macro stops.	

You are ready to use the macro as soon as you have entered the instructions and have assigned the macro a name. Since this is a fairly complicated macro, you will want to use the single step mode, press **[ALT]-[HELP]** to verify that you have entered the correct instructions.

Before using the typing alternative, you must position the worksheet cursor in the correct starting position. Each command in the macro is the same as keyboard input with respect to the *current active cell*. Thus commands such as {**right**} move the cursor one cell to the right from its current position, and **/RE** erase the contents of the cell under the worksheet cursor. Position the worksheet cursor on the first cell in an address (cell A3 in Table B-4, for example). Then begin executing the macro by typing **[ALT]** and the appropriate letter.

As you can see from Table B-6, the instructions are a cryptic set of letters. To make them easier to understand, commands are typed in upper case letters while cell references and named keys (words in brackets) are in lowercase. Similar functions (printer setup, copying, etc.) have been grouped together on a single line, and line-by-line notes are provided to the left of the macro.

The first line of the macro sets up the printer. Among other things, it clears the current printer setting, enters the code for compressed typing, and specifies the range of cells to be printed.

The second line of the macro copies each cell into its proper position in the master mailing label.

The third line prints the mailing label. There is no need to specify Setup commands or the print range because that was done in the first line of the macro. Notice that this line contains three L's. In order to correctly position the print head for printing the next label, each L advances the paper in the printer by one line. You will have to adjust your macro to the size of the labels you are using.

At the end of the copying sequence (line 3), the worksheet cursor is in the Zip Code column. The fourth command moves the cursor down one row to the next address.

The Copy command in the fifth row of the macro copies the Zip Code for the new address into cell F16. If you have just printed the last entry in the list, this command copies a blank. Whether or not F16 contains a number or a blank is crucial to the test to decide whether all the names in the list have been printed. The test is on the next line.

In the sixth row the macro function, **/XIf16 < >0**, asks the question, "Is the value in F16 (where you've been copying Zip Codes) different from zero?" If it is, the **/XI** function is TRUE, and 1-2-3 continues processing commands *on the sixth line*. The worksheet cursor moves to the beginning of the worksheet line with {end}{left}, and the macro function /XGh6 sends 1-2-3 off to cell H6 to begin creating an address label for the next address in the list.

If, however, the value in F16 is equal to zero (as it would be after processing the last entry in the list), the function /XIf16<>0 is FALSE. Lotus quits reading instructions in the sixth row and moves *immediately* to the next row. This row places the word **DONE!!!** in the cell below the last Zip Code.

The typing alternative now moves down one row, where it finds a blank cell. Since this is a non-label cell, processing of the keyboard macro stops.

SUMMARY

You have just gone through a short description of two keyboard macros. The first example, was simple and straightforward while the second was more complicated and made extensive use of special features.

After these examples, a number of general comments are in order. First, you must enter into the macro the *exact* sequence of keystrokes required to produce the action you desire. Doing this can be a bit tricky, so run through the sequence key-by-key while writing down each key-stroke. You may have to repeat this several times.

You should also follow the pattern set in the example and place related commands and functions on the same line. Be sure to write a short description of the action performed by each line. Finally, use the **[ALT]-[HELP]** feature to identify mistakes in your macro. You can name the macro after you enter the first line, and use **[ALT]-[HELP]** to check each line as you enter it into the macro. Alternatively, you can wait until the macro is complete and then step through it character-by-character.

Since the commands in keyboard macros are actually entered as text, it is a simple matter to edit changes with the **[EDIT]** key. Just remember that each line must begin with a letter of the alphabet or a forced text entry.

With the typing alternative, you can become as fancy as you wish. You can date stamp each label with the @TODAY function. You can print the address in regular type and the return address in compressed type, or you can include a message on the address label. There is very little you *can't* do with 1-2-3's typing alternative.

---

* Some material in this appendix first appeared in *What If...A User's Guide to Spreadsheets on the IBM PC* by Andrew T. Williams, John Wiley & Sons, Inc., New York, 1984.

APPENDIX C
HOW TO USE SYMPHONY'S TELECOMMUNICATIONS ENVIRONMENT

INTRODUCTION

One of the most useful of Symphony's five environments is the *Comm* (for telecommunications) environment. With this environment, you can establish a communications link with another microcomputer or a remote mainframe. You can communicate with an operator at the other end of the line, and you can use the facilities of an electronic database such as the Source or the Dow Jones News/Retrieval service. You can transfer files between computers and, if Symphony is running on microcomputers at each end of a communications link, you can transfer information directly from one worksheet into another.

There are three things you will need to do before you can use Symphony for telecommunications. First, you must have the appropriate hardware to connect your microcomputer to the telephone lines. Secondly, you must use the Install Program to create a driver set for your telecommunications hardware. And, finally, you must prepare a communications settings sheet.

Modems

To connect your computer to the phone lines, you will need a device called a *modem*. A modem converts electronic information into sounds that can be understood by the modem at the other end of the line.

Modems come in two types: direct-connect and acoustical. The direct-connect type is easiest to use because Symphony can dial the number for you or answer an incoming call automatically. Direct-connect modems can also transmit data faster than acoustical modems. With an acoustic modem, you have to dial the number yourself and then place the telephone handset into two rubber cups that hold it firmly in place.

Direct connect modems come in two types. One type is placed outside your computer and is connected to it by a cable. It is called an "external" modem. The other type is an "internal" modem. It is on a printed circuit board, which plugs into one of the expansion slots inside you computer. All acoustical modems that aren't built-in to a particular personal computer are external.

If your modem is an external modem, you need a place to connect the cable that runs from the modem to your computer. This connection is called a "communications port" or sometimes a "serial port". Each modem comes with its own manual. Read that manual to familiarize yourself with the operation and requirements of your particular modem.

After making your modem selection, use the Symphony Install program diskette to create a driver set to match your hardware. Follow the prompts and make the appropriate selections.

SETTING COMMUNICATIONS PARAMETERS

The final task in setting up Symphony for communications is to specify a Settings sheet. The individual choices which define a communications link are called *communications parameters* and a full set of parameters is called a *protocol*. To specify your protocol, type **[ALT]-[TYPE]** and select Comm to display a Communications window. Then press **[MENU]** to display the main Comm command menu. The choices on that menu are:

Phone   Log on   Transmit-Range   File-Transfer   Break   Settings

In a moment, you will come back to the first five of these choices, but for now select Settings. When you do, Symphony displays the settings sheet shown in Figure C-1. Like other settings sheets, this one displays settings which define a particular action. (Other settings sheets include those to specify graphs, databases, and the Print command.)

You can define and save multiple settings sheets. In fact, since the sheet contains a phone number, communication protocol, and log on sequences, you should create a *separate* settings sheet for each computer with which you communicate.

```
 Speed and type of transmission                                        MENU
 Interface  Phone  Terminal  Send  Break  Handshaking  Capture  Login  Name  Quit
 ----------------------------------------------------------------------------
 :  Interface             Terminal                 Send                      :
 :    Baud:      110       Screen:    Window         EOL:       \n           :
 :    Parity:    None      Echo:      No             Delay:     0            :
 :    Length:    7         Linefeed:  No             Response:  \j           :
 :    Stop bits: 1         Backspace: Backspace    Break:       60           :
 :  Phone                  Wrap:      Yes           Handshaking              :
 :    Type:      Pulse     Delay:     0               Inbound:  Yes          :
 :    Dial:      60        Translation:               Outbound: Yes          :
 :    Answer:    15          (none)                 Capture:                 :
 :    Number:                                         Range:    No           :
 :                                                    Printer:  No           :
 '===================================================Communications Settings:=='
```

Figure C1. Default communications settings sheet.

Because there is no universally recognized standard for communications protocols, Symphony provides an opportunity to set a large number of parameters in order to make the system adaptable to all situations. Your choices are:

Interface	**Phone**	**Terminal**	**Send**	**Break**
Handshaking	**Capture**	**Log on**	**Name**	**Quit**

At first, this large array of choices is formidable, but the only choices you *must* make are Interface and Phone. You can ignore the other options because the default choices made by Symphony are correct for most situations.

Interface

Begin specifying your communications parameters by selecting Interface. The following four choices will appear in the control panel:

Baud   Parity   Length   Stop-bits

Each of these choices determines an important parameter concerning the way data is transmitted from one computer to another. In essence, these settings determine the "language" used for communications.

A crucial point is that the settings for baud rate, parity, length, and stop-bits **must** be the same on both the sending *and* receiving computers. Thus, you must coordinate your parameter settings with the operator of any other computer you are communicating with. In some cases, a telephone conversation just before telecommunications can be used to check the settings. If you are communicating with a mainframe computer or an electronic database, the operator of the system will supply a manual which tells you how to use the system and at what levels to set the parameters. Read that manual before attempting to communicate with the system.

Select each of the following choices in turn, and set each parameter to the proper level.

Baud Baud is a measure of how fast data is transmitted from one computer to another. The setting you select depends upon the capabilities of the modems at *both* ends of the line. A higher baud rate means that it takes less time to transmit a document of a given length. It also means that the probability of transmission errors is higher.

Typical baud rates for communicating over telephone lines are 300 baud (Symphony's choice 3) and 1200 baud (Symphony's choice 5). Select the number that corresponds to the baud rate at which you want to communicate. When you make a selection, the baud rate appears opposite the word "Baud" in the first column of the Setting Sheet.

Parity Parity determines the type of error checking used when data is transmitted. Your options are 1 (none), 2 (odd), and 3 (even). Even (3) is a common setting for this parameter.

Length When data is transmitted, it is broken up into groups called *words* which are either seven or eight bits long. The length option lets you select 1 for seven-bit words or 2 for eight-bit words.

Stop-Bits Stop-Bits determine the number of bits sent after each data word. Stop-bits act like a period at the end of a sentence; they tell the receiving computer that an entire word has been sent. Your options are 1 and 2 for one and two stop-bits respectively.

This completes the specification of the interface parameters. Now, select Quit to return to the Settings menu where you can make your next choice: Phone.

Phone

Select Phone from the Settings command menu, and the the following choices appear:

Type   Dial-Time   Answer-Time   Number

You only need to set Type and Number. The defaults of 60 seconds for Dial-Time (how long Symphony tries to dial a number) and 15 seconds for Answer-Time (how long Symphony tries to answer an incoming call) are adequate for most communications situations.

Type You're choice depends on whether you have Pulse or Tone phone service. The distinction is between phones that select numbers by "dialing" a rotary dial and those that select numbers by "beeping" with push buttons. Beeping (tone) is faster, so that is the preferred option. Try it even if you have a standard rotary dial telephone since the rotary dial phone can be used on a tone line. If Tone doesn't work, then use the Pulse option.

Number When you select this option you are prompted for a phone number. Remember to include a 9 or other digit if a one must be dialed to obtain access to an outside line. When the number has been correctly entered, press **[ENTER]** to return to the Settings menu.

Figure C-2 on the following page shows a settings sheet that has been set to 1200 baud, even parity, seven-bit words, and two stop bits. The phone number, 9-234-1234, has also been entered.

AUTOMATIC LOG ON SEQUENCE (OPTIONAL)

If you are communicating with a mainframe computer or an electronic database, you will have to go through a *log on sequence* before you can use the system. The log on sequence consists of a dialogue between you and the host computer. The host computer asks questions about what service you would like and, perhaps, about the equipment you are using. You respond by supplying the appropriate answer to each question. On many systems, you will also be asked to supply a personal password which gives you access to the host computer. If you don't supply it, you will be denied access.

Specifying a log on sequence as part of a settings sheet is entirely *optional* since you can also type this information from the keyboard each time you've

```
Speed and type of transmission                                  MENU
Interface  Phone  Terminal  Send  Break  Handshaking  Capture  Login  Name  Quit
'------------------------------------------------------------------------.
:  Interface          Terminal            Send                           :
:    Baud:     1200    Screen:   Window    EOL:      \m                   :
:    Parity:   Even    Echo:     No        Delay:    0                    :
:    Length:   7       Linefeed: No        Response: \j                   :
:    Stop bits: 2      Backspace: Backspace  Break:    60                 :
:  Phone               Wrap:     Yes       Handshaking                    :
:    Type:     Pulse   Delay:    0          Inbound:  Yes                 :
:    Dial:     60      Translation:         Outbound: Yes                 :
:    Answer:   15        (none)            Capture:                       :
:    Number:   9-234-1234                    Range:    No                 :
:                                            Printer:  No                 :
'=================================================Communications Settings:=='
```

Figure C2. Settings sheet with parameters set.

established a connection with a host computer. In fact, you should run through the log on sequence manually the first few times you use a remote computer in order to get the sequence right. Once you do get it right, you can avoid a great deal of repetitive typing by telling Symphony what the dialogue will be, and then letting Symphony go through the log on sequence automatically. Automatic log on is easier and more accurate that manual log on, so set up Symphony to do it for each host computer with which you communicate.

To specify the log on sequence, select Log on from the main Settings command menu. The screen changes to look like Figure C-3 and your menu choices are:

Maximum-Time   Repeat-Time   A B C D E F G H I J   New Quit

The first two options are Maximum-Time and Repeat-Time. Maximum-Time specifies the number of seconds Symphony waits for the entire log on procedure to succeed before signaling an error if unable to make a connection. Repeat-Time specifies the number of seconds Symphony waits before repeating a given exchange. (Repeat-Time only matters if the Count is 2 or more.) Symphony begins by setting these times to 0, and you must experiment to find the appropriate values for a particular log on sequence for a

```
/
/
/  Number of seconds to wait for log-in to succeed                    MENU
/  Maximum-Time  Repeat-Time  A  B  C  D  E  F  G  H  I  J  New  Quit
/ ,--------------------------------------------------------------------,
| :                                                                    :
| :  Count  Send  (maximum time 0)              Receive (repeat time 0):
| : A 1                                                                :
| : B 1                                                                :
| : C 1                                                                :
| : D 1                                                                :
| : E 1                                                                :
| : F 1                                                                :
| : G 1                                                                :
| : H 1                                                                :
| : I 1                                                                :
| : J 1                                                                :
| '===========================================================Login Settings:=='
```

Figure C3. Login settings sheet.

particular host computer. Begin by setting Maximum-Time at 60 and Repeat-Time at 15. Then, if necessary, adjust the values.

The letters A to J give you access to ten lines of dialogue (or, as Symphony calls them, "exchanges"). This is ample room for all log on sequences. Select A for the first line and the following menu choices are displayed. Select each of these four options in turn to completely specify the dialogue for row A.

Count   Send   Receive   Quit

Count The Count is the number of times Symphony repeats a line of dialogue. It is sometimes necessary to repeat a line before the host computer accepts your log on, so select a number such as 2 or 3. The Repeat-Time, which you set to 15 seconds in the previous section, determines how long Symphony waits for a response to a Send line. If necessary, you can adjust the Repeat-Time.

Send Specify the sequence of characters (up to 30) to be sent to the host computer. When specifying these characters, you must use the decimal ASCII code (American Standard Code for Information Interchange) for any control key used in the sequence.

For example, you often need to end a set of characters with the **[ENTER]** key. To include the **[ENTER]** key in a line of dialogue, place the decimal ASCII code for **[ENTER]**, \ **013**, at the appropriate point in the sequence (see Figure C-4). Also see Appendix B of the Symphony *Reference Manual* for more information about ASCII codes.

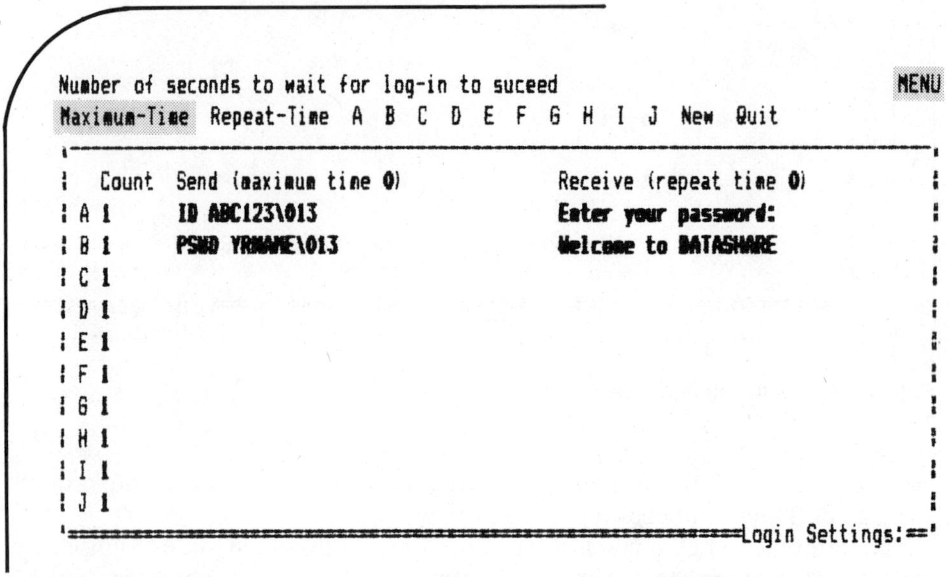

```
Number of seconds to wait for log-in to suceed                    MENU
Maximum-Time  Repeat-Time  A  B  C  D  E  F  G  H  I  J  New  Quit
¦──────────────────────────────────────────────────────────────────¦
¦  Count  Send (maximum time 0)              Receive (repeat time 0) ¦
¦ A 1       ID ABC123\013                    Enter your password:    ¦
¦ B 1       PSWD YRNAME\013                  Welcome to DATASHARE     ¦
¦ C 1                                                                ¦
¦ D 1                                                                ¦
¦ E 1                                                                ¦
¦ F 1                                                                ¦
¦ G 1                                                                ¦
¦ H 1                                                                ¦
¦ I 1                                                                ¦
¦ J 1                                                                ¦
'================================================Login Settings:=='
```

Figure C4. Login settings sheet with dialogue on lines A and B. Note 013 used in place of [ENTER].

Receive Next, select Receive and specify the characters the host computer sends back to your computer in response to the characters you just specified with Send. Symphony will verify this part of the dialogue before sending the next set of characters.

Quit Quit ends the specification of line A and returns you to the Log on menu where you can select B to specify the next line of dialogue.

Continue specifying lines of dialogue (up to 10) until you have completed the conversation necessary to log on to a particular host computer. If you make a mistake in the dialogue, you will discover your error when you next try to log on to the system. At that time, return to this menu, and revise the incorrect dialogue.

SAVING A SETTINGS SHEET

Once you have specified a settings sheet, you are ready to use it to establish a communication link with the host computer: but before you do, save the settings for use in future communications sessions. Do this by selecting Name from the Settings menu. The following submenu appears:

Retrieve   Save   Erase   Phone-and-Log on

Save Save is the option you choose to save a settings sheet. The process is just like the one you go through with File Save to save a worksheet file, except that the settings are saved in a file with a .CCF extension.

When you select Save, Symphony displays all of the named settings sheets on the directory that was current when you started the session (A: \ , for example). Select one of these names or type in your own. A good filename identifies the host computer to which the settings apply. Finally, press **[ENTER]** and your communications settings are saved. You can now use the Settings Name command to use these settings at any time.

The other choices on this submenu are Retrieve, Erase, and Phone-and-Log on.

Retrieve

Retrieve displays a menu of named settings sheets in the control panel. Choose the one you want to use, and it will become the current settings sheet.

Erase Erase erases a settings file.

Phone-and-Log on This option calls up a settings sheet and automatically dials the specified phone number. Then, if you have provided a log on sequence, proceeds to log on automatically. Provided you have specified all the required information in you log on sequence, you can establish a connection with a host computer with a single key stroke.

ESTABLISHING A COMMUNICATIONS LINK

Using A Direct Connect Modem

Once you have specified the communication parameters on a Setting Sheet (or recalled a named Setting Sheet), you are ready to establish a communications link with another computer. If you have a direct connect modem, there are two ways to do this.

The first is to use the Phone-and-Log on command on the Name submenu described at the end of the last section. When you use this command, names of the stored settings sheets are displayed in the control panel. When you select a name, Symphony dials the specified phone number and, if there is one on the settings sheet, submits a log on in conversation.

When the appropriate settings sheet is already in memory, select Phone from the Comm main menu and the following submenu choices appear:

Call   Wait-Mode   Answer   Hangup
Data-Mode   Voice-Mode

Selecting Call displays the phone number specified on the current settings sheet. To use it, press **[ENTER]**. If you want to call another number (but use the same communications parameters), press **[ESC]**, type in the number you wish to call, and then press **[ENTER]**.

When Symphony establishes a connection with the remote computer, it returns you to the Comm window. If you have specified a log on sequence, select Log on and send your sequence. If you haven't specified a log on in sequence, use the keys on your keyboard to log on.

If the attempt to establish a communications link fails because the number is busy, because there is an error in the log on sequence, or because of a failure in the hardware (most commonly, a loose connection between pieces of equipment), Symphony displays a message and returns to the Comm window. If you get an error message (flashing ERROR in the mode indicator), you must acknowledge the message by pressing either **[ESC]** or **[ENTER]**.

Using an Acoustic Modem

If you have an acoustic modem connected to your computer, you will have to manually dial the telephone number of the remote computer.Otherwise, using an acoustic modem is much the same as establishing a link with a direct connect modem.

The first step is to enter the Comm window and make sure that the current settings sheet is the appropriate one for the communications you wish to do. If it isn't, use Name to load the appropriate settings sheet or modify the current Setting Sheet to contain the correct parameters. Then return to the main Comm window menu.

Next, manually dial the telephone number of the remote computer. When the remote computer "answers", you will hear a high-pitched tone. This is called a "carrier," and it indicates that the host computer is ready to communicate. Place the telephone handset into the rubber cradles on the acoustic modem. Press down on the handset to firmly seat it in the cradles.

You can now proceed with the log on sequence, if one is required. If you have stored a log on conversation, you can use it by selecting Log on from the main Comm window menu.

If you fail to establish a communications link, Symphony will display a message to that effect. If you receive an error message (flashing ERROR in the mode indicator), respond by pressing either the **[ESC]** or the **[ENTER]** key.

TRANSMITTING INFORMATION

Although you can "chat" with the computer at the other end of the line by typing messages on the keyboard, the real use of a communications link is to transfer information from one computer to another. There are two general ways to transfer information with the Symphony Comm environment. One is to transmit *complete files* (such as worksheet files) and the other is to transmit information from a *range of cells* on the current Symphony spreadsheet.

Transmitting Files

To send a file to a remote computer, select File-Transfer from the main Comm menu. Then select Send, and you will be prompted for the name of the file to transmit. Note that Symphony assumes the file is stored in the current directory. If it isn't, you must supply the appropriate drive designation or path name. Once the file to send has been specified, transmission takes place, and a message appears on the screen telling you how large the file is in bytes and how many bytes have been transmitted. As the file is transmitted, the number of bytes transmitted increases until the entire file has been sent.

If the remote computer has the appropriate software, sending files with the "XMODEM" protocol is the best way to assure that the data being transferred is error free. Files transferred under this protocol are subject to special error checking procedures which verify the accuracy of the transmission. If the remote computer is running Symphony, there is no problem. If it isn't, you must verify that the software being used by the other computer is capable of transferring files under the XMODEM protocol.

To transfer a file under the XMODEM protocol, you *must* set the Interface parameters on the Setting sheet to a Length 2 (8 bits), Parity 1 (none), and Stop-Bits 1 (1 stop-bit). Once done, selecting File-Transfer from the Comm main menu automatically results in transfer under the XMODEM protocol.

Transmitting Ranges of Cells

The alternative to transmitting an entire file is to transmit the information in a range of cells on the current Symphony worksheet. If the remote computer is running Symphony at the time of the transmission, the information can be captured directly into a worksheet.

To transmit a range, select Transmit-Range from the Comm main menu. You are then prompted to specify the range of cells you wish to transmit. You can point to the cells or you can speed that process by naming the range before you begin the communications session. If the range is named, you can supply the range name in response to the *Range to send:* prompt.

Information transmitted from a range of cells on a worksheet is transmitted as *long labels*, regardless of its original form.

RECEIVING INFORMATION

Just as there are several ways to send information from one computer to another, there are several ways to receive information.

The simplest way is to have the information appear on the screen as it is received. New information is added below existing information and when the screen is full, rows at the top scroll off as new rows are added at the bottom. However, any information not visible on the screen is *lost*, so this method is useful only when you don't mind losing what has been received. Such situations occur when when you are looking through a database for the information you require, or when you are "chatting" with the operator at the other end of the line.

Using File-Transfer To Receive Files

If you are using the File-Transfer option on the main Comm menu to receive a file, the file will be automatically saved to a diskette. In setting up the File-Transfer Receive option, you have an opportunity to assign a filename to the incoming file and to specify the full path name to designate the diskette or directory where the file is to be stored.

Using Capture To Receive Information

In many cases, the information you receive from the remote computer won't be in the form of files, but rather in the form of text. This is true when you download from a mainframe computer or when you use an electronic database to provide information.

To record this information for use later, you *must* capture the information into a range of cells on the current worksheet. Begin by choosing the Capture option of the Settings command and defining a Capture range. The Capture range is the place where information is stored as it is received. You can also have the information captured to your printer at the same time. If you select this option, the incoming information will be printed as it is received.

Captured information is entered into the cells of the Capture Range as *text*. Furthermore, if the text extends across cell boundaries, it is broken up into labels that are as wide as each column. Therefore, the current column width in the Capture range determines the length of each label. If you are receiving text, make the columns wide so you can use the Doc environment to edit the material. If you are receiving numbers (as text), set each column width so that a single number will be entered into each cell.

Obviously, numbers received as text cannot be used by Symphony in calculations. However, Symphony does have a number of @ functions and a Data environment command called Parse that can be used to convert text into numbers. See the Symphony *How To* manual for details.

You can capture information to either a Capture range, the printer or both at the same time. Furthermore, once you have specified the Capture range on the settings sheet, you can enable and disable the function by using the **[CAPTURE]** function key.

ENDING A COMMUNICATIONS SESSION

There are several ways you can end a communications session. Mainframes and databases often require you to go through a dialogue to end a session. Type the appropriate responses from the keyboard, and when the remote computer signs off, select Hangup from the Comm command menu and Symphony will disconnect from the phone line.

If you are communicating with another microcomputer, simply let the operator on the other end know you are ending the session ("over and out," is a popular sign-off phrase), and then select Hangup from the Comm command menu.

If you must end a communication quickly in mid-session, select Break from the Comm command menu. This command sends a series of characters that stops communications.

A final alternative is to physically hang up the phone if you are using an acoustical modem, or to turn off the power to an external direct connect modem. This breaks the telephone link between the two computers and cancels the conversation. Like hanging up on a friend, this is not a recommended alternative, but sometimes it is the only action some computers will understand.

SOME COMMON COMMUNICATIONS PROBLEMS

If the material you are receiving is coming across garbled, verify that the communications parameters have been set to the same values at *both* the sending and receiving end. If they haven't, reset the parameters and try again.

If you are having trouble establishing a connection with the phone line or if your communications is interrupted for no apparent reason, check the cable connections. A loose connection in one of the cables that connect the computer to the modem or the modem to the phone line is one of the most common communications problems. If possible, have the operator at the other end check those connections as well.

If Symphony fails to move down one line after you reach the right edge of the screen, you will need to use the Terminal option on the Settings menu to set the Linefeed to Yes. Then when you get to the end of a line, Symphony will automatically move down one line.

A similar problem can occur when you are sending information from a range. Unless the computer on the other end is setup to respond with a \ j at the end of each line it receives, Symphony will send only one line and then refuse to send any more. To correct this problem, choose Send from the Settings menu and delete all the Response characters. Symphony will now send each line without waiting for the \ j response character from the receiving computer.

Finally, a common set of problems has to do with a feature of telecommunications called "echo." Some computers return (or echo) to the sending computer each character as it is transmitted. This is a form of error checking, but for it to work properly, the sending computer must not display keystrokes as they are typed, otherwise every letter would appear twice (as in "ttwwiiccee"). If you observe this happening, enter the Terminal command on the Settings menu and turn Echo off.

The opposite problem may occur if the remote computer doesn't echo. In this case, what you type doesn't appear on your screen. Again, enter the Settings command and choose Echo. This time turn it on.

In general, if there is something strange about the way characters appear on the screen, the first thing to check is Echo.

SUMMARY

You are now ready to use Symphony to establish a communications link between your computer and a remote computer. Remember to set the communications parameters and to select the type of phone service you will be using. If the remote computer requires a log on dialogue, you can simplify your communications tasks by entering the dialogue into a Log on sheet. Symphony then submits the dialogue whenever you log on to the computer.

Don't forget to use the Name command on the Settings menu to create a settings sheet for each remote computer with which you communicate. You can then establish a communications link by simply selecting Phone-and-Log on with the Name command. Symphony then automatically dials the number of the remote computer and submits any log on sequence you have specified. No matter which features you choose to use, Symphony's Comm environment will be a powerful addition to your electronic tool kit.

Index

absolute cell reference, 214
  Copy command and, 132
  creation of, 215
  database and, 258
Access System, 18
active cell, defined, 33
AND criteria in database, 256
arithmetic operators, 203
arrow keys, 29, 37, 41
  END key and, 39
asterisk, 254
AUTO123 filename, 147

B & W option under Graph
    command, 298
backup copies of diskettes, 145,
    231
BKSP key, 37
blank characters, Data Sort
    command, and, 246
borders, printing and, 185, 199
Borders option under Print
    command, 199
built-in (@) functions, 4, 44, 50,
    201-212
  arithmetic, 203
  date, 208
  financial, 209
  logical, 206
  mathematical, 209
  special, 210-212
  statistical, 204, 271
  trigonometric, 209

CALC function, 65
CAP LOCK key, 29
cell(s), 32
  anchor, 95
  entries in, 43-46
  expanding cursor and, 95
  Range commands and, 54, 90
cell references, 213-217
  database and, 258
  Copy command and, 130
Clear option under Print
    command, 180
Color option under Graph
    command, 298
Column-Width command, 58, 64,
    73
  Worksheet, 58, 73
  tree diagram for, 74
Combine option of File
    command, 153
commands, 2. See also specific
    command
  menu for, 56

command line, 34
  cursor in, 20, 35, 37
  defined, 19
command tree. See also specific
    command
  use of, 57
control panel, 32-35
Copy command, 3, 122-133
  cell references and, 130
  Range names and, 109
  ranges defined under, 124
  tree diagram for, 124
  use of, 138
CTRL-BREAK, 28
CTRL-C, 28
cursor
  command line, 20, 35
  control of, 37
  expanding, 92
  worksheet, 32, 38
cursor control keys, 37
  context-determined, 39
  primary, 38
  secondary, 41

Data commands. See also specific
    command
  tree diagram for, 238
  use of, 277
Data Distribution command, 273
  tree diagram for, 275
Data Extract command, 262
Data Fill command, 217
  tree diagram for, 218
Data Query command, 248-259
  tree diagram for, 249
Data Sort command, 242-248
  data range and, 244
  tree diagram for, 243
Data Table, 278
  modification of, 226
  One Way, 219
  tree diagram for, 222
  Two-Way, 224, 279
Data Table command, 218
database
  commands for, 237-280. See
      also specific command
  construction of, 248
  criteria for, 251-259
  defined, 4, 239
  field names in, 240
  omitted and rearranged, 264
  function of, 241
  options of, 217
  parameters for, 244
  records in 241

statistical function in, 271
Date format, 62
date functions, 208
Date Prompt, 17
default page, printing and, 175
default settings for commands, 56
Default command, 67
  tree diagram for, 68
DEL key, 38
Delete command, 4, 58, 71
  tree diagram for, 72
Delete option under Data Query
    command, 266
Directory command, 161
  tree diagram for, 162
Disk-Manager, 22
Disk Operating System (DOS), 14
  installation of, 16
display of entries, Global Format
    command and, 61
dollar sign, absolute cell
    reference and, 215
DOS (Disk Operating System), 14
  installation of, 16
drivers, device, 16

electronic spreadsheet, defined, 1
END key, 37
  ARROW key and, 39
  HOME key and, 40
entries, types of, 43-46
entry line cursor, 35, 37
entry space, worksheet
    construction and, 228
environments in Symphony, 10.
    See also Symphony
Erase command, 55, 58
  File, 160
  Range, 99
  tree diagram for, 100
  Worksheet, 75
  tree diagram for, 75
error messages, 36
error trapping in worksheet
    construction, 229
escape key, 28
expanding cursor, 92
Extract command, 262

field
  in database, 241
  defined, 5
field names in database, 240
files
  listing of, 165
  names of, 146, 232
  organization of, 148